IMAGES
of America

MIDDLETOWN REVISITED

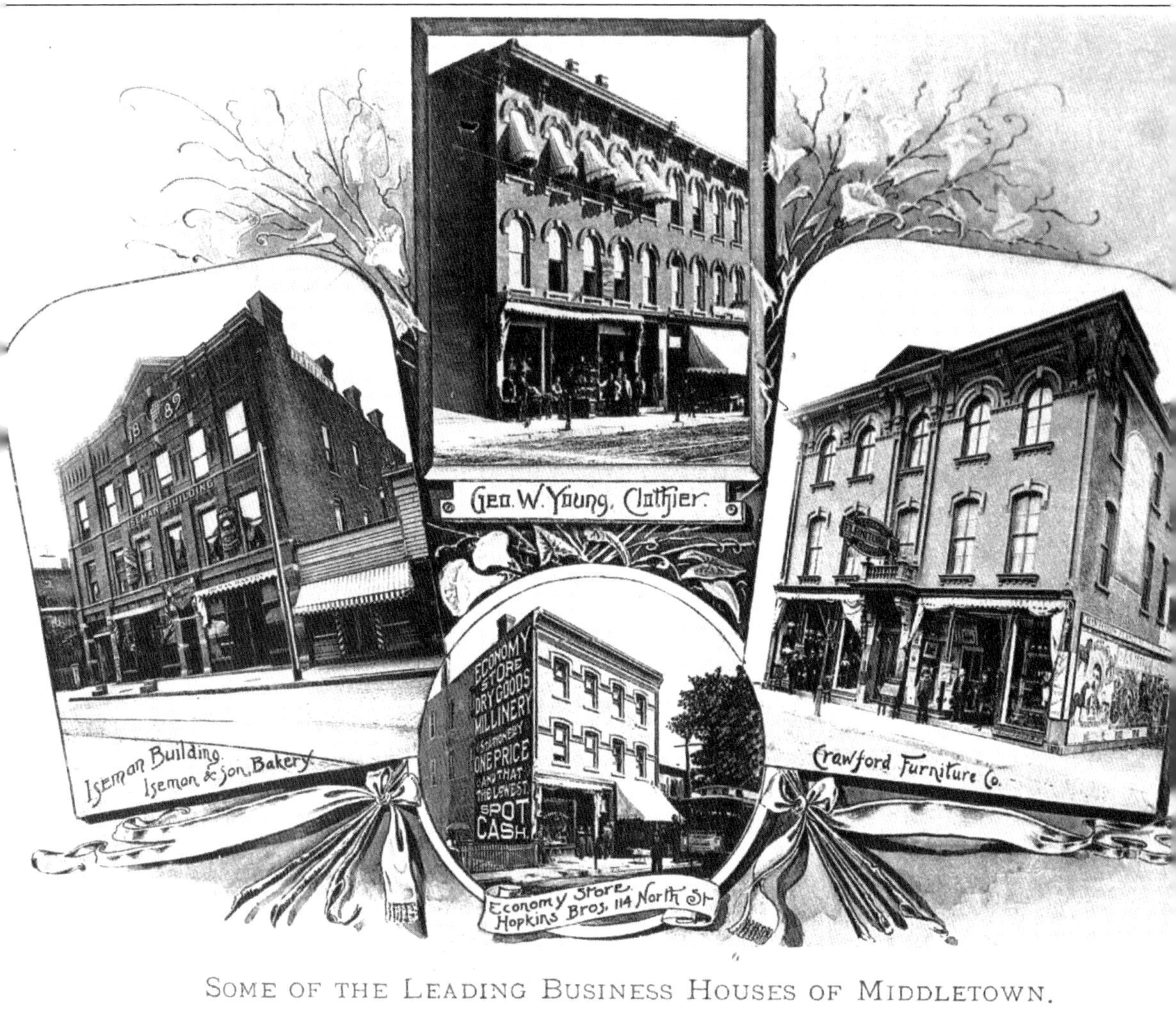

A promotional illustration shows some of the city's outstanding businesses around the beginning of the 20th century. The Iseman Building on James Street still stands.

On the cover: The heart of Middletown, Franklin Square, is seen here as it looked in 1934. Whelan Drug Company, also known as the United Cigar Store, was a fixture on the corner of North and East Main Streets for many years. The building survives today and is occupied by a fire and police store. There are a lot of people on the streets on what looks to be a fine, warm day. (Courtesy of the Historical Society of Middletown.)

IMAGES
of America

MIDDLETOWN REVISITED

Marvin H. Cohen

ARCADIA
PUBLISHING

ISBN 978-0-7385-5741-0

Published by Arcadia Publishing
Charleston, South Carolina

Printed in the United States of America

Library of Congress Catalog Card Number: 2007937771

For all general information contact Arcadia Publishing at:
Telephone 843-853-2070
Fax 843-853-0044
E-mail sales@arcadiapublishing.com
For customer service and orders:
Toll-Free 1-888-313-2665

Visit us on the Internet at www.arcadiapublishing.com

Contents

ACKNOWLEDGMENTS

I would like to thank all my friends and colleagues at the Historical Society of Middletown and the Wallkill Precinct who assisted and encouraged me with this book. I'd also like to give a special thank you to Dorothy Hunt-Ingrassia, Gwen Deserto, and Ann P. Vail for their help.

All of the photographs in this book were selected from the archives of the Historical Society of Middletown. Primary photographers were Truman J. Moon, well-known educator; William G. Embler, managing editor of the *Middletown Times-Herald*; and Paul Weisshaar, amateur local photographer.

INTRODUCTION

This book, the second Images of America volume on Middletown, tries to cover the period from the 1920s to the 1960s. A few earlier photographs, however, are included.

Middletown had many industries, factories, businesses, and stores that deserve to be remembered. A vibrant and busy downtown, as well as a number of neighborhoods with their own homes and stores, was a feature of the city.

There were numerous industries, some of which are shown in this book, others that seemingly were not recorded. We recall the aroma of baking bread at the Spaulding Bakery on Sprague Avenue, the sweet smell of flavoring made at Polak's Frutal Works. We remember Ideal Wrapping Machine Company on Sprague Avenue, which manufactured machines to wrap candy. Master Rule on Mulberry Street, Avon Products on James Street, and Middletown Footwear and Clemson Lawn Mowers on Railroad Avenue are a few more of our businesses that are now gone.

National chain stores such as Sears Roebuck and Montgomery Ward were downtown, as were A&P supermarkets and Grand Union. Postal Telegraph and Western Union were here as well.

As we pass through the streets of Middletown, we note buildings that have been rehabilitated, buildings that are derelict, and vacant lots where buildings once stood. Perhaps this book will fill in some of the blanks and enable us to realize what once was there.

Middletown is still a thriving small city in the center of Orange County. We may no longer have our numerous dairy farms, our railroads, or our heavy industry, but we have progressed in other ways, as a desirable community in which to live and raise a family.

One

The Heart of the City

If any one place could be deemed the heart of Middletown, it would be Franklin Square. It is not known how the name came about. The building on the square with the busts of Benjamin Franklin was built long after the name was applied to the intersection.

The junction of North and South Streets as well as East Main and West Main Streets has long been the hub of downtown. This area seems to have been a favorite place for photographers to gather. Many old buildings remain, others succumbed to changing times and still others are being rehabilitated today. Presented in this chapter are a number of photographs of Franklin Square as it once was.

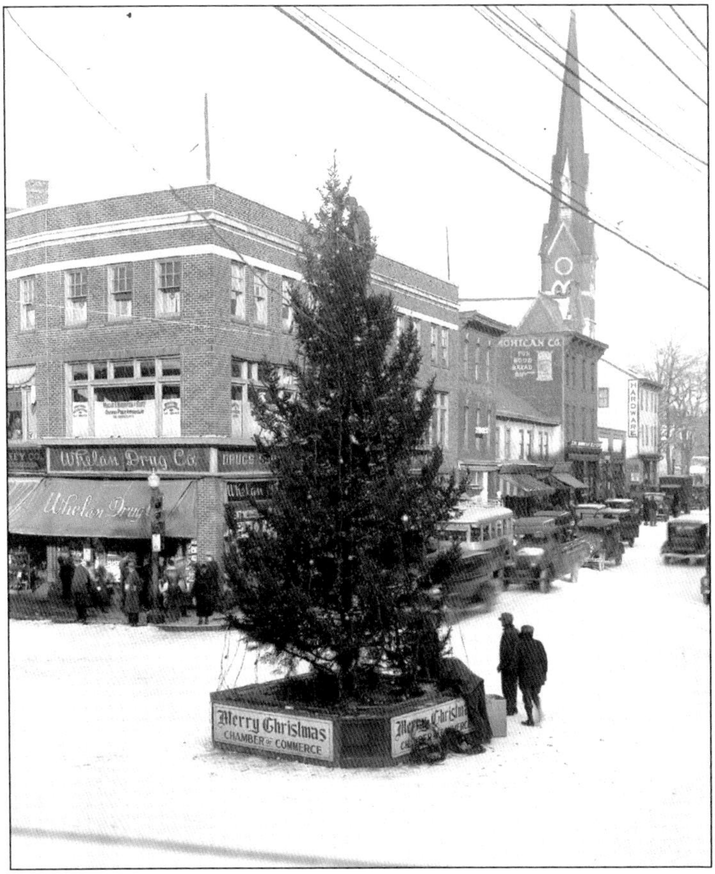

The city's Christmas tree is being decorated in 1934. Erected by the chamber of commerce each year, the tree was placed in the center of Franklin Square. It looks like snow is on the ground as workmen scale the tree to place the lights.

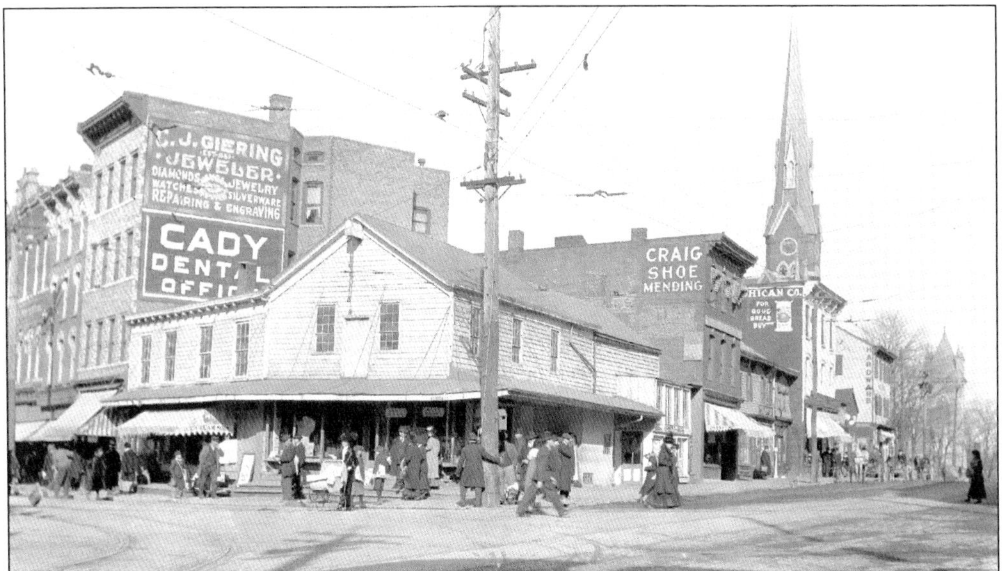

This view of Franklin Square shows the time before automobiles existed. A lady pushes a wicker baby carriage across North Street.

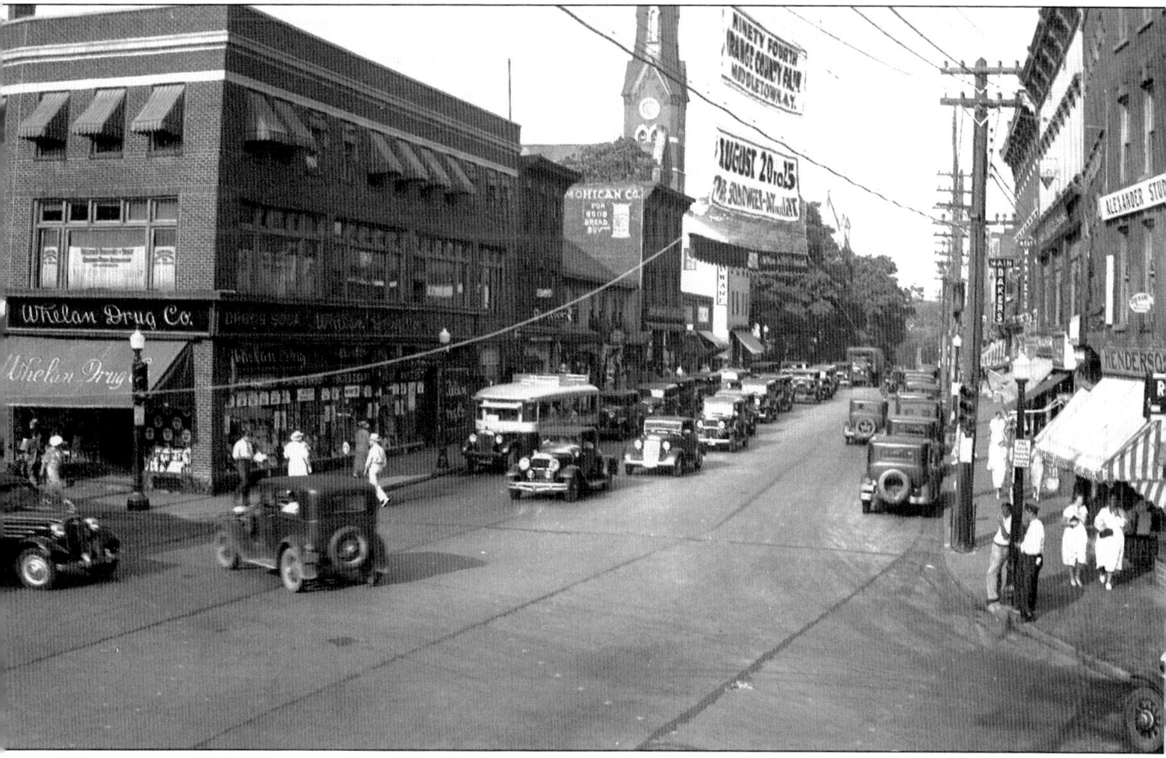

The center of Middletown, Franklin Square, looked like this in 1934. Visible on the right is Joe Henderson's men's store with Ben Alexander's photography studio above. In the background is Main Bakers. On the other side of the street is Whelan's Drugs, the Mohican Market, and Pelton's Hardware Store.

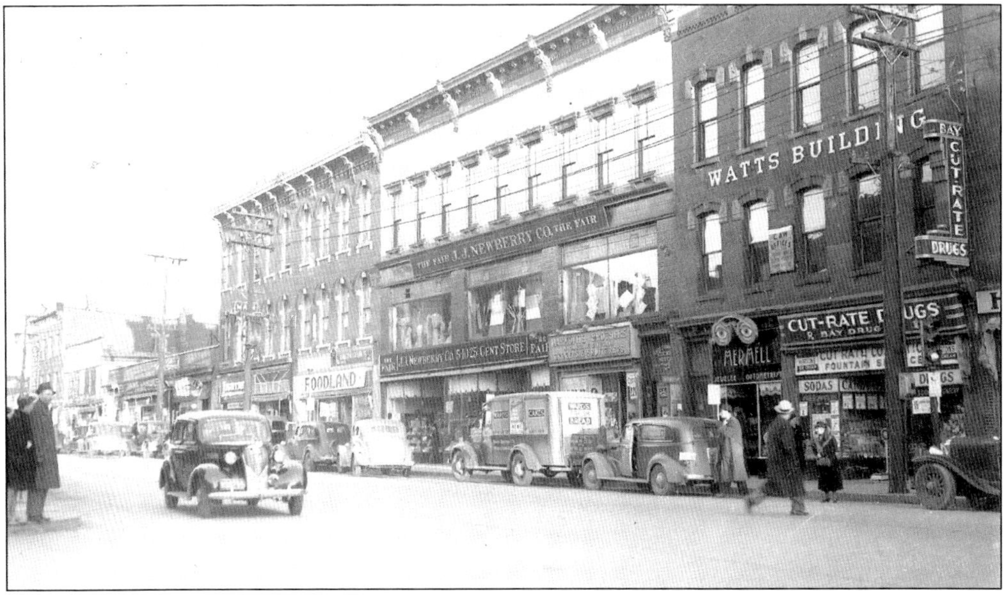

East Main Street looked like this in 1938. Prominent in this photograph is J. J. Newberry's, always called the "Fair Store," Mermell Optical, and Bay Drugs. Other businesses shown include Foodland and Grand Union.

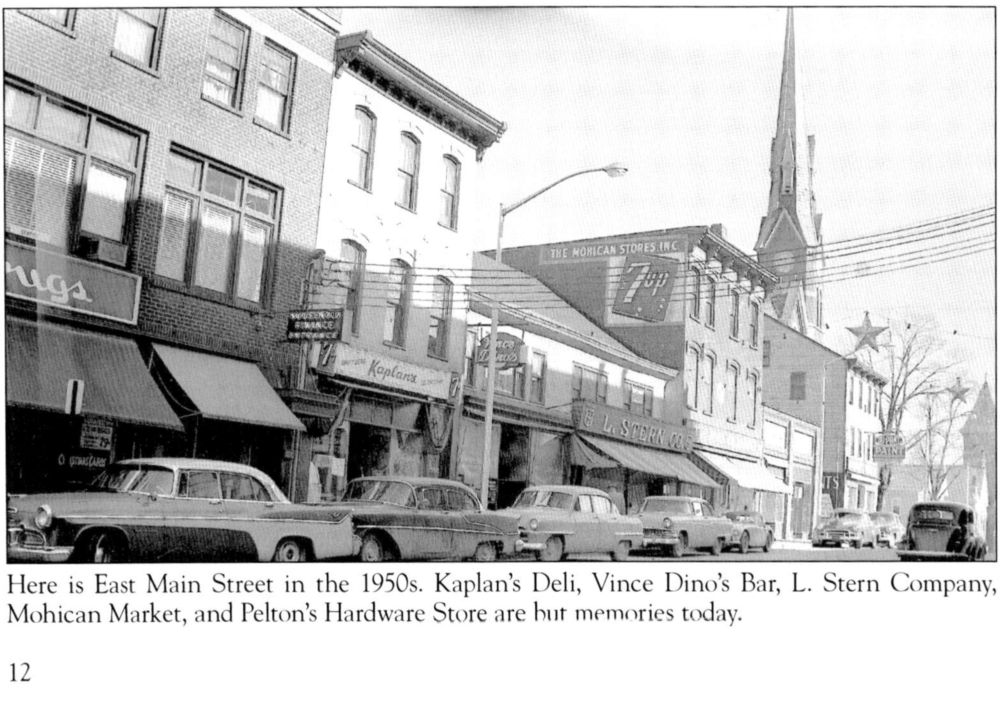

Here is East Main Street in the 1950s. Kaplan's Deli, Vince Dino's Bar, L. Stern Company, Mohican Market, and Pelton's Hardware Store are but memories today.

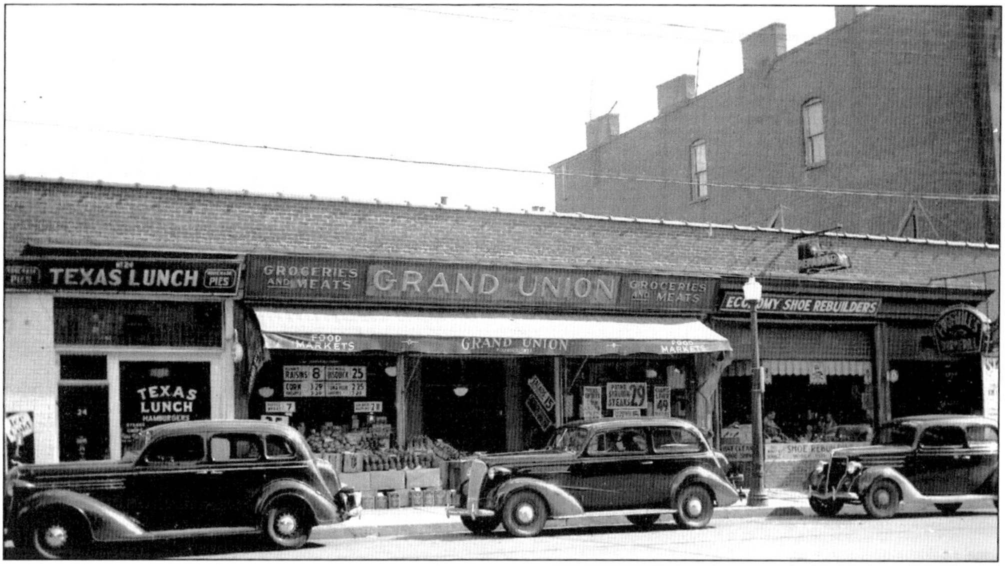

This 1938 view of East Main Street shows the Grand Union store, the Texas Lunch, and Economy Shoe Rebuilders. Freehill's Tavern is next door. The cars at the curb, from left to right, are a Dodge, Chevrolet, and Ford.

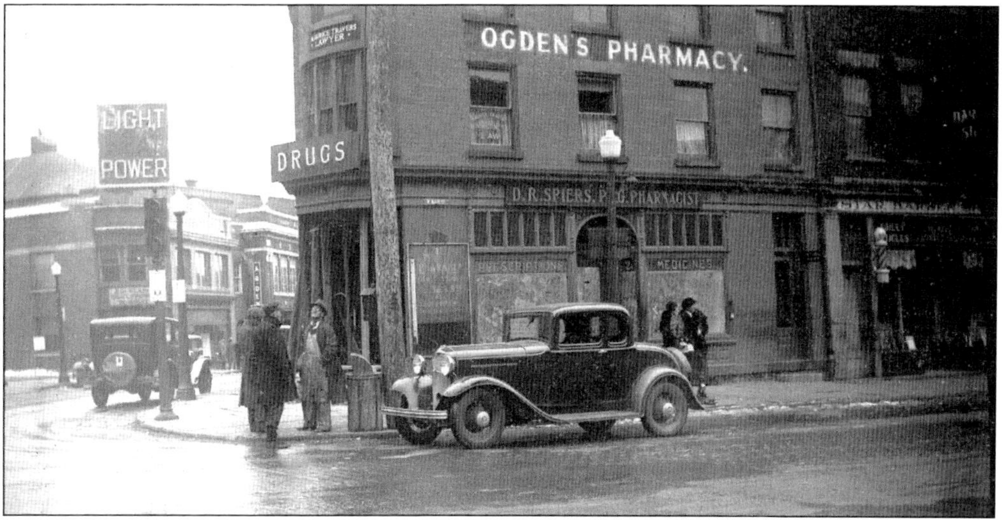

This photograph shows Franklin Square on a rainy day in 1932. Ogden's Pharmacy occupies the historic building at the corner of South and West Main Streets. Attorney Maurice Travers has his offices above. The Rockland Light and Power building can be seen on South Street.

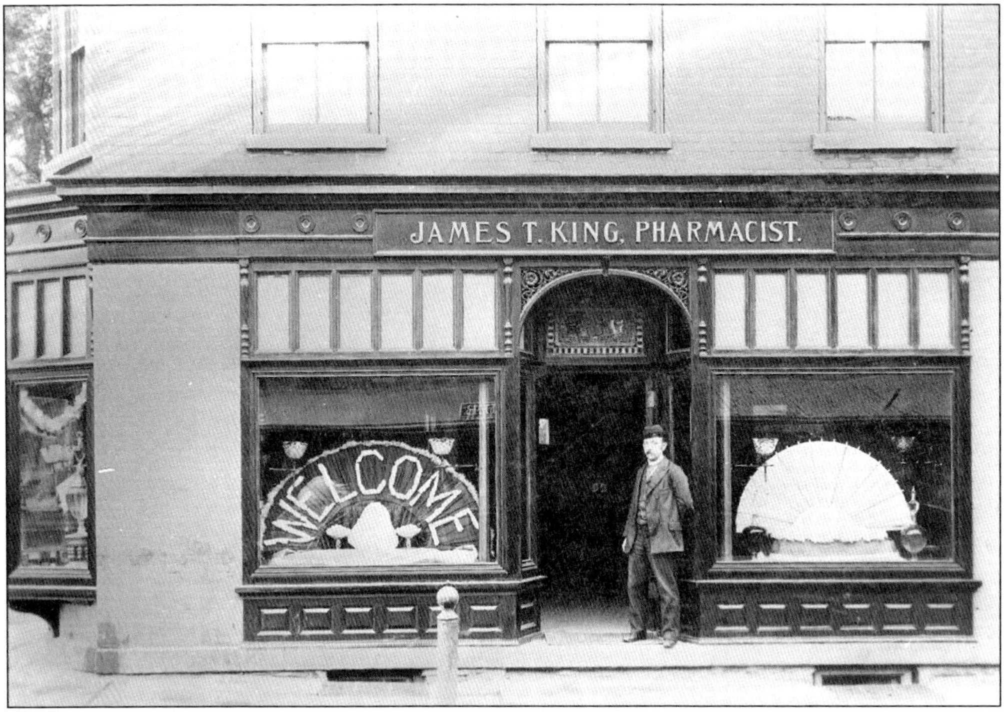

James T. King was operating the drug store on the square when this photograph was taken.

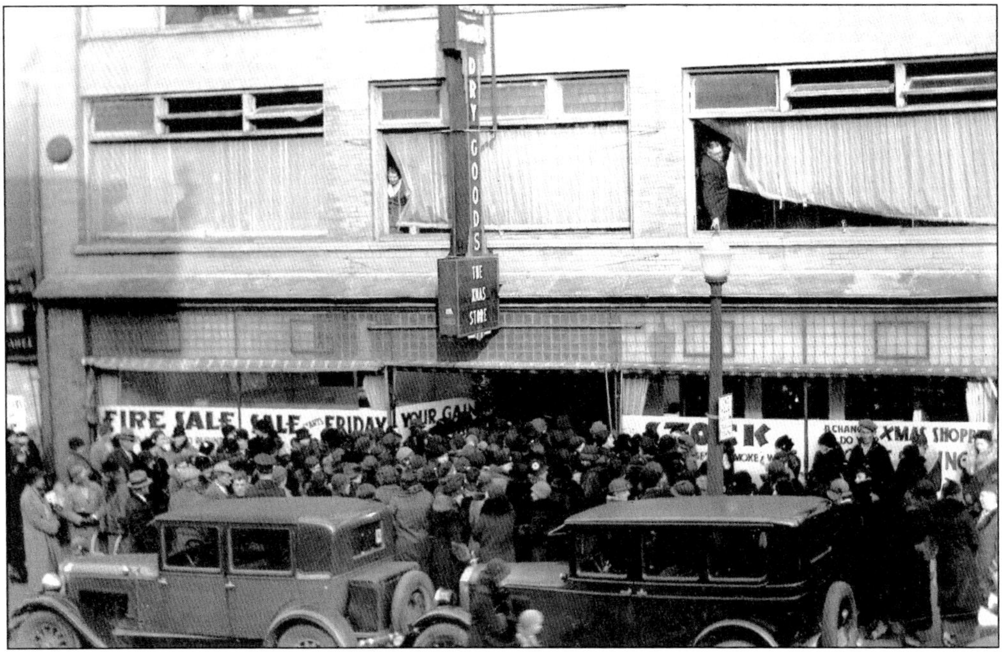

One of Middletown's oldest businesses was Carson and Towner Dry Goods Company, at 7–11 West Main Street. On November 29, 1933, with the store filled with Christmas merchandise, there was a smoky fire in the building next door. Two days later, large crowds gathered for a fire sale. The photograph shows the opening of the store at 9:00 a.m. on Friday, December 1, 1933. The site today is occupied by the Olde Erie Brew Pub.

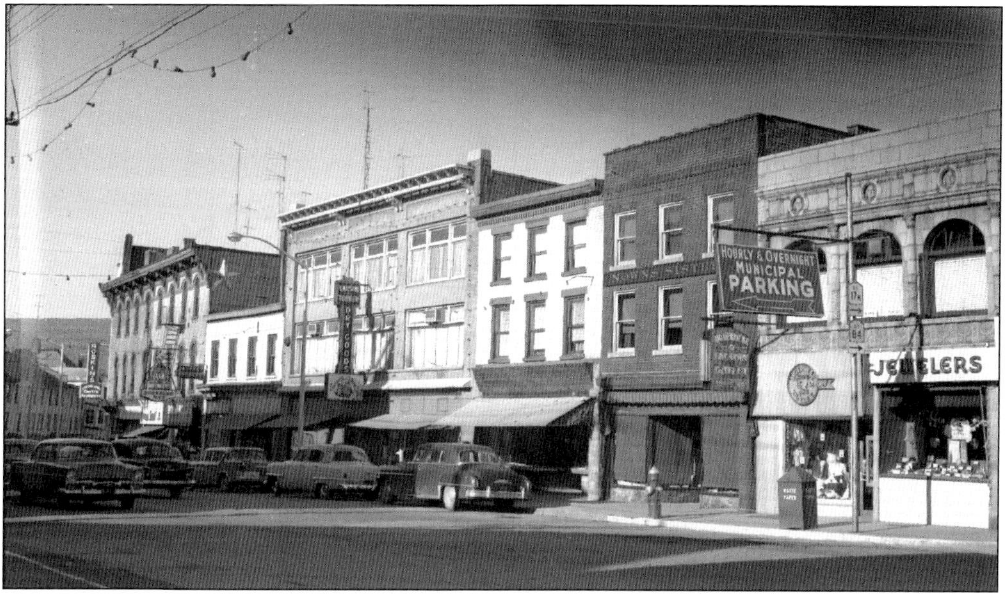

This view of West Main Street was taken at Christmastime in the 1950s.

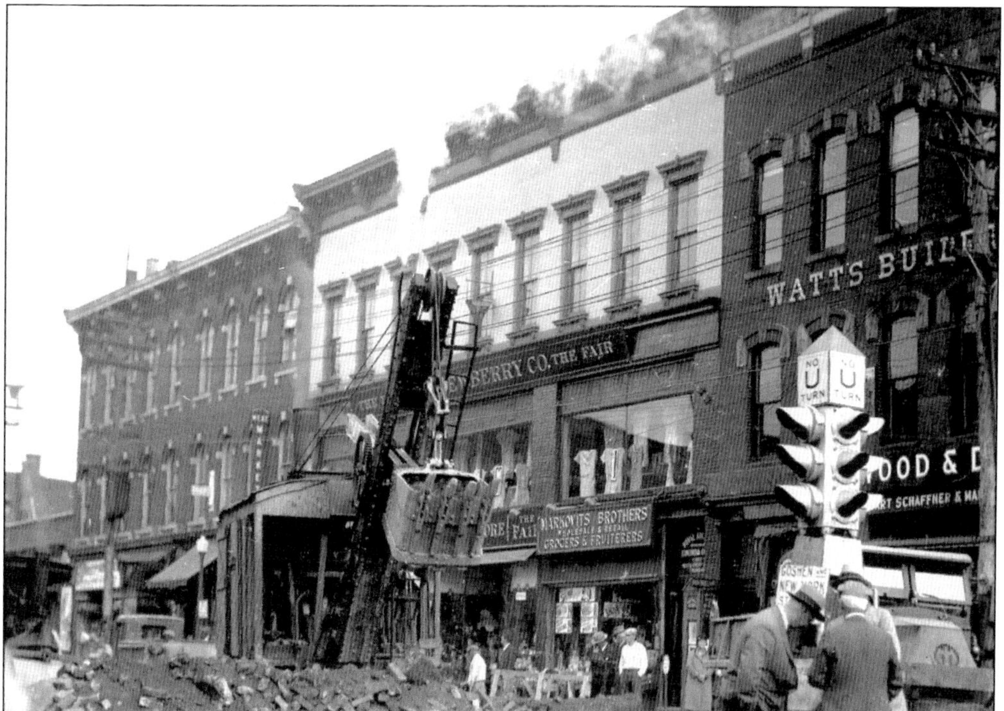

A steam shovel digs up East Main Street as a group of sidewalk superintendents watch. Shown is the Markovits Brothers grocery store and Wood and Doty men's clothing store. Wood and Doty later moved to North Street.

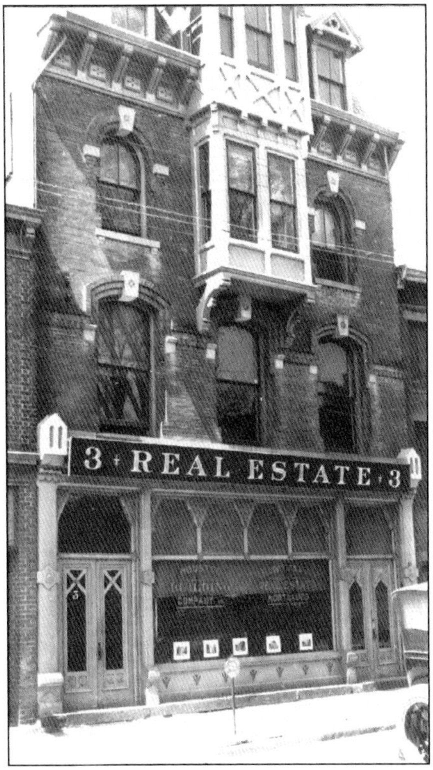

The distinctive building at 3 South Street was recently renovated. This 1915 photograph shows R. H. Houston Real Estate on the first floor. Next door, at 5 South Street were the Hupmobile dealership and the law offices of A. C. N. Thompson.

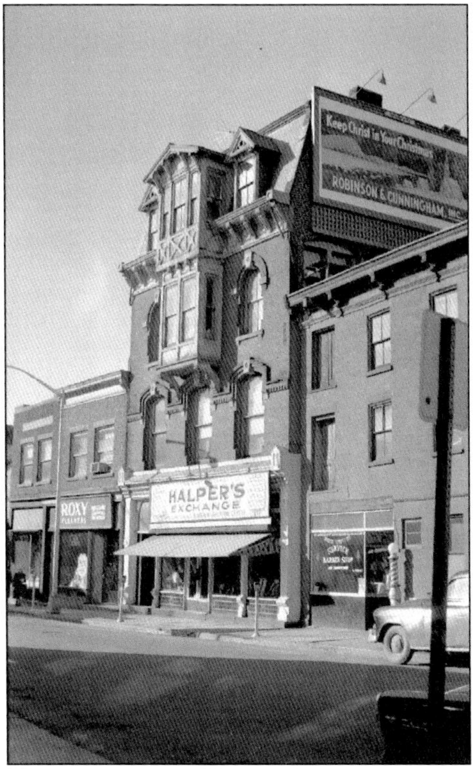

The Houston building now houses Halper's Exchange in this 1950s photograph. The billboard overhead bears a message from Robinson and Cunningham, a local stationery store.

Two

A Walk Up North Street

North Street has long been regarded as the primary business street of Middletown. Stretching from Franklin Square to the city limits, North Street has always been a center of commerce. In this chapter, many of the buildings and businesses of the street will be viewed, beginning at Franklin Square and walking north. As one strolls along the busy sidewalks, one will pass the intersection of Orchard and Depot Streets, cross the Erie Railroad tracks, pass the corner of Courtland Street and Railroad Avenue, and shortly reach Wickham Avenue. A little further, and one will reach Low Avenue and begin to retrace their steps. Note that Low Avenue was not named for its elevation but for Judge Henry R. Low and is pronounced like "cow."

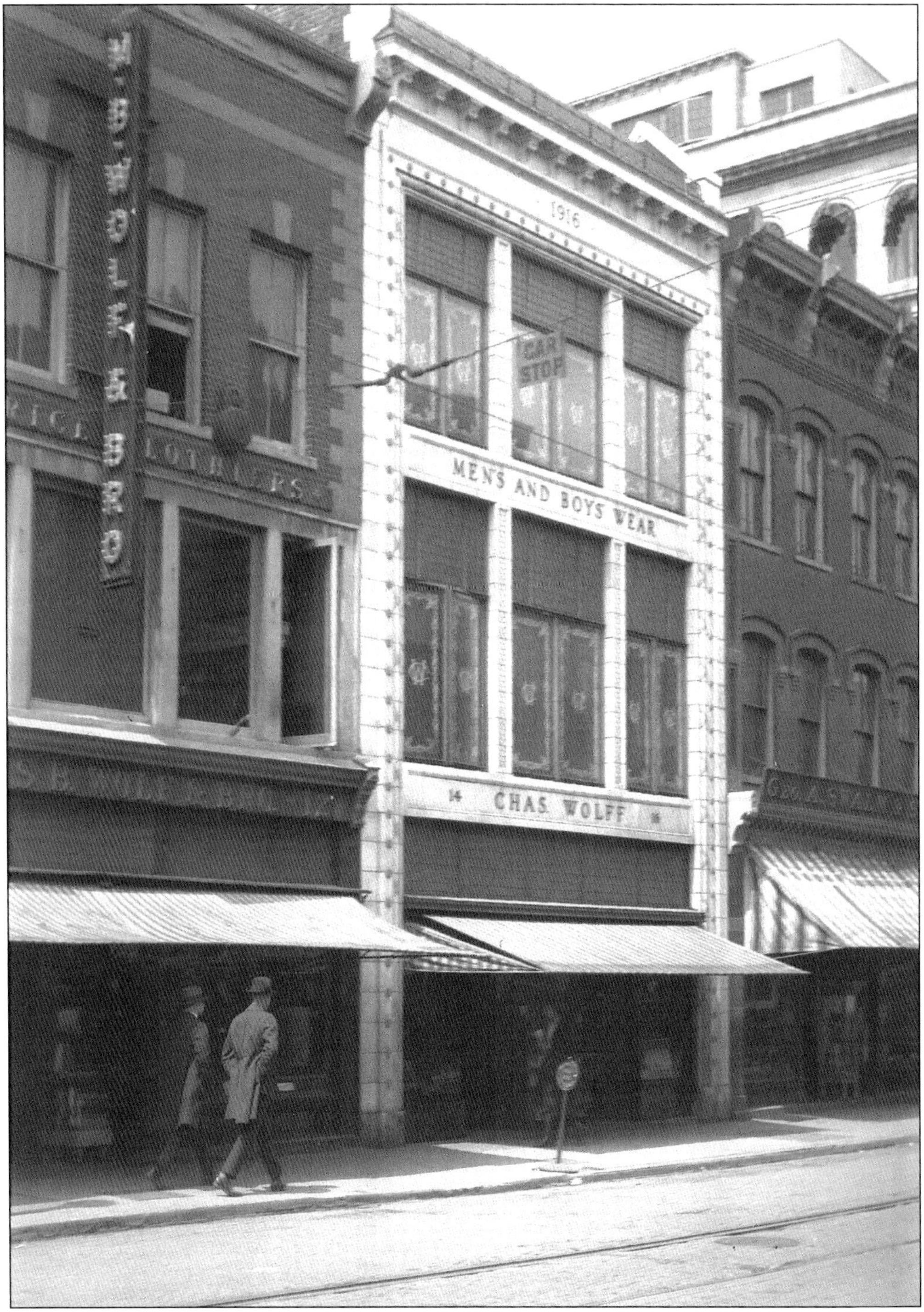

This view of the west side of North Street was taken in the 1920s. The Charles Wolff building looks much the same today, but the lettering was changed to read "Kassel Bros." The M. B. Wolf store became Wood and Doty. The sign in the center of the photograph, which reads "car stop," was for the trolley cars or street railway. The building is currently being rehabilitated.

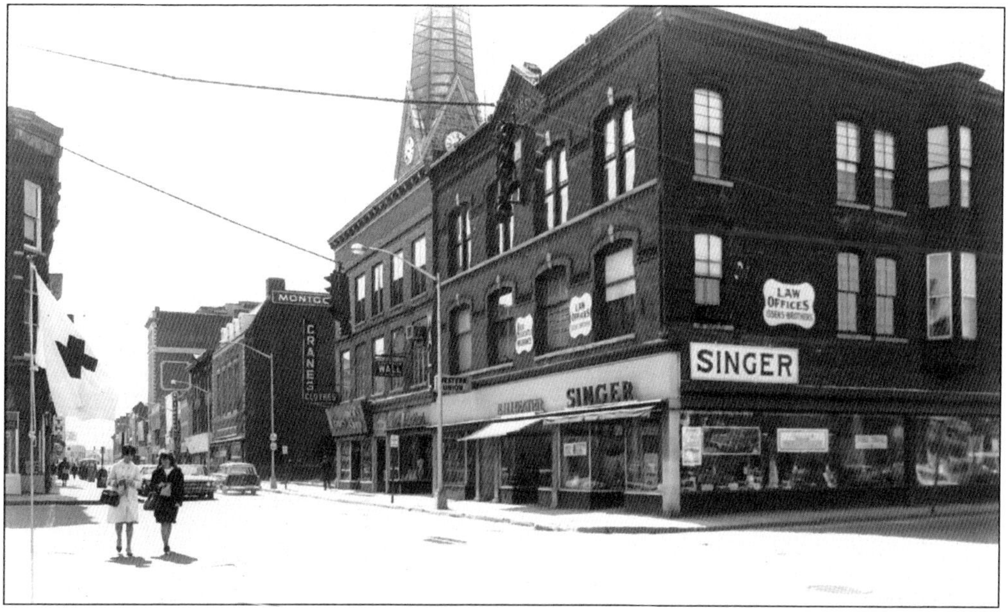

Shown is the corner of North and Depot Streets in the 1960s. The Singer Sewing Machine store was formerly S. T. Randall's radio and music shop. The building to the left housed Crane's Clothes, formerly Phil Wall's United Clothiers. The radio station WALL was located on the second floor along with Isseks Brothers Law Offices. These buildings were destroyed in a major fire in 1976, and the area is now a part of Grace Church's property.

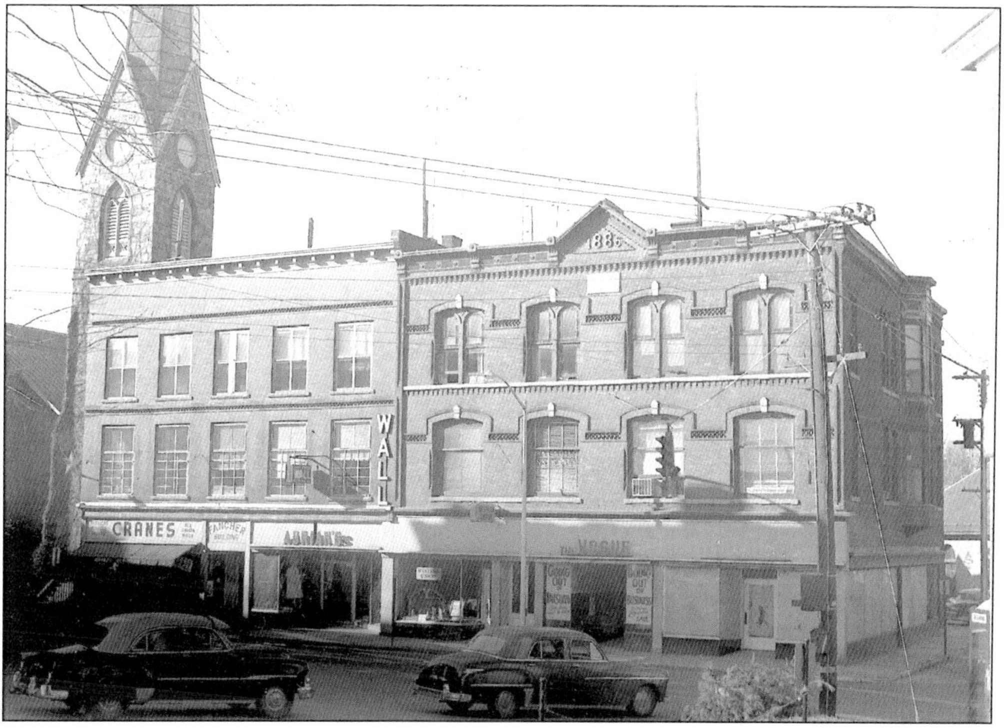

This is another view of the Fancher Building. Now the corner store is vacant, the Vogue store is going out of business, but Western Union Telegraph and Crane's Clothes remain open.

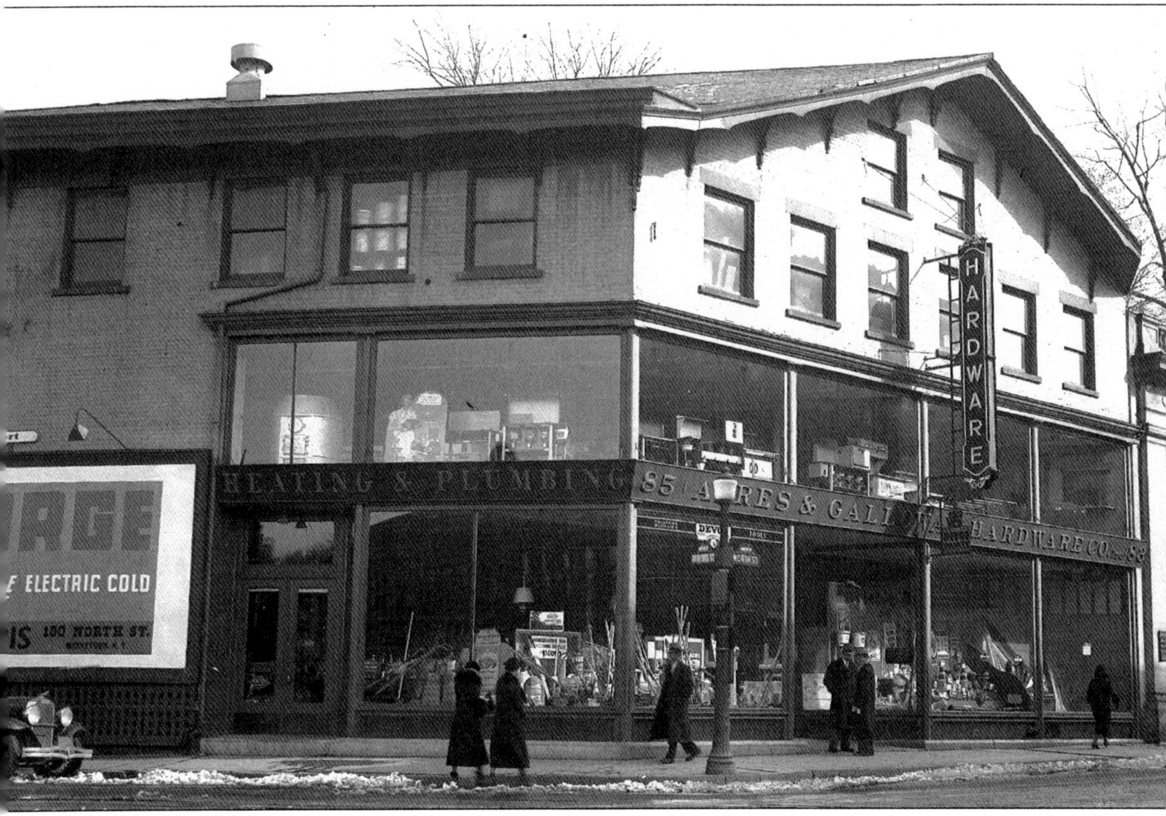

This vintage scene does not look much different today. Ayres and Galloway Hardware Company, one of Middletown's oldest businesses, remains in operation in the 21st century.

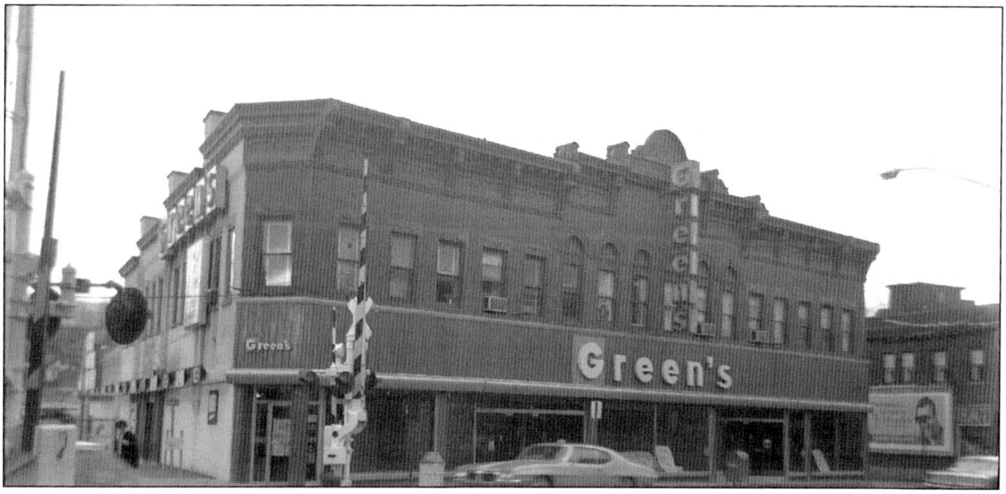

Green's Department Store was an institution on North Street for many years. The building still stands, but Green's Department Store is no longer in business. In this 1972 photograph, the store has just closed and moved to the Orange Plaza Shopping Center.

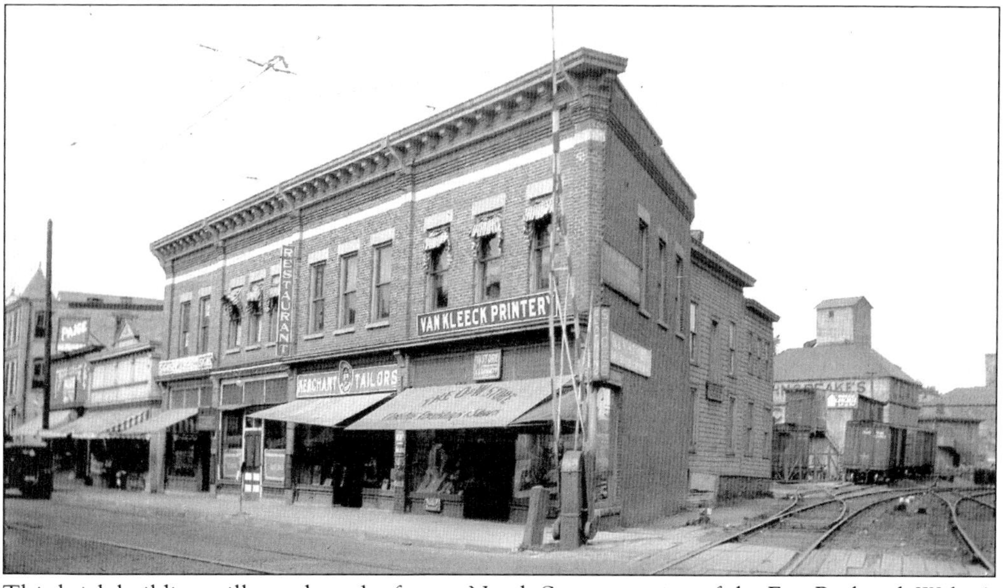

This brick building still stands at the former North Street crossing of the Erie Railroad. Weber's Army and Navy Store long occupied the ground floor in the foreground. Beakes Coal Company, seen along the railroad tracks, later became H. D. Gould Lumber Company. In the background, Empire Garage is selling Paige automobiles.

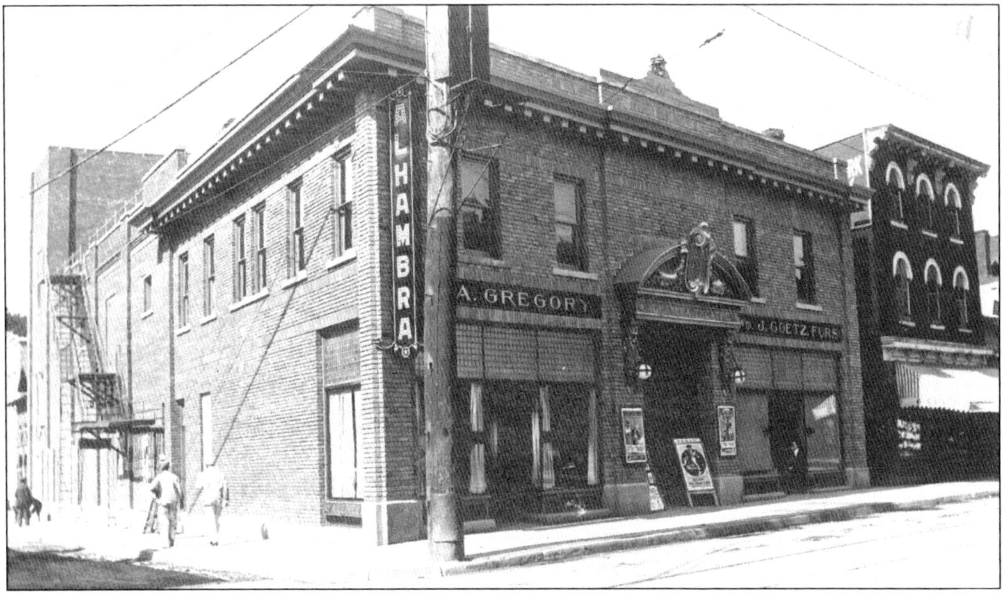

The Alhambra was Middletown's other theater after the Paramount, State, and Stratton. Located at the corner of North and John Streets, the building still survives. In this undated view, stores flank the entrance to the theater.

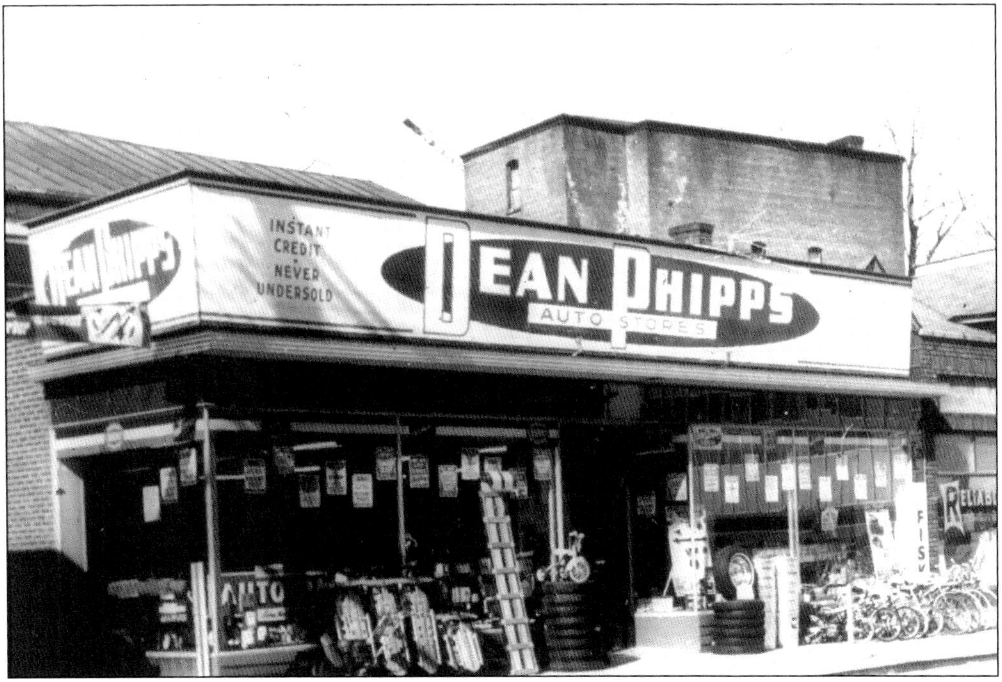

The Dean Phipps automotive chain had a store at 120 North Street, across from Sears Roebuck in this 1950 scene.

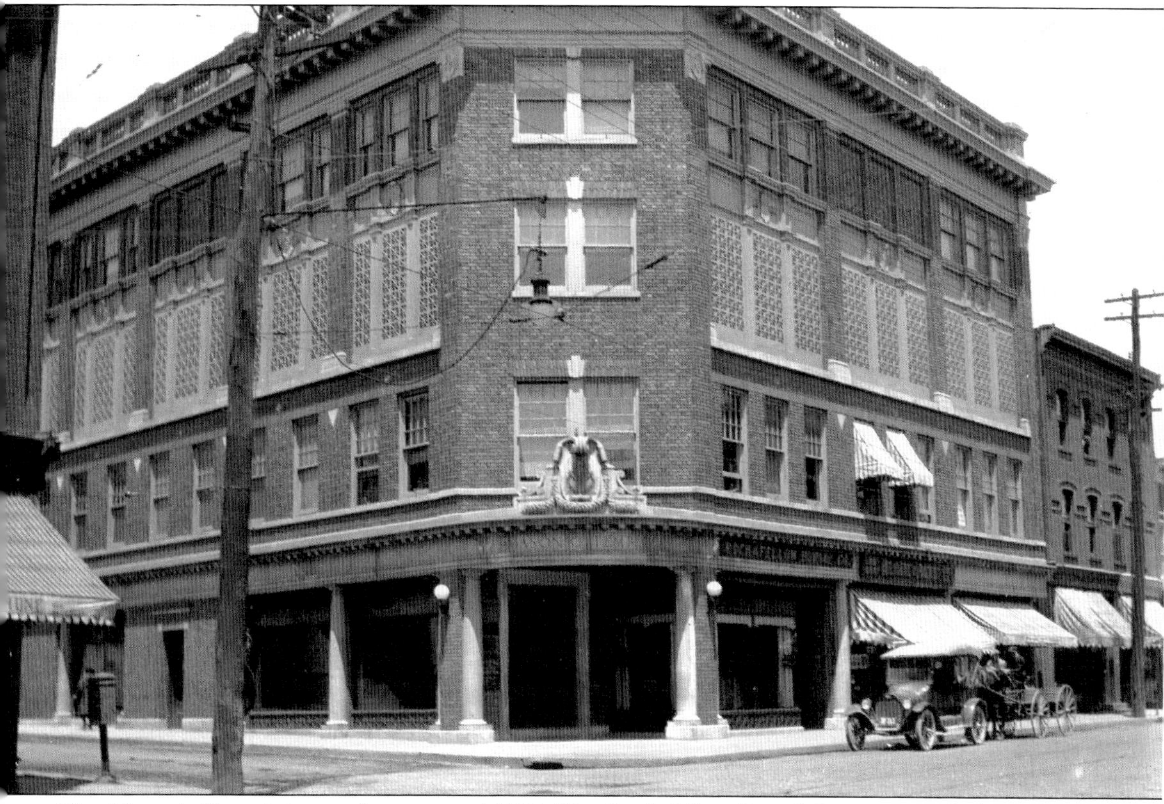

The Masonic Temple is seen here around 1922. The Rockefellow Burial Company and a branch of the A&P are on the first floor. The structure was ravaged by a serious fire in 1922 and was rebuilt. The ornate building still serves Hoffman Lodge today.

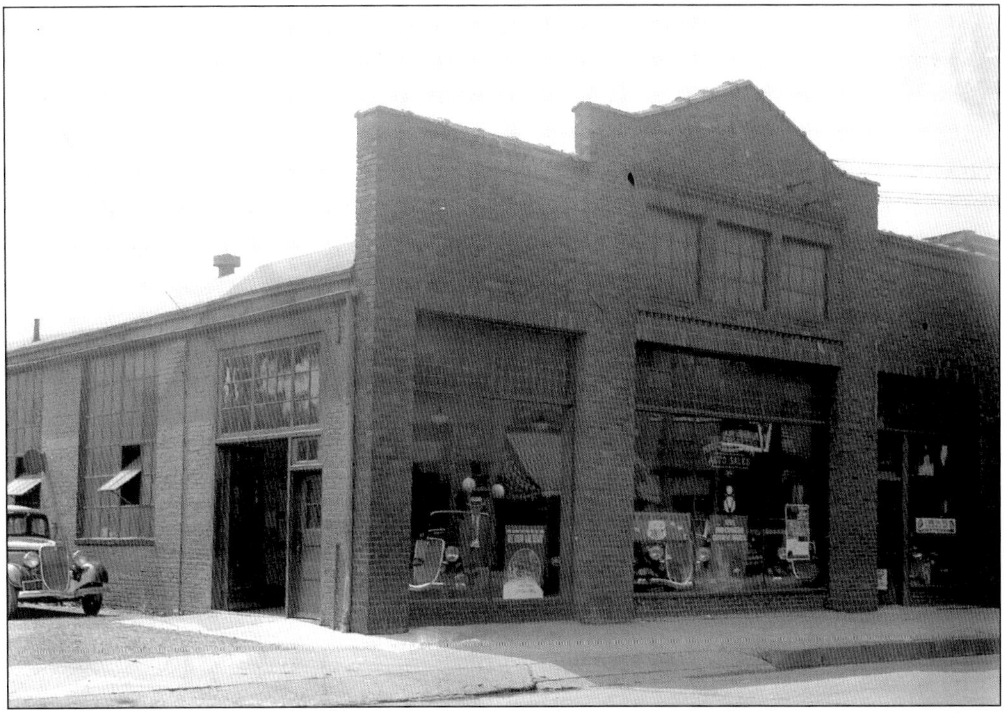

In years past, most automobile dealers preferred to locate near the center of the city. Shown here is Middletown Auto Sales at 131 North Street. On display are new 1934 Ford cars. The business later became Vee Motors, and when it relocated its showroom, the structure became Markovits Brothers Foodmart. The supermarket was destroyed in a fire on December 31, 1963, and the site today is a parking lot.

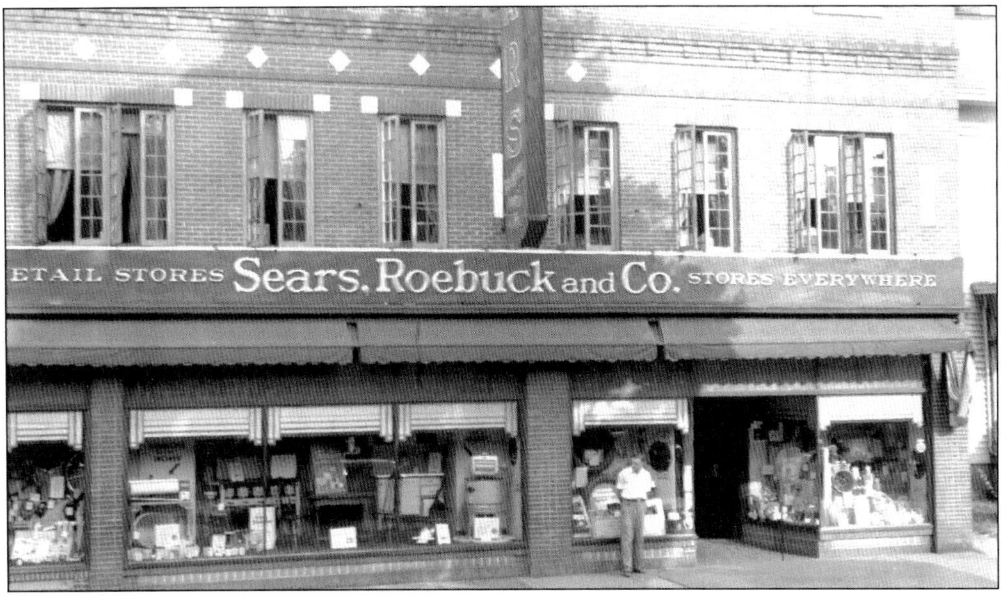

Sears, Roebuck and Company operated this store at 121 North Street. The two-story building is now Elliott's Furniture. Not to be outdone, Montgomery Ward also opened a store on North Street that is now vacant.

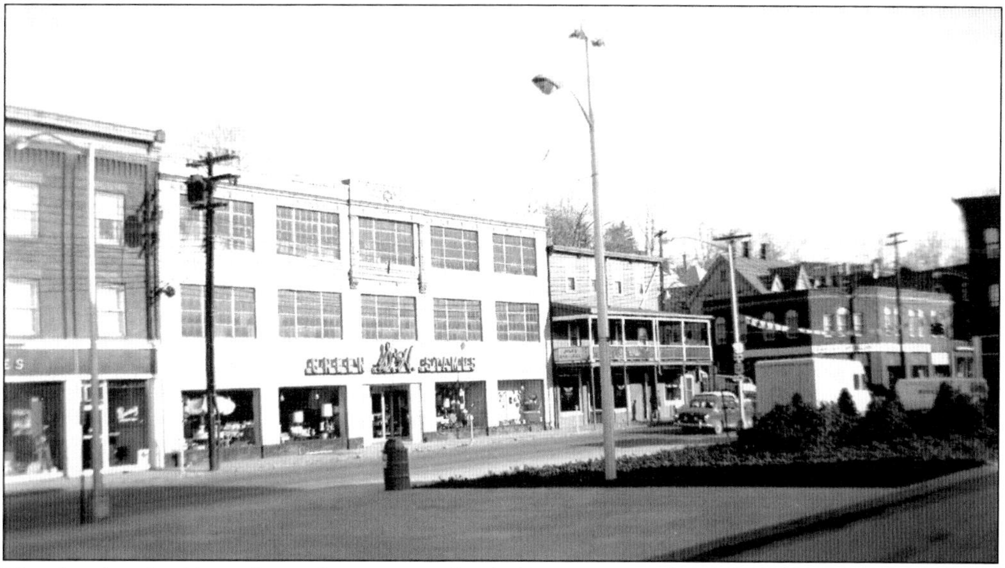

The familiar building shown here is on North Street across from the Chase Bank. Built by H. M. Stanton in 1927, this structure served as Middletown's Chevrolet dealership for many years. Internal ramps allowed cars to access the second and third floors. At the time of the photograph, it was occupied by S&H Green Stamps. Today the building is used as a warehouse by Kandel Brothers Electric Sales. The structure on the right with the balcony housed Jule's Bar and Grill.

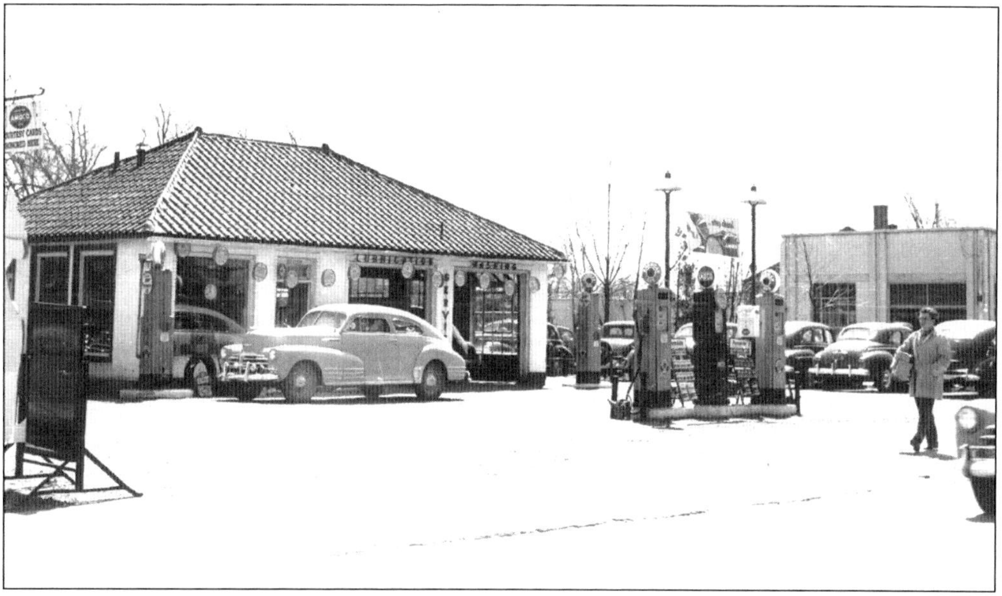

In 1951, there were two gasoline stations on North Street where the Chase Bank stands today. Shown is a typical neighborhood American Oil Company, or Amoco, station. The building next door was a Shell station. Both were removed to build the County National Bank building in 1959.

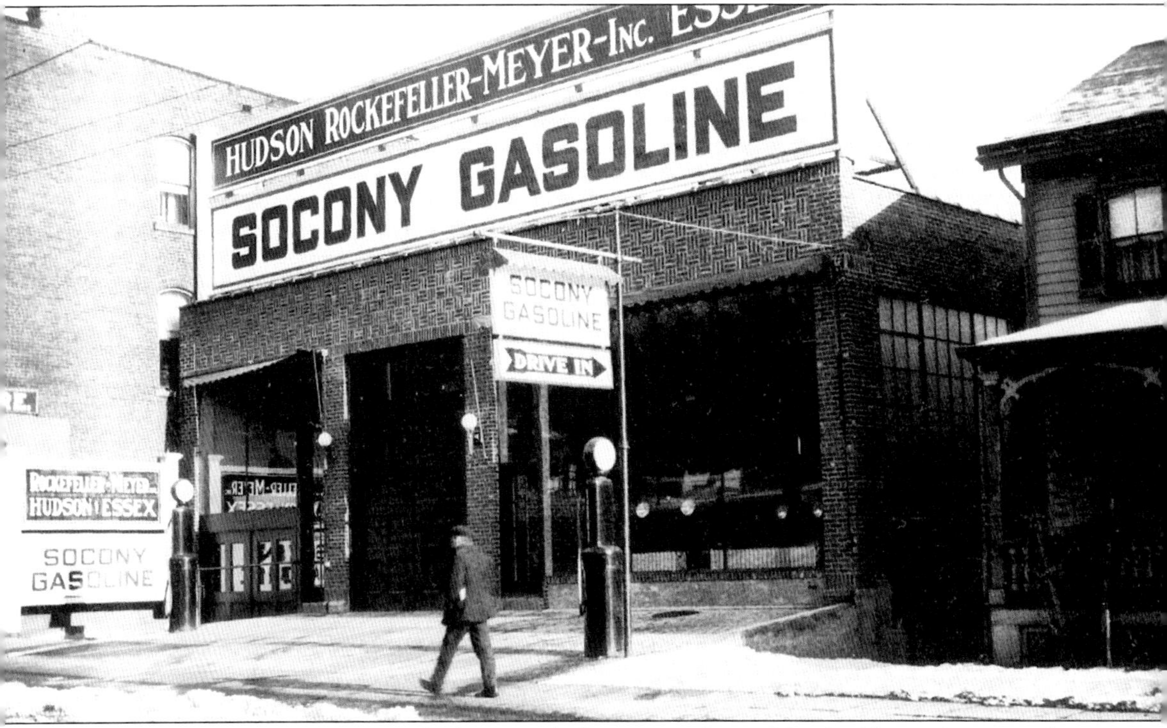

The structure shown here has had a myriad of owners and uses. This building is known today as the home of Kandel Brothers Electric at 151 North Street. In this photograph, Rockefeller-Meyer sold Hudson and Essex automobiles and Socony gasoline. Other car dealers later occupied this site. It was also the home of the Times-Herald Record newspaper for a brief time. Socony was the acronym for Standard Oil Company of New York, later known as Mobil Oil Company.

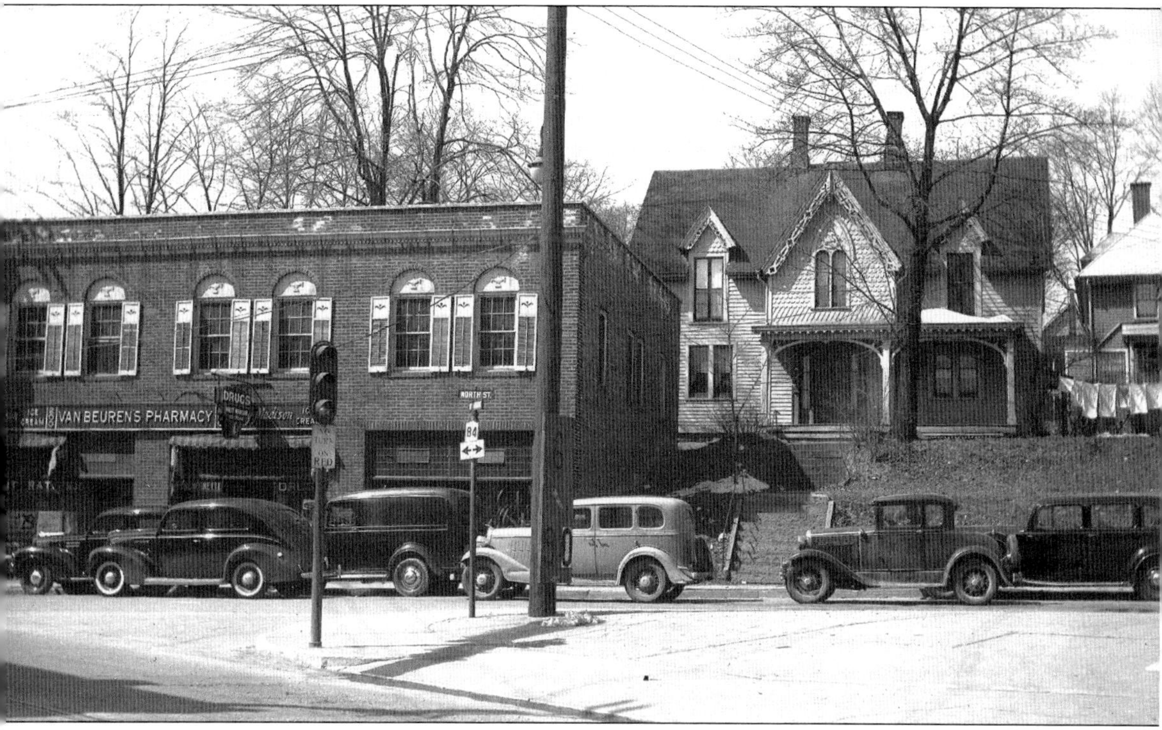

North Street near the corner of Wickham Avenue today is known as Park Circle. In this mid-1930s scene, the Chattle house is seen overlooking North Street. VanBeuren's Pharmacy is ready to fill a prescription or provide a delicious ice-cream sundae.

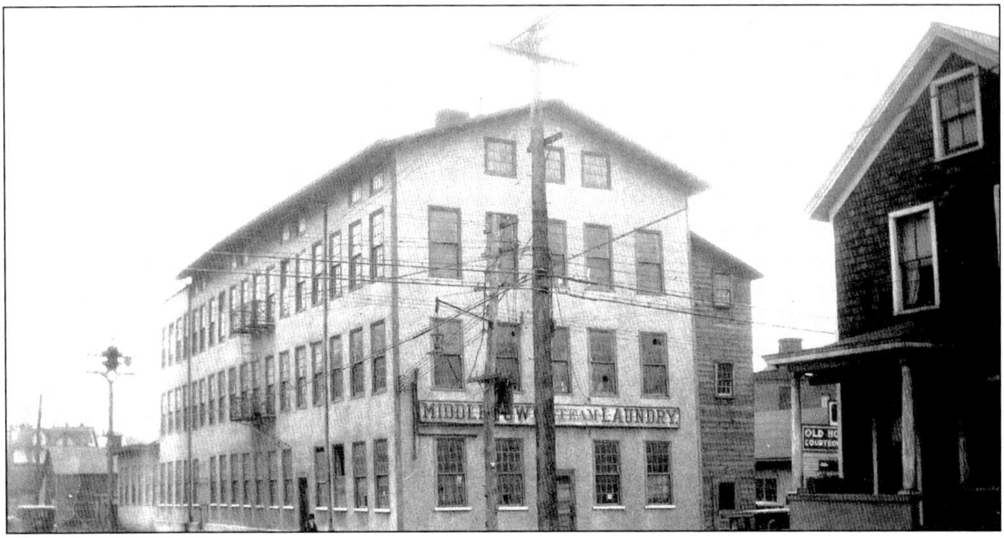

The scene shown here has changed out of all recognition. This is North Street and Low Avenue about 1927. In 1929, Barney Cohen built a gasoline service station on the site of the Middletown Steam Laundry.

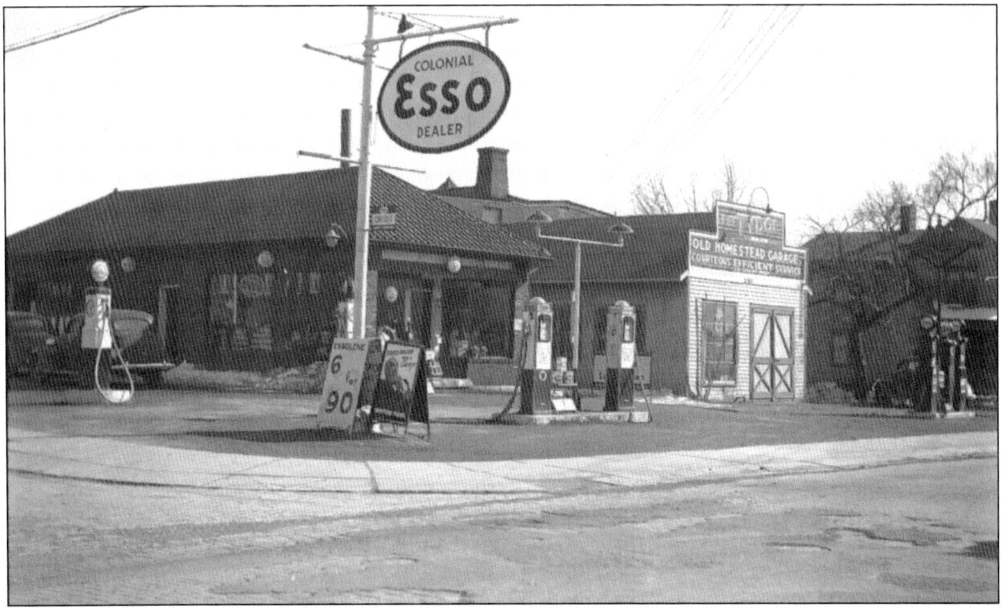

This photograph is of Barney's Esso Service in 1938. In those days, one could buy six gallons of gasoline for 90¢. Note the Old Homestead Garage, visible in both photographs, operated by Joseph N. Grant. Grant was a veteran mechanic who would work on any automobile, no matter how old, as long as it was not a Ford. A sign hung prominently inside stating "We Do Not Work on Fords."

Three

Some Street Scenes

Middletown, of course, boasted many other streets than North Street and Franklin Square. There were neighborhood stores and small businesses, light and heavy industry, factories, and residences scattered throughout the community.

Many street scenes were captured by amateur photographers. Businesses, theaters, houses of worship, homes, and events were captured on film for people to enjoy many years later. Particularly interesting are the scenes Truman Moon captured of "before and after." Moon could be depended upon to record the ever-changing scenes of Middletown. A number of other gentlemen also photographed the city, and many today are indebted to them for the images in this chapter.

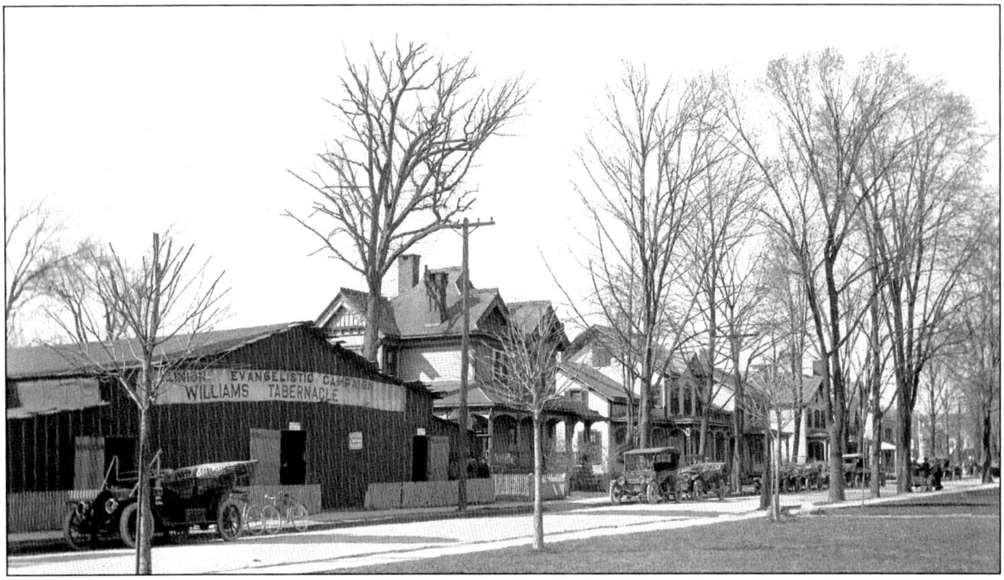

William's Tabernacle was located on Grove Street near the corner of Railroad Avenue and was built in 1915. Truman Moon recorded the construction of the building in April of that year.

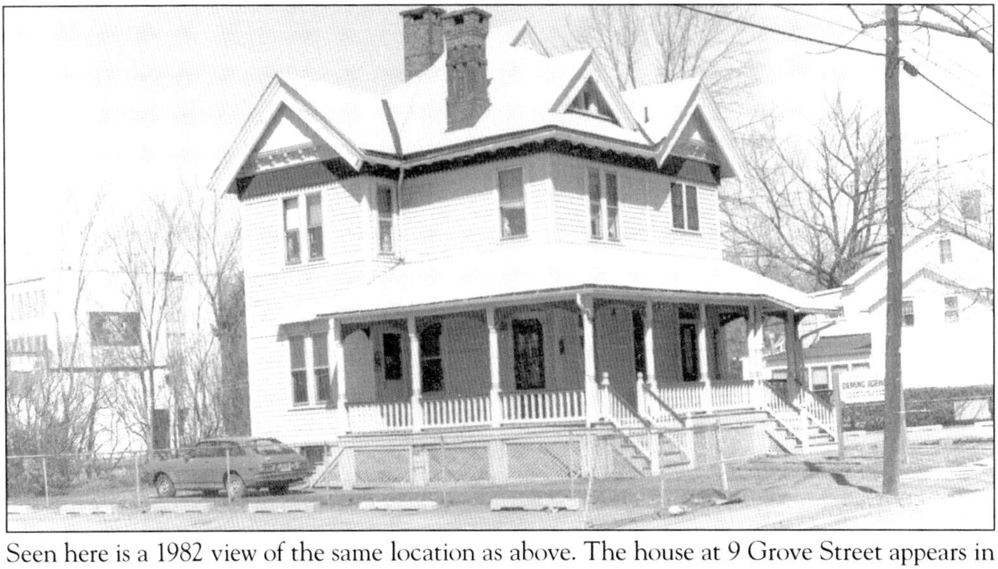
Seen here is a 1982 view of the same location as above. The house at 9 Grove Street appears in both photographs.

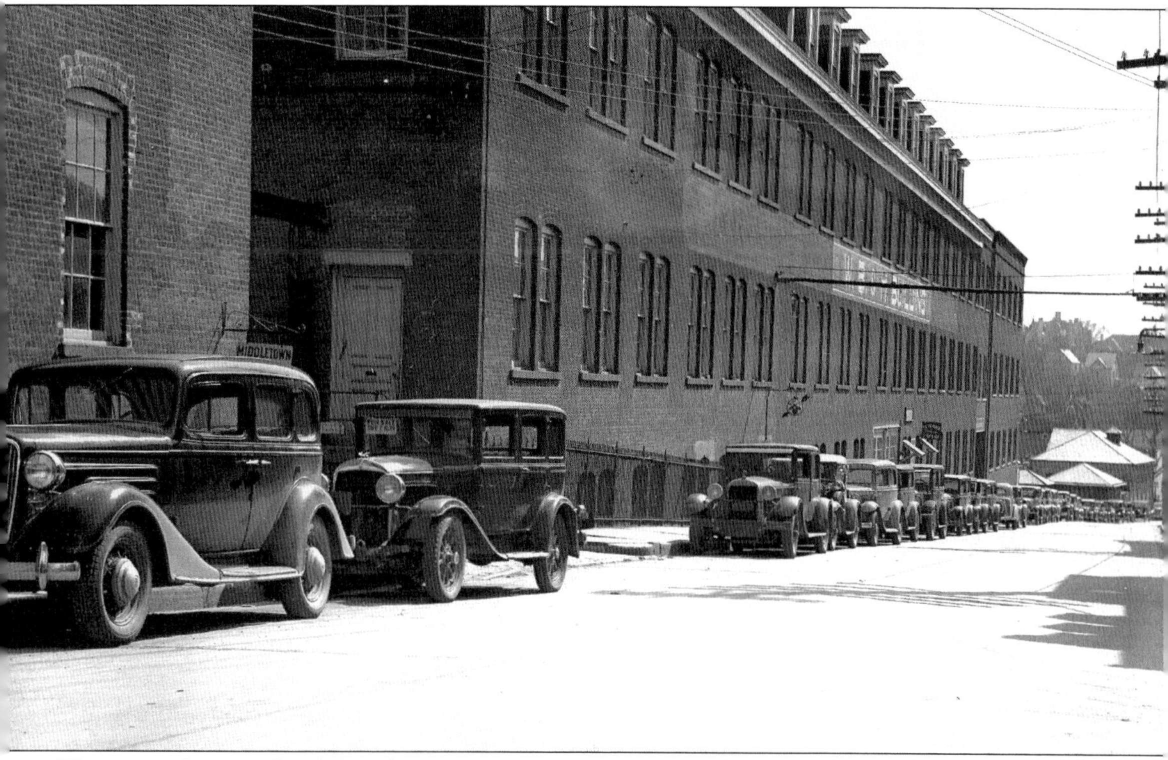

This is a photograph of Canal Street in 1935. The WB&H building, formerly the Borden Condensery, still stands. The street has been considerably widened since then.

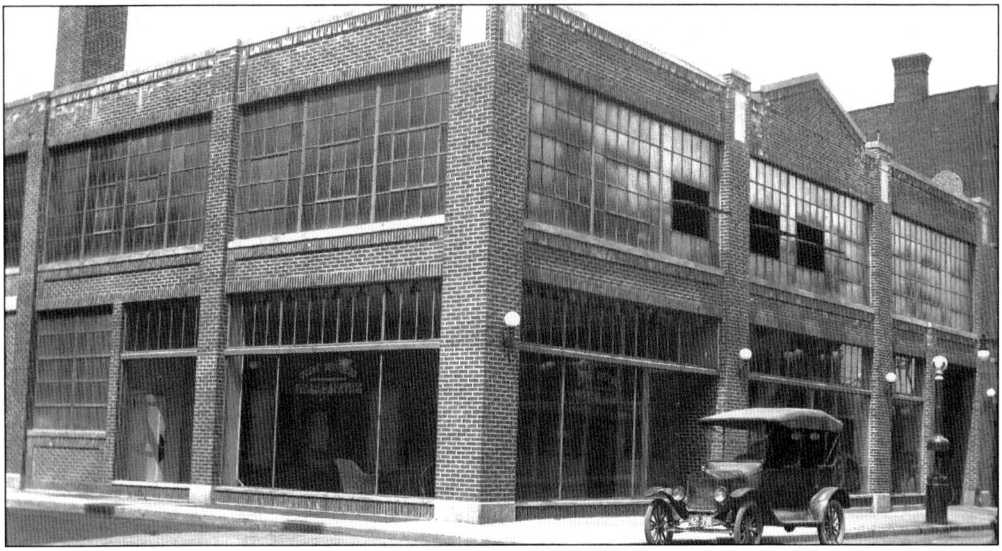

Middletown's Avon building was completely renovated in 2007. The building, on James Street at the corner of Henry Street, is shown in 1922 soon after being built. The structure was an automobile dealership known as Case-Kane Motors, Middletown's Dodge dealer. An internal ramp allowed cars to drive to the second floor.

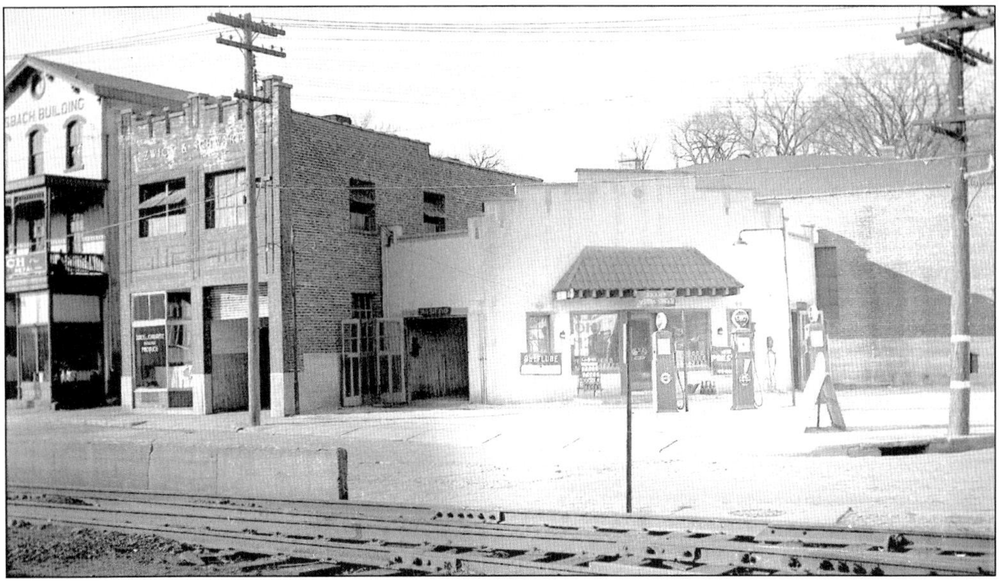

This photograph shows the corner of Union and Franklin Streets in the 1930s. The small building is now an automobile repair shop.

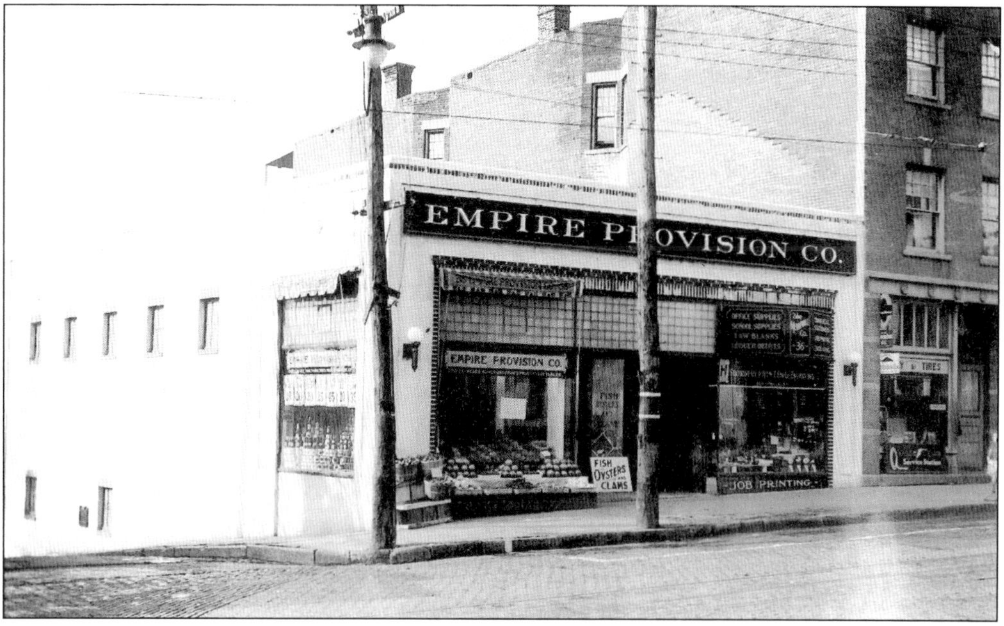

Here East Main Street and the corner of William Street intersect. The Empire Provision Company building now houses City Footwear. In the building to the right is Cavender's Tire Company.

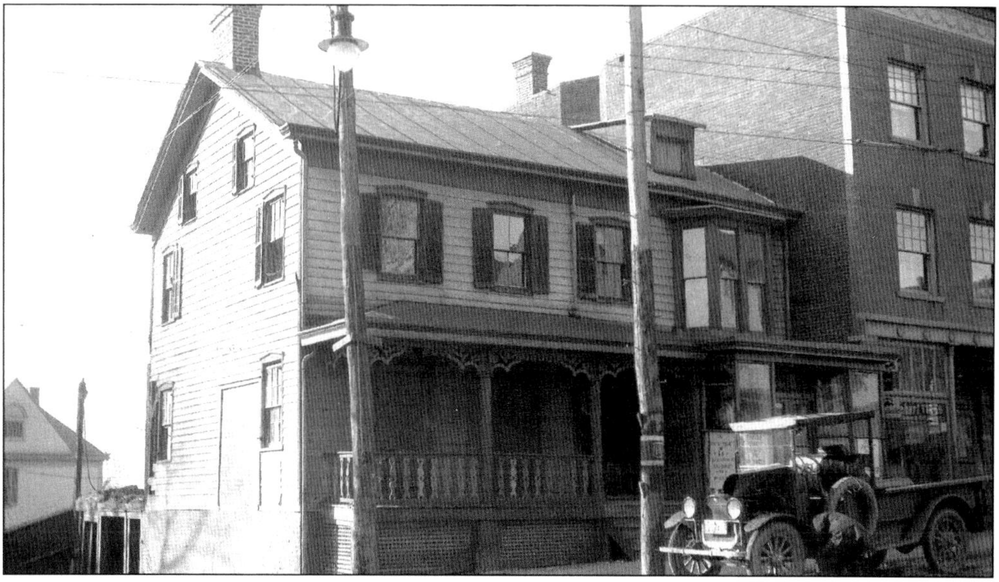

The same scene as above is seen here before the Empire Provision building was erected.

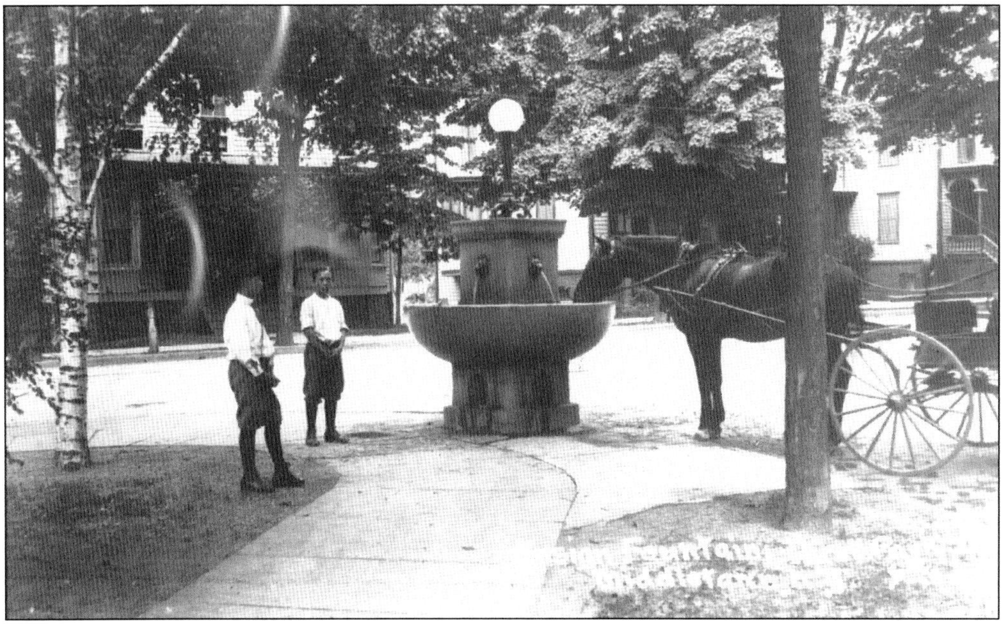

Middletown's drinking fountain for horses stood at the corner of Wickham Avenue and Grove Street adjoining Thrall Park. The indentations at the bottom were for dogs. Just visible is a tin cup for people. The fountain was presented to the city by the National Humane Alliance in 1903. The boy on the left is Roy Wilson, who went on to become chief of police of the New York, Ontario and Western Railway. The lower portion of the fountain remains in Thrall Park if one knows where to look.

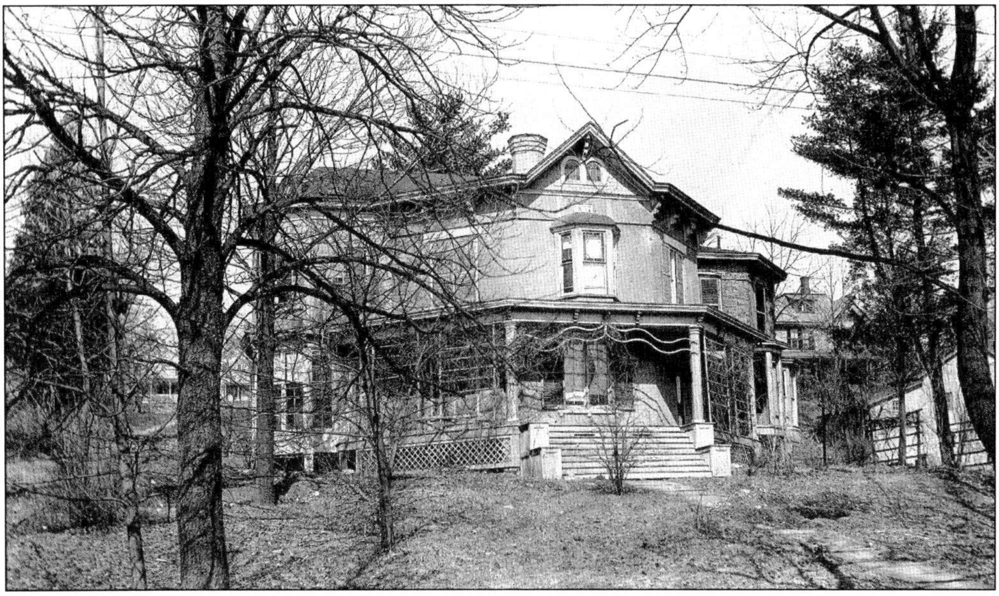

Middletown's only octagon house was located on Sybil Ridge, between Division Street and Beacon Street. The home of dress reformer Lydia Sayer and her husband John Hasbrouck, a newspaper editor, the building was torn down to build Memorial Junior High School. The name Sybil Ridge refers to Lydia's national publication the *Sybil*, which advocated women's dress reform in the hoop-skirt era. Division Street was later renamed Linden Avenue.

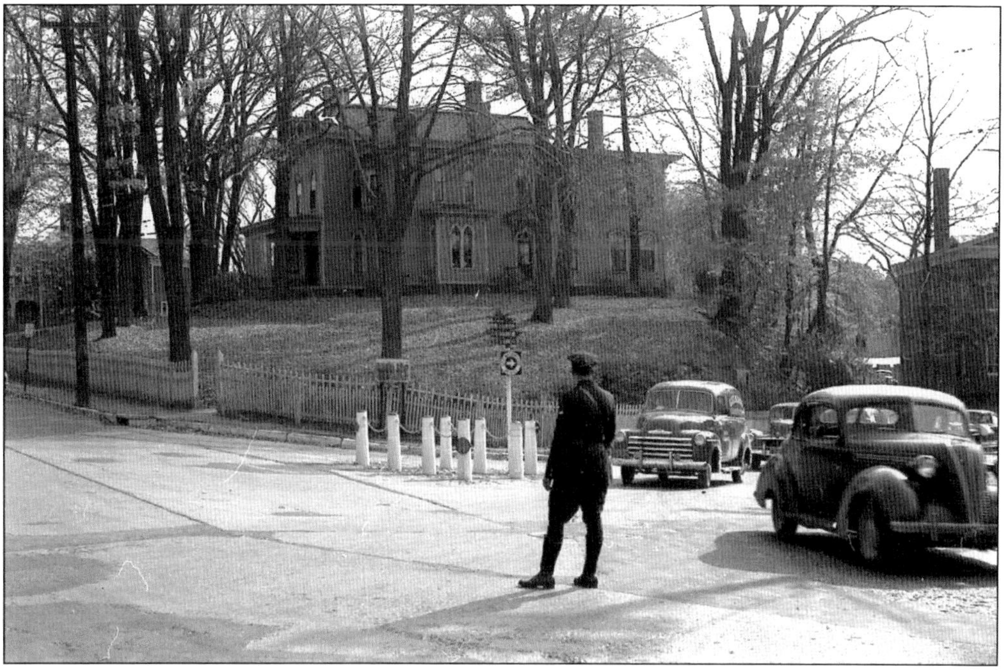

A policeman directs traffic at Academy and East Main Streets as Route 17 traffic flows through the city. In the background is the Schwartz house, torn down to build an automobile dealership in 1956. Benton Avenue School is shown above the vintage Hudson coupe.

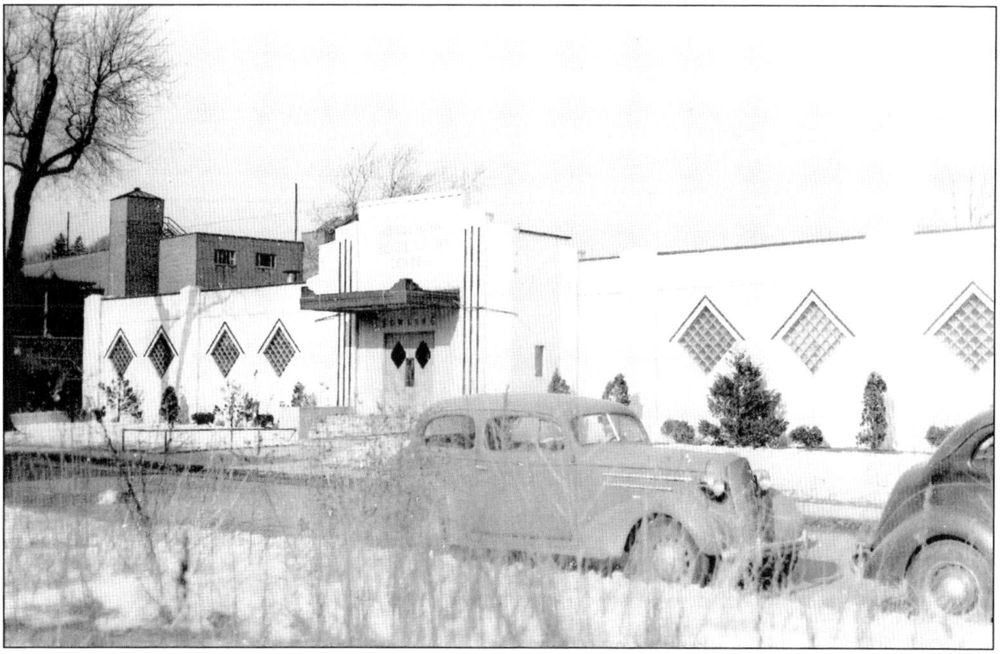

The Middletown Recreation Center on Railroad Avenue in March 1946. Today known as Middletown Lanes, the building remains the city's local bowling alley.

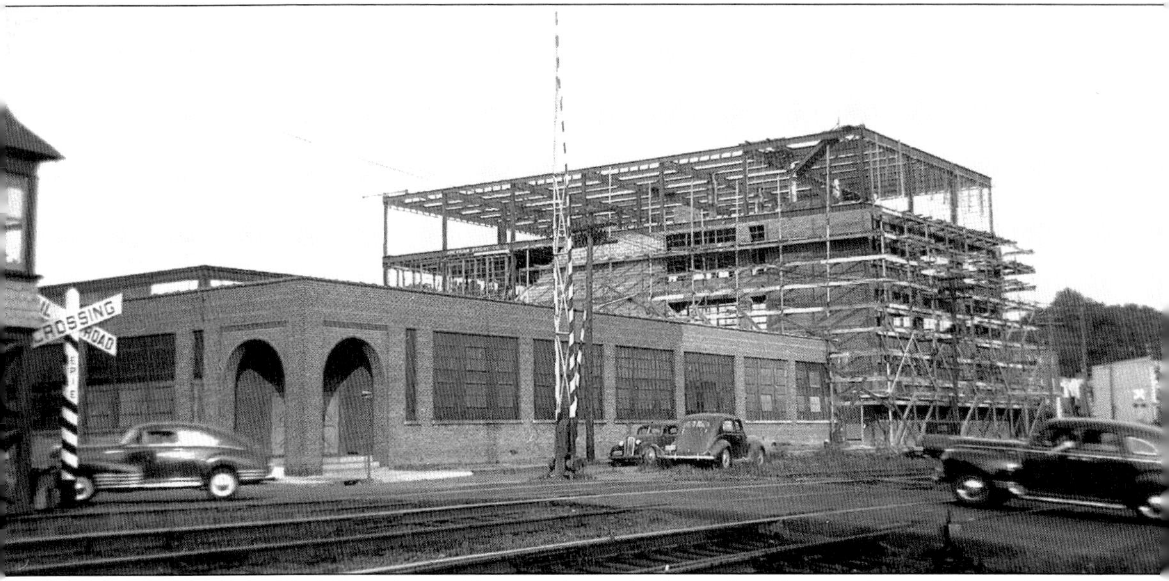

It is the spring of 1947, and an addition is being built on the Clemson Lawn Mower plant on Railroad Avenue. The building still stands and is now Bright Chair Company, but much else is gone. Montgomery Street remains but no longer crosses the Erie Railroad, as the tracks, the crossing gates, and the gate tower are all history.

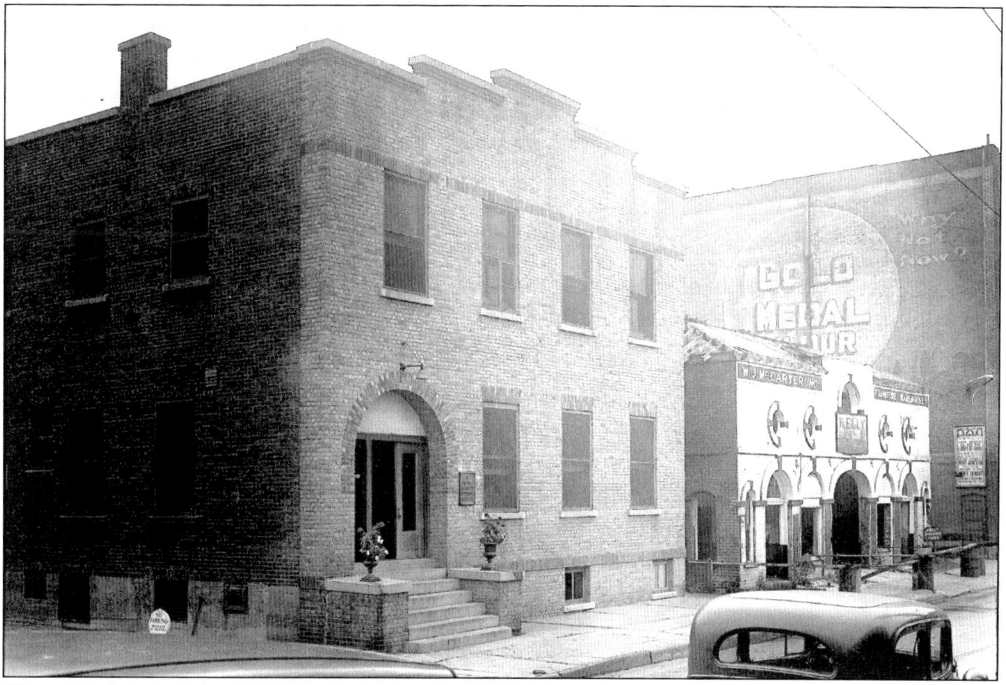

This is a photograph of John Street in 1935. The headquarters of the Orange County Telephone Company is shown in the foreground with the former Scott's Livery Stable beyond. These buildings were razed to build a new telephone company office that opened in 1938 and is still in use today.

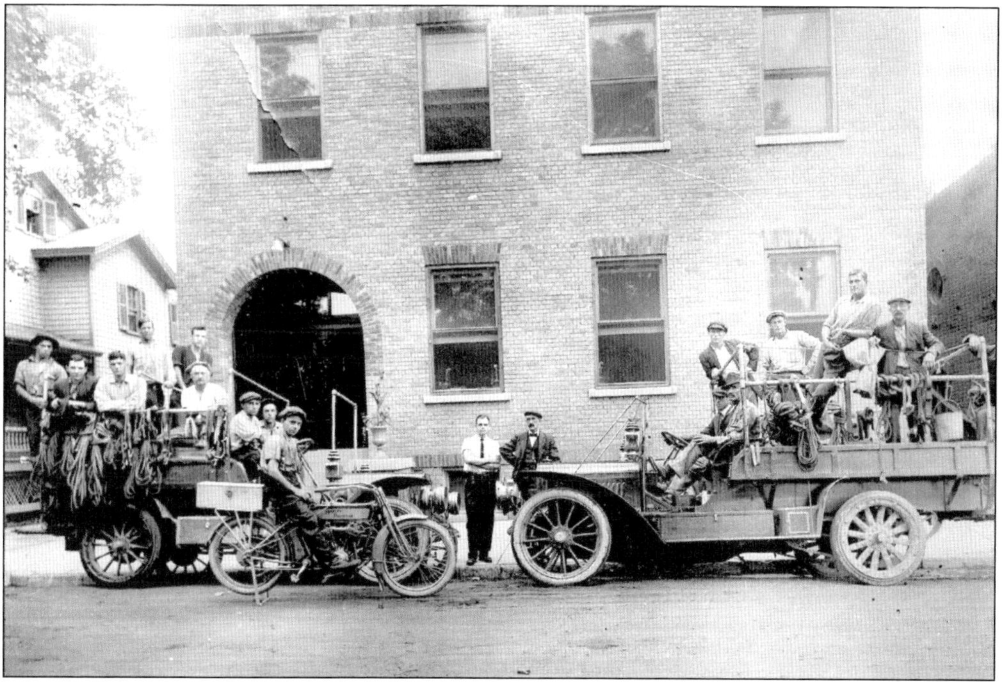

Orange County Telephone Company's trucks are posed in front of the old headquarters of the company on John Street in this *c.* 1910 photograph.

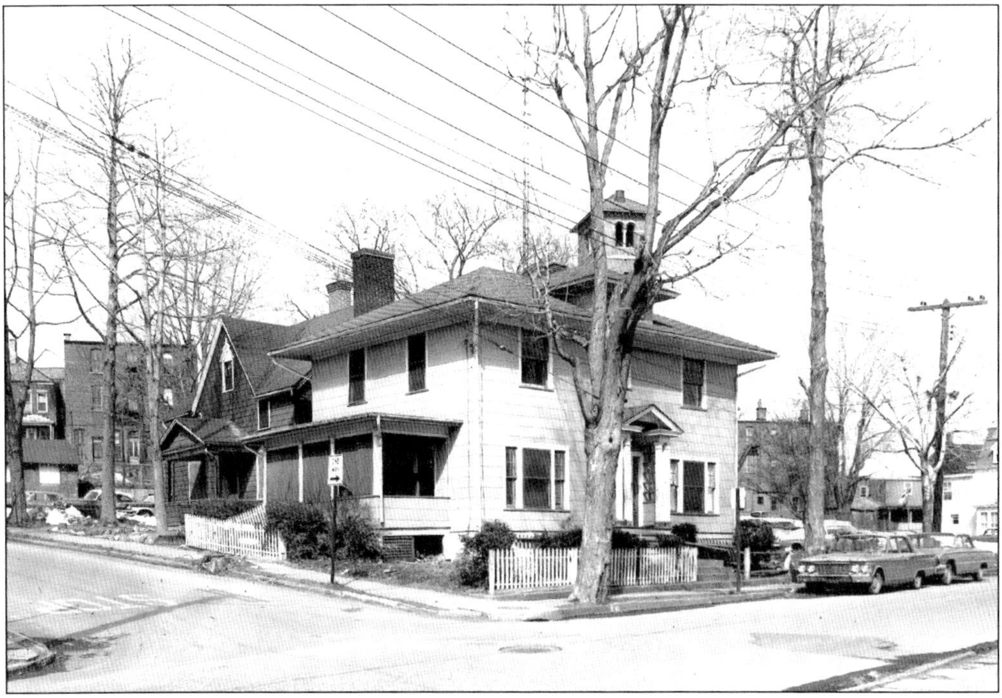

This home stood at the corner of East Avenue and William Street. This is now part of the rear parking lot of Webb Horton Church. There was a scheme to construct a home for the aged called Presbyterian Manor Apartments on this site, which did not come to fruition. Both this house and the one above it on William Street were razed at the same time.

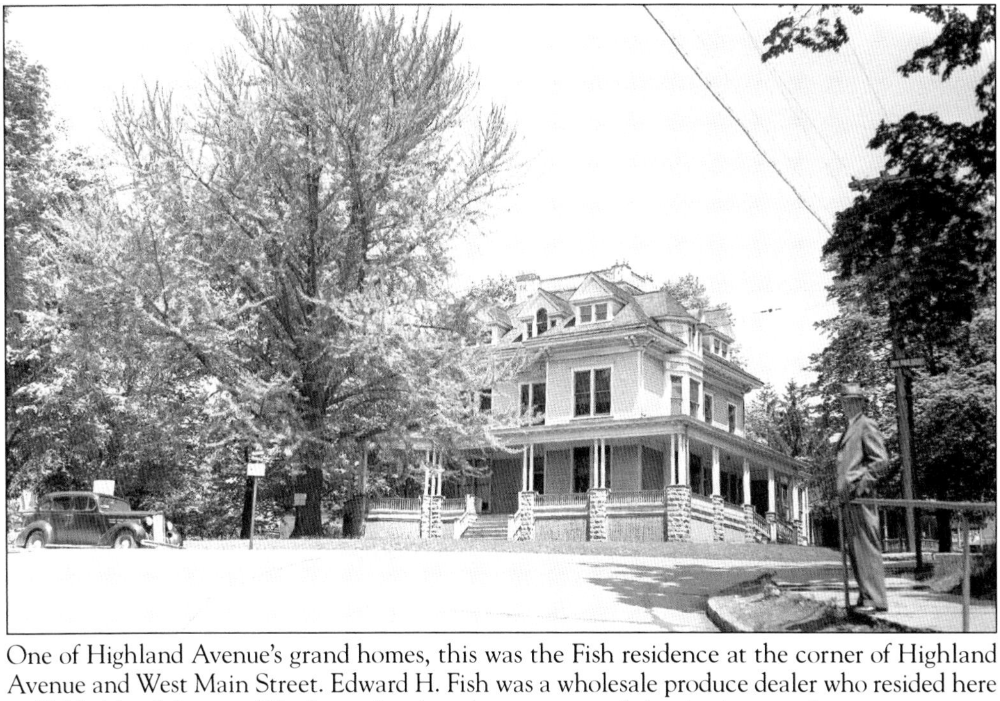

One of Highland Avenue's grand homes, this was the Fish residence at the corner of Highland Avenue and West Main Street. Edward H. Fish was a wholesale produce dealer who resided here at 27 Highland Avenue. The house has long been gone, and the site is now a lawn.

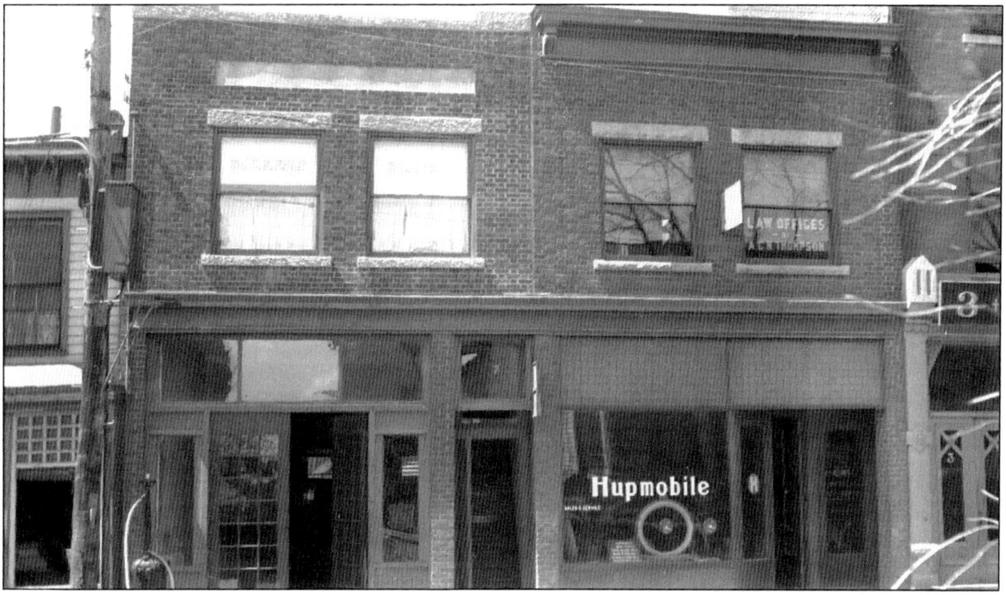

The building at 7 South Street housed the local Hupmobile dealer in this 1920s photograph. Notice the gasoline pump at the curb. On the second floor were the offices of dentist S. M. Holt and attorney A. C. N. Thompson.

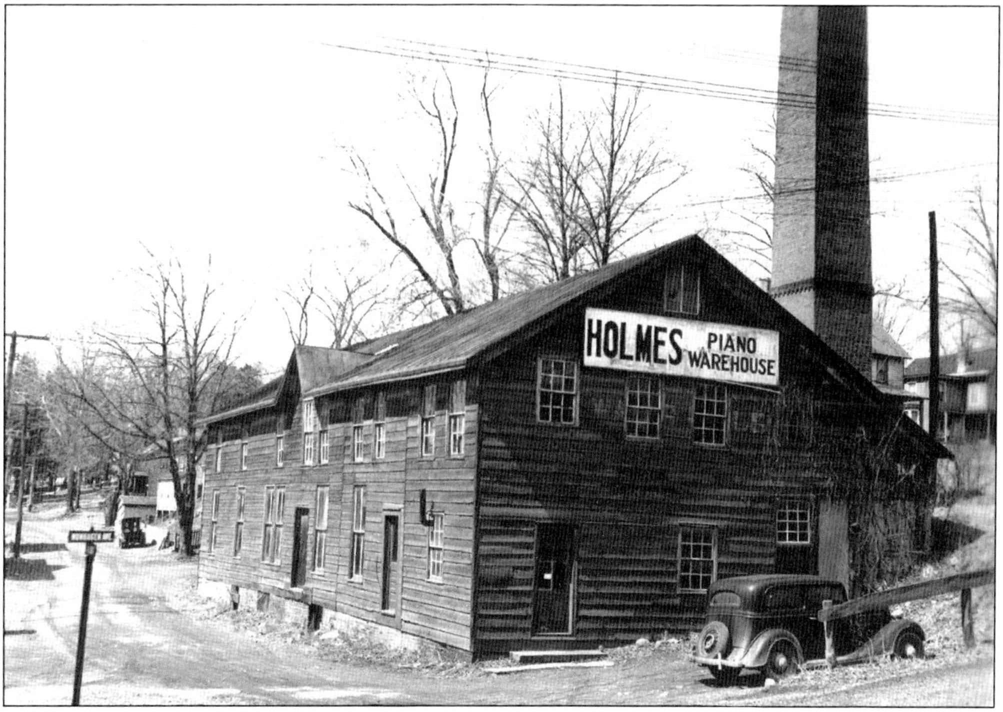

Still in existence today, this old building was originally the Houston Brothers Mill at the corner of Monhagen Avenue and Mill Street. Shown as Holmes Piano Warehouse in the 1930s, the brick chimney has since been removed, and the building modernized.

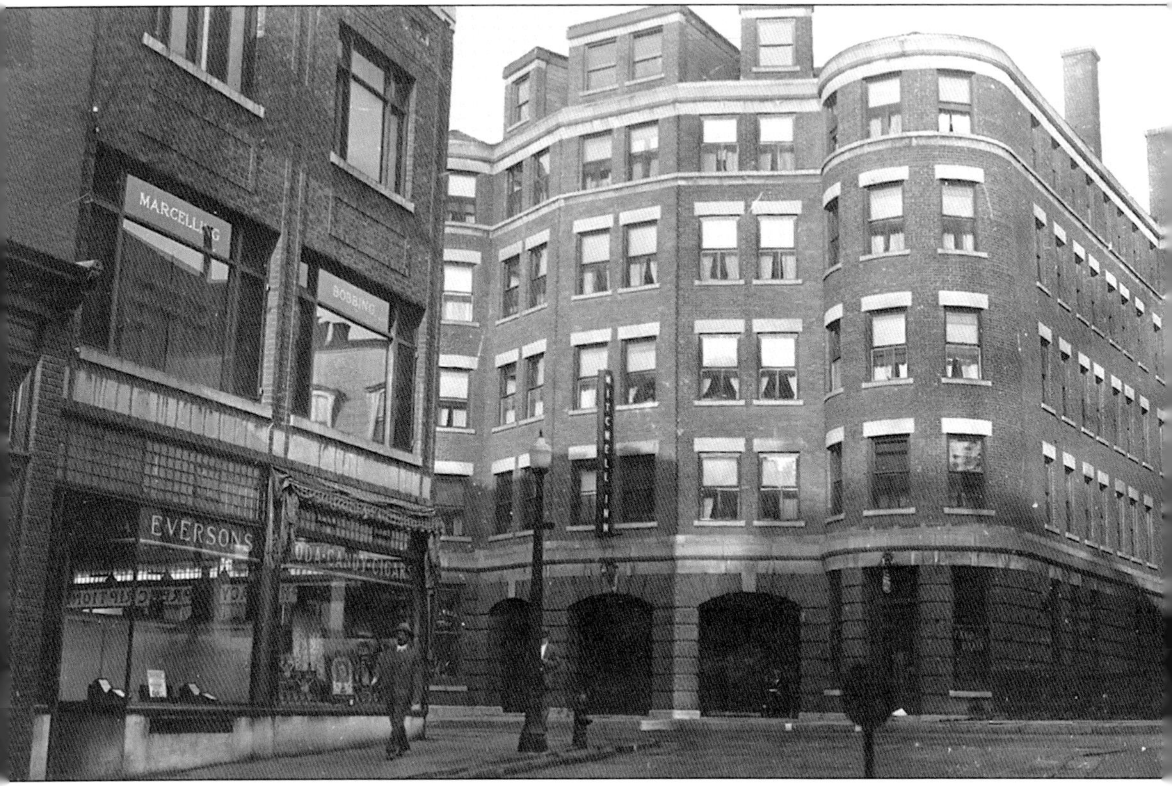

Taken from King Street, this photograph is a classic view of Middletown's premier hotel, the Mitchell Inn. On the left, Everson's Drug Store can be seen, with the Luxor Beauty Salon on the second floor.

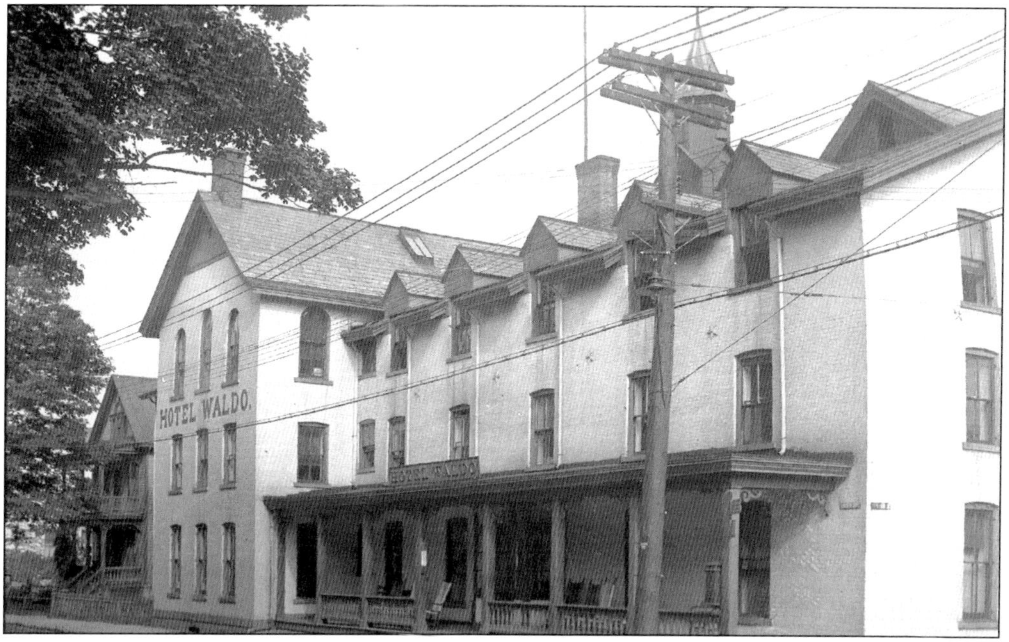

The Hotel Waldo stood on Linden Avenue at the corner of Franklin Street. The Hotel Waldo was long known as a traveling man's hotel. In earlier years, it had a broad veranda on the rear overlooking the Erie Railroad yards and station.

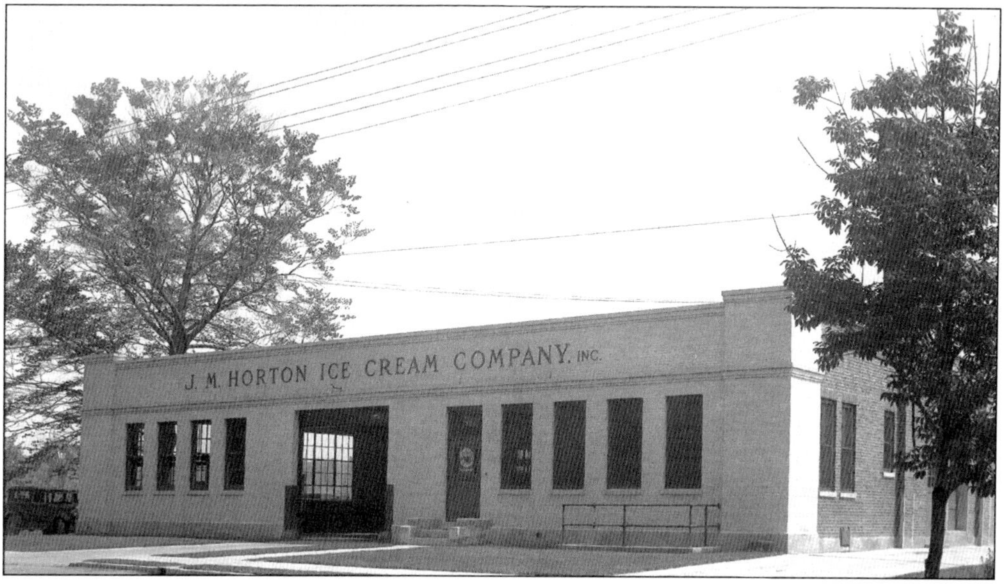

Located at 188 Monhagen Avenue, the Horton Ice Cream building was built in 1933. Later converted to an industry called Filtronics, the structure was destroyed in a major fire on August 23, 1992.

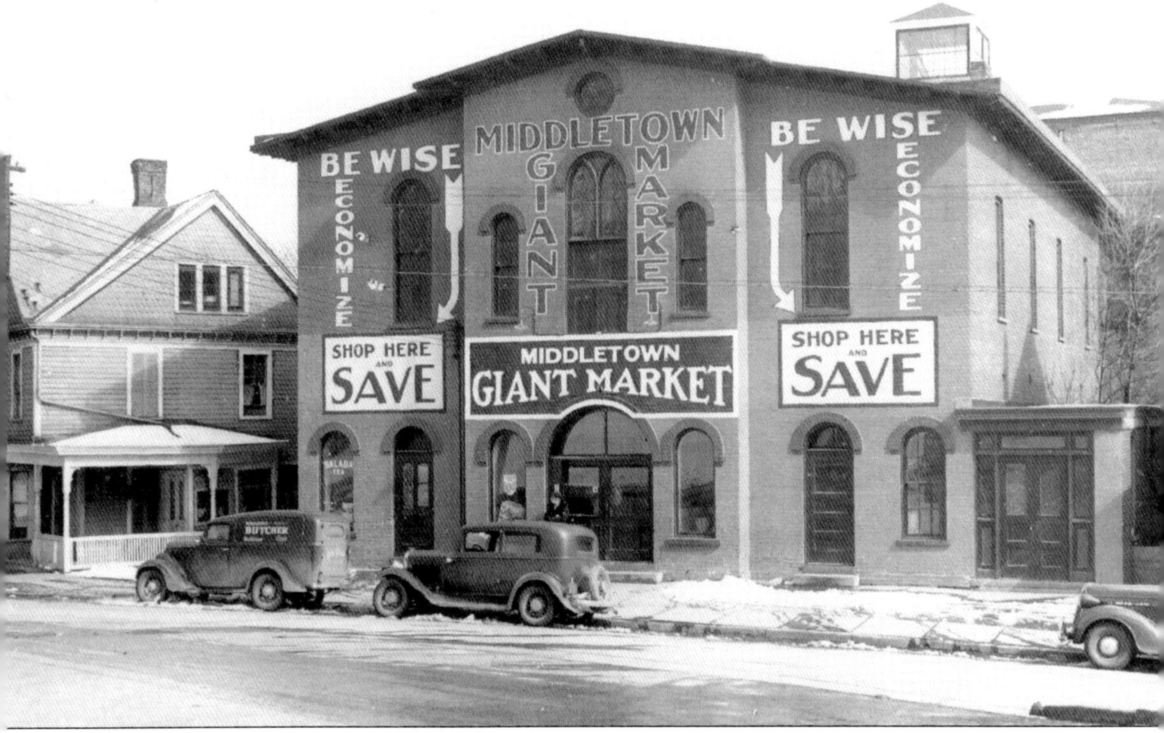

The historic building shown here was known as Linden Hall. A Civil War–era structure, it housed lectures and political rallies. Here it is shown in the 1930s, as an early supermarket. Linden Hall was located near the corner of Linden and Wickham Avenues and was torn down in the 1960s. At one time, it was also called Slauson Hall.

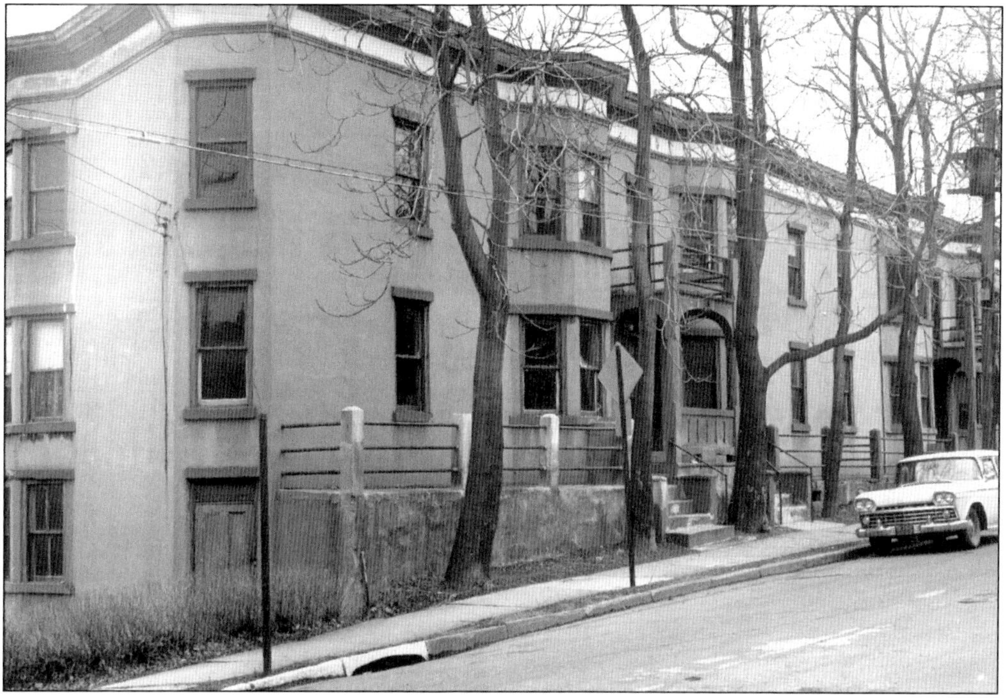

The Linden Block stood on the corner of Linden Avenue and Wisner Avenue. One of the city's apartment houses, it gradually became run down and was condemned. Habitat for Humanity recently erected two new homes on this site.

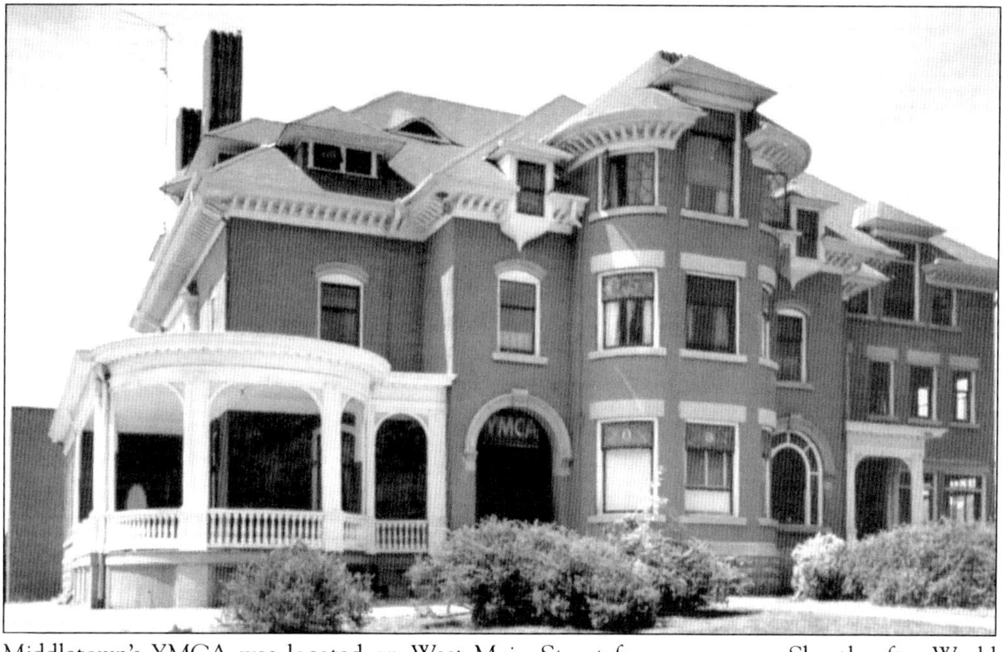

Middletown's YMCA was located on West Main Street for many years. Shortly after World War II, it moved to the large home of George N. Clemson on Highland Avenue. The photograph shows the Clemson home as it looked in the possession of the YMCA. The institution is still on the same site but in a much newer building.

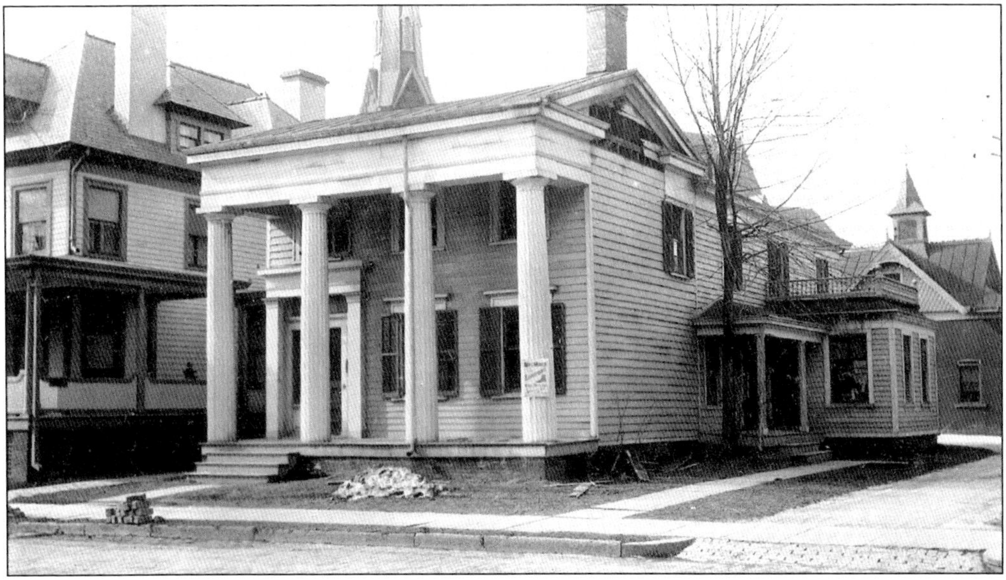

The distinctive building at 20 Orchard Street is shown with its original round columns. These were later replaced with square columns. This was the home of the Old Orchard Club, a men's association. The club later moved to West Main Street, and the building became the Colonnade Tea Room. Other tenants were the Colonial Gift Shop and later, Ross Insurance Agency.

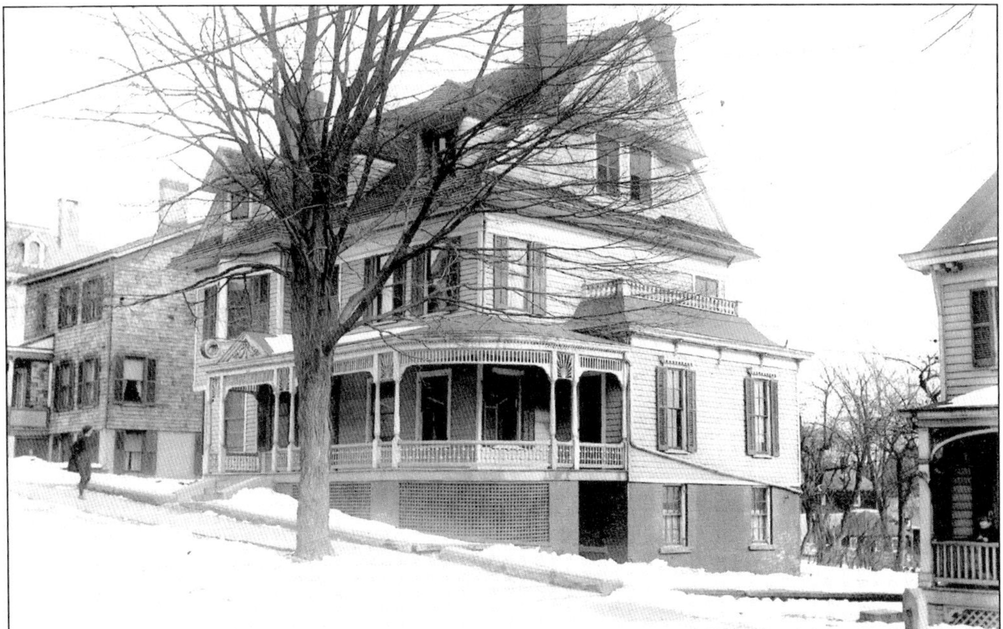

This home was located on South Street going up the hill from Fulton Street. The Harry Ogden home, it was later bought by the Loyal Order of Moose and became their clubhouse. The buildings shown were torn down under urban renewal.

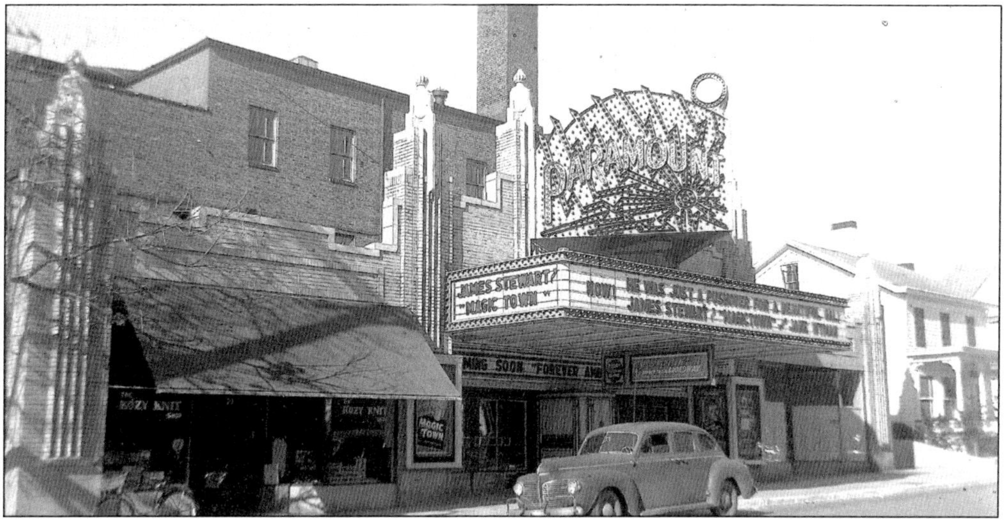

Middletown's Paramount Theater on South Street is fortunately still standing. This photograph shows the historic showplace around 1950. It looks much the same today, with the exception of the ornate Paramount sign. The building is now owned by the City of Middletown and is used for shows and presentations.

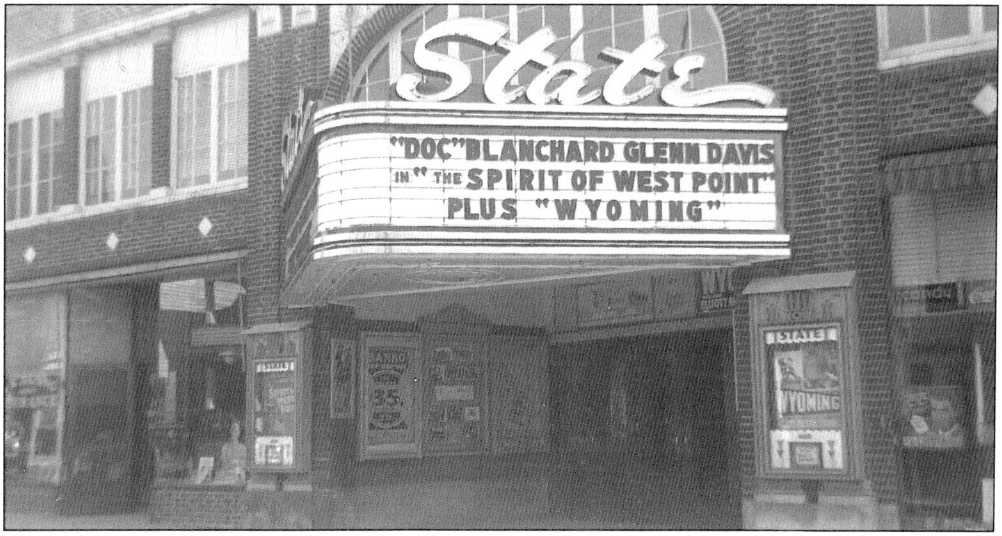

The State Theater was across the street from the Paramount Theater as seen in this photograph taken at the same time as the one above. The State Theater was torn down, and the site is now a parking lot.

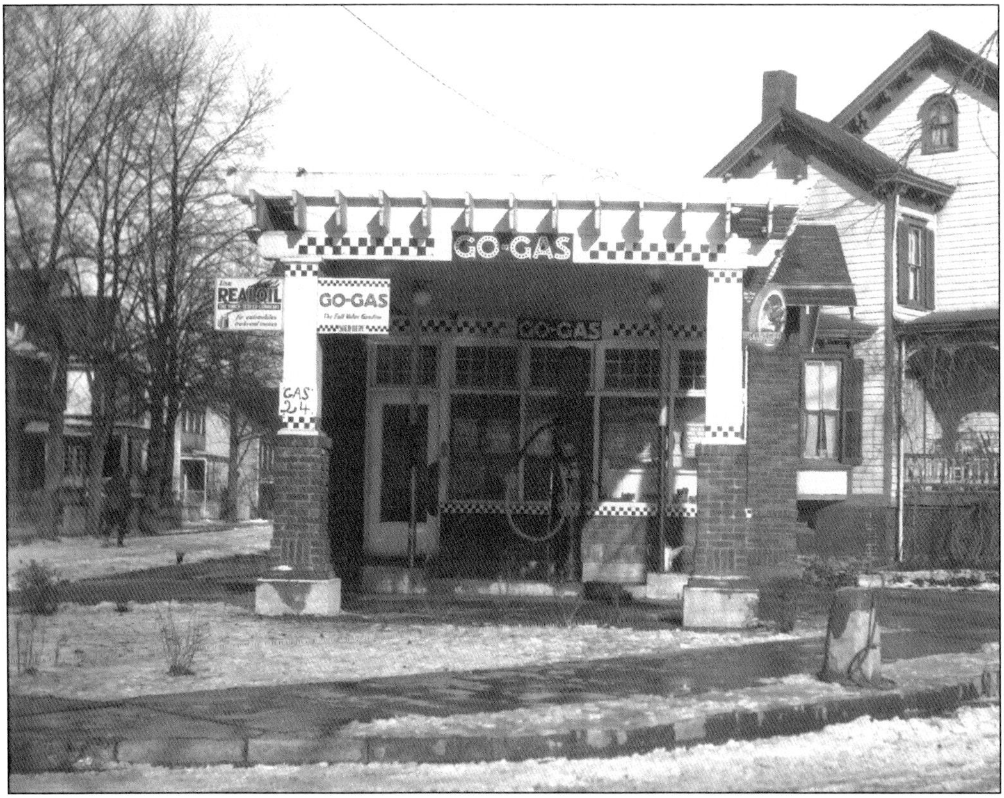

Go-Gas was being sold for 24¢ a gallon when this photograph was taken. The building at the corner of Wickham Avenue and Smith Street is still in use as an automobile repair shop.

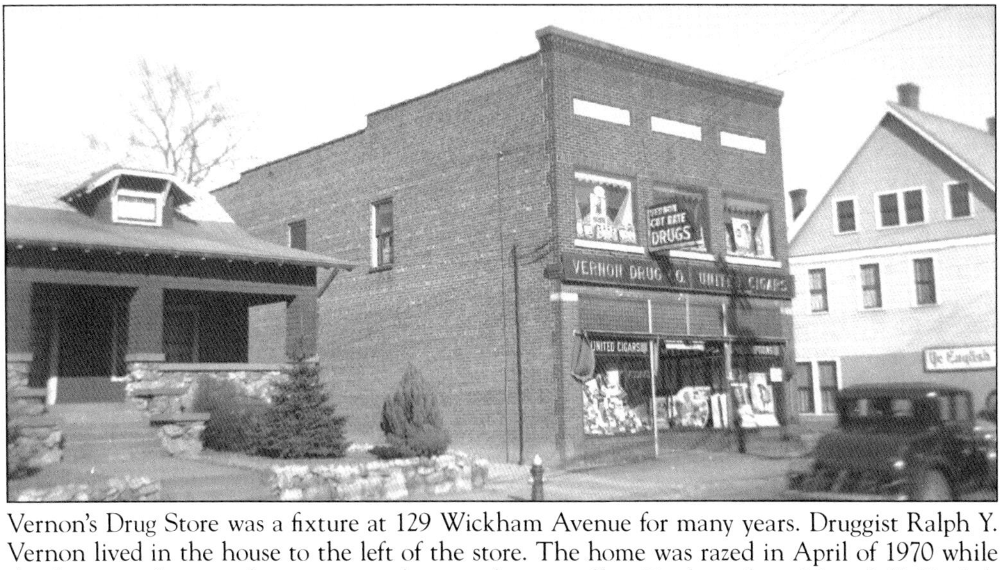

Vernon's Drug Store was a fixture at 129 Wickham Avenue for many years. Druggist Ralph Y. Vernon lived in the house to the left of the store. The home was razed in April of 1970 while the drug store has now been converted to a real estate office. To the right is Mauro's Ye English Tavern on the corner of Wickham and Low Avenues.

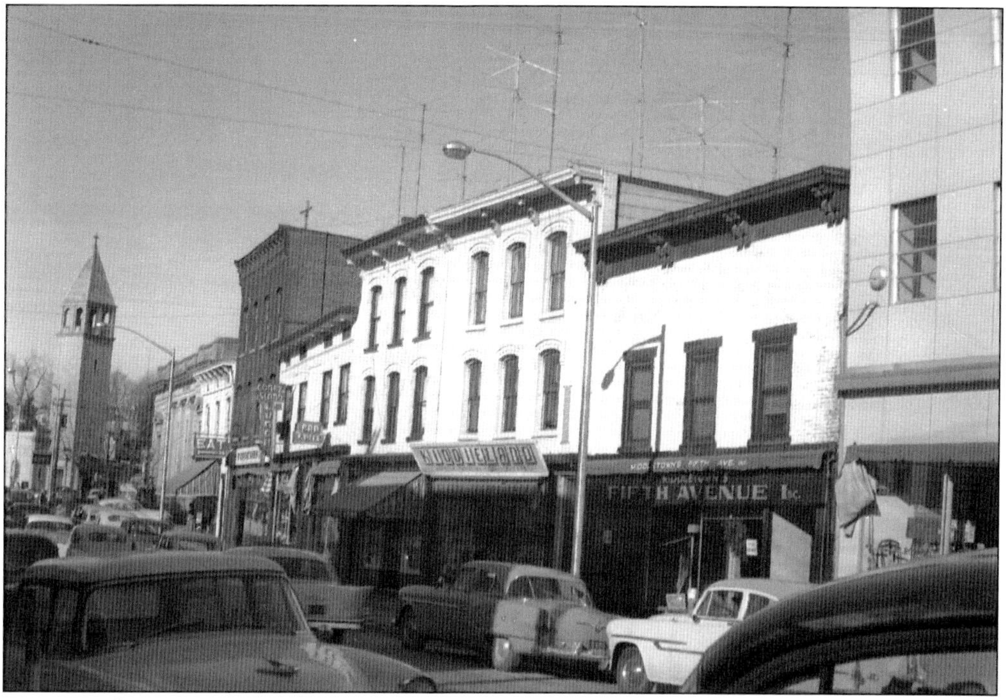

A view of West Main Street in the 1950s shows several long-gone businesses including Middletown's Fifth Avenue and Kiddieland. The Coney Island Restaurant has since moved to Railroad Avenue after a fire destroyed its building.

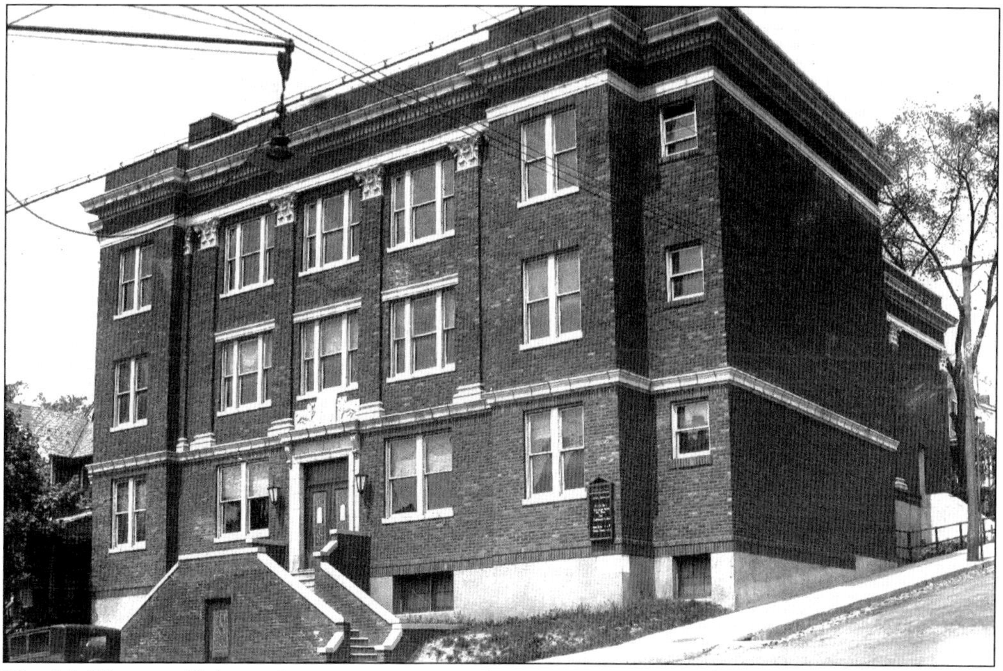

The Middletown Hebrew Association met in this synagogue on Linden Avenue at the corner of John Street. The building was built in 1925 and served the congregation until Temple Sinai was built on Highland Avenue in 1969.

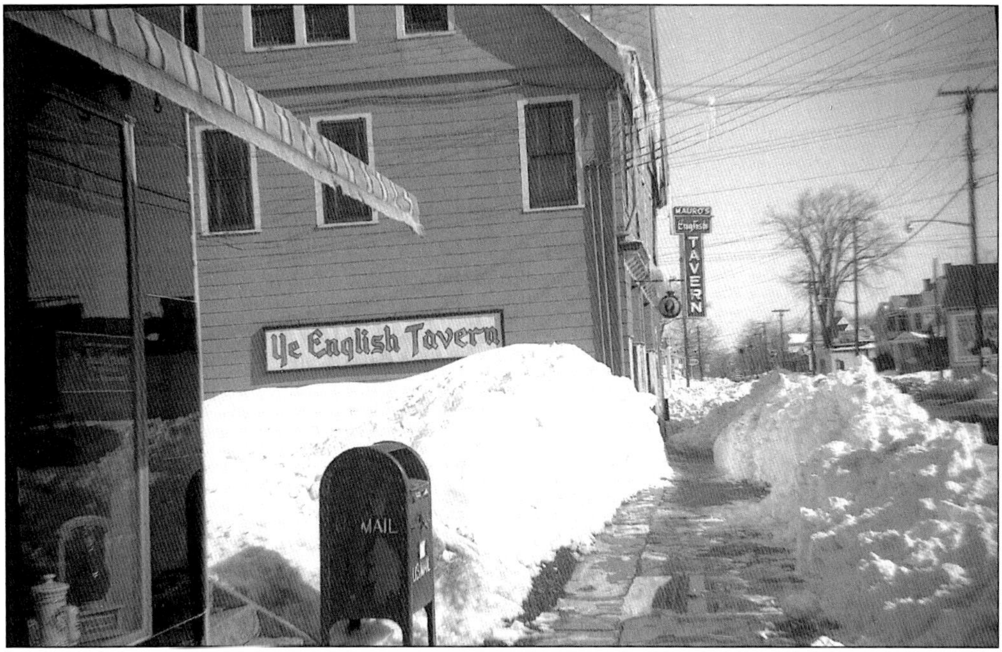

This view is from one standing in front of Vernon's Drug Store on Wickham Avenue after a heavy snowfall. Mauro's Ye English Tavern is just ahead.

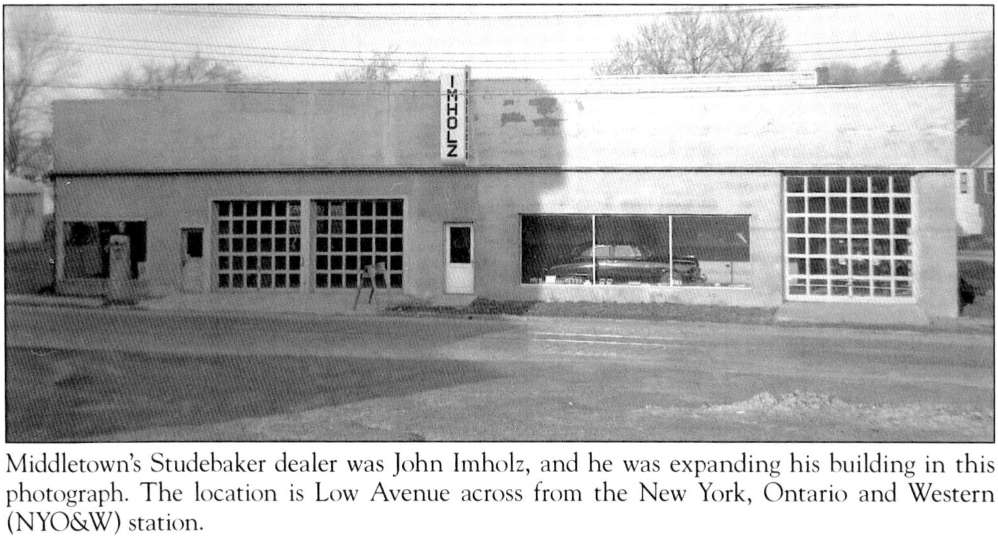

Middletown's Studebaker dealer was John Imholz, and he was expanding his building in this photograph. The location is Low Avenue across from the New York, Ontario and Western (NYO&W) station.

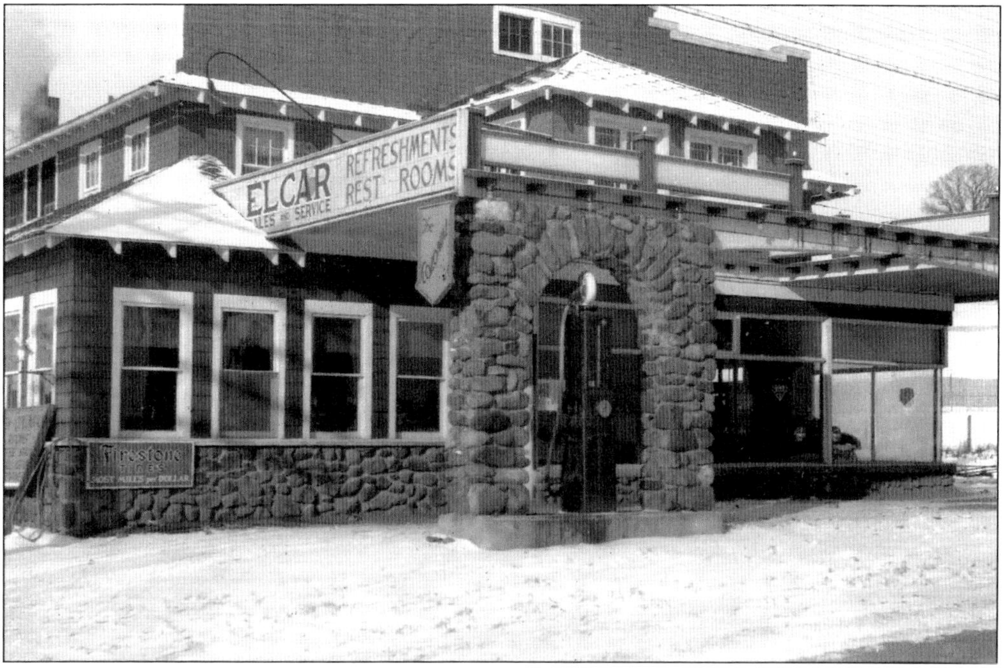

The Colonial Garage stood on the Goshen State Road across from Wilson Field. In this photograph they are selling Elcar automobiles, which were manufactured from 1916 to 1931. Today that area would be called Route 17-M or Dolson Avenue Extension. In later years other car dealers utilized this building until it was torn down when the area was redeveloped.

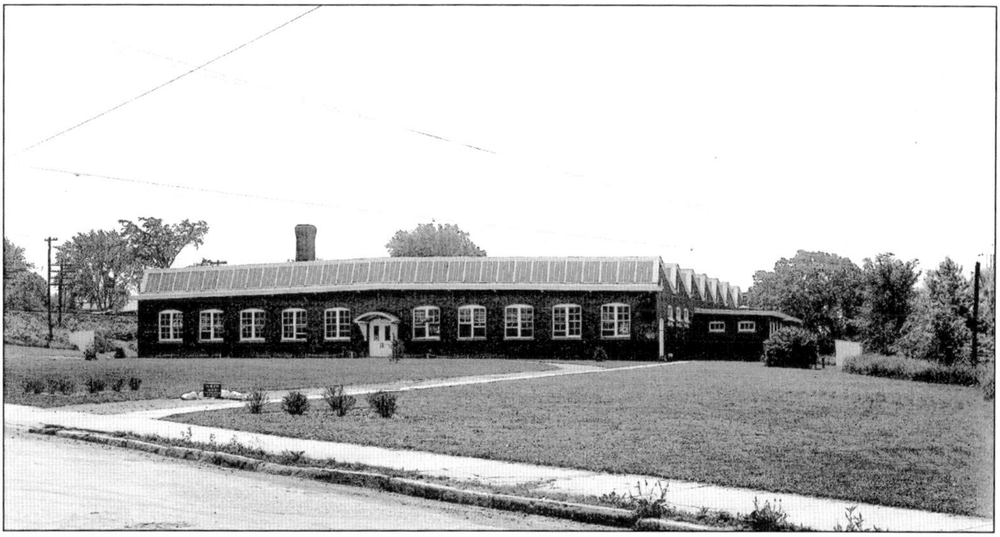

Harold H. Smith, a former mayor, built this brick and steel structure on Genung Street in 1919 for the Dundee Textile Corporation of New York, which operated the plant until forced by the Depression to close in January 1936. Benjamin Rubin opened the Middletown Rollerdrome in June 1938 and continued until the advent of World War II. In the early 1950s, the building was acquired by the Kieley and Mueller Company, which manufactured automated valves for industrial use. The structure is still in use today.

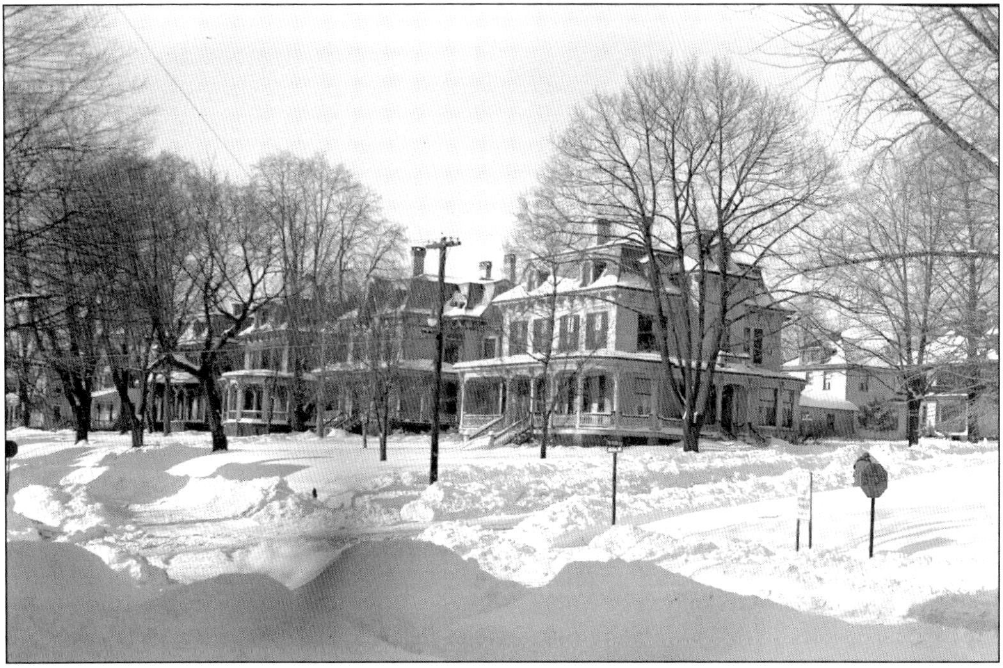

Truman Moon took this snowy picture at the corner of Highland Avenue and West Main Street. He referred to this intersection as "Jordan's Corners."

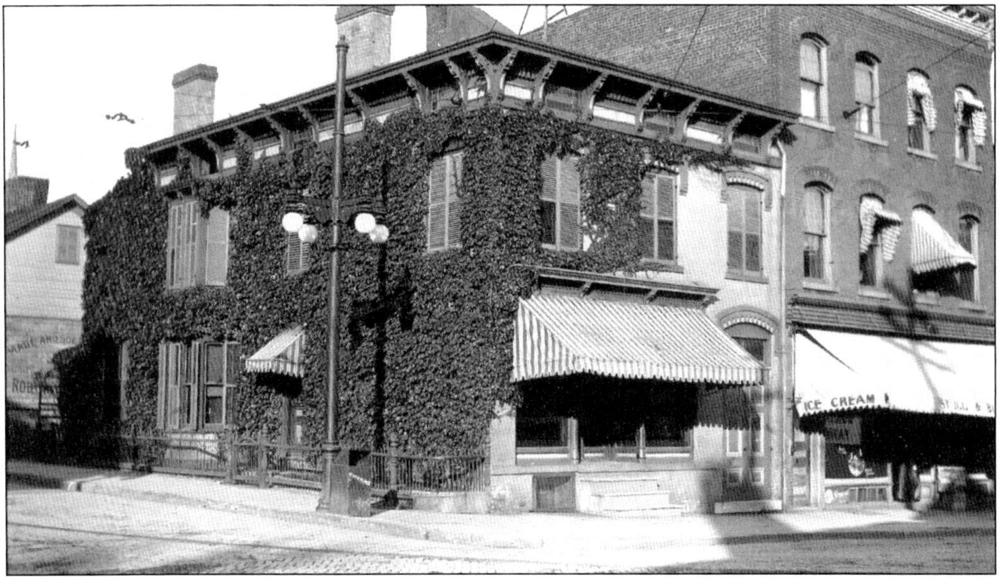

Mentley's Jewelry Store was located at the corner of West Main and James Streets for many years. The store is shown here in 1920 covered with ivy.

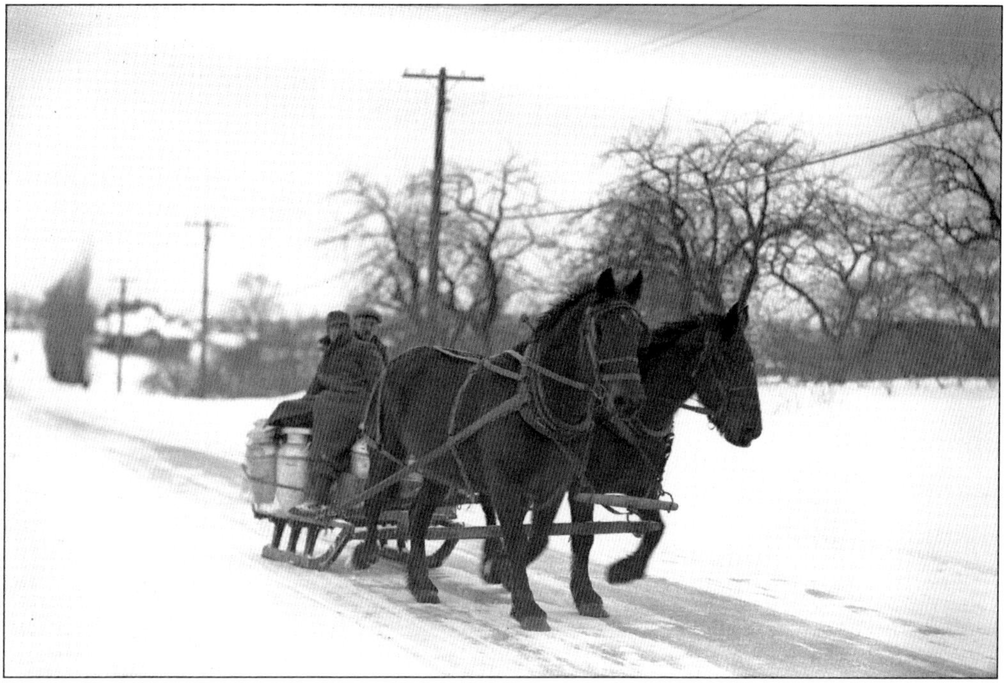

No matter what the weather, farmers had to get their milk to the creamery. Here is a team of horses and cutter driving along what may be the Mount Hope Road on their way to one of Middletown's dairies.

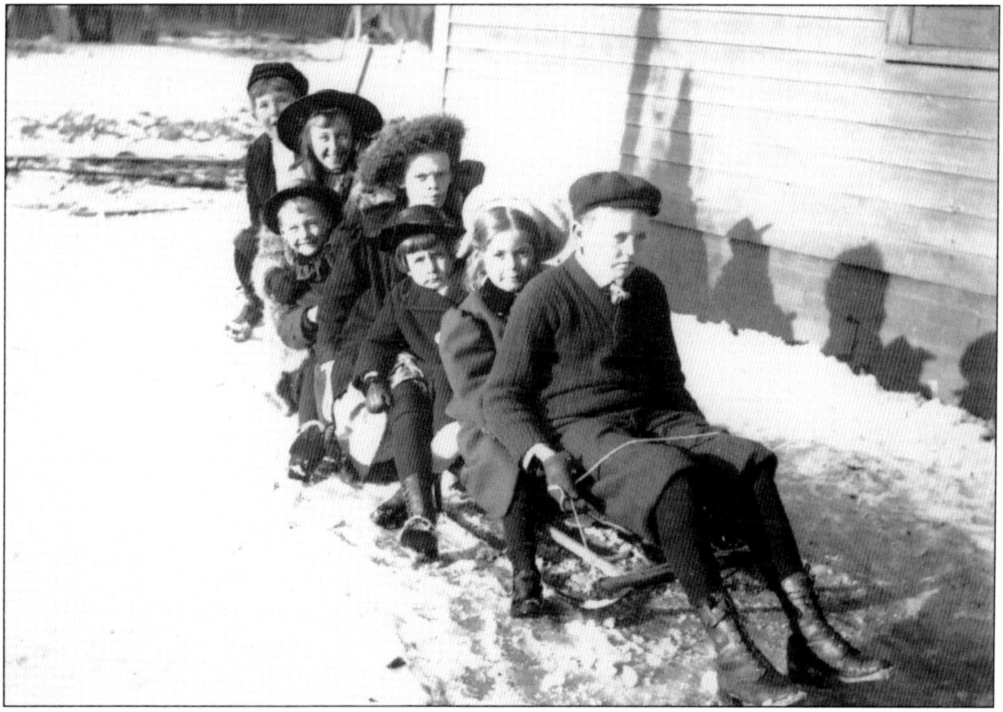

How many kids can fit on a sleigh? A boy with black stockings prepares to steer while the other kids hang on. The girls outnumber the boys in this photograph.

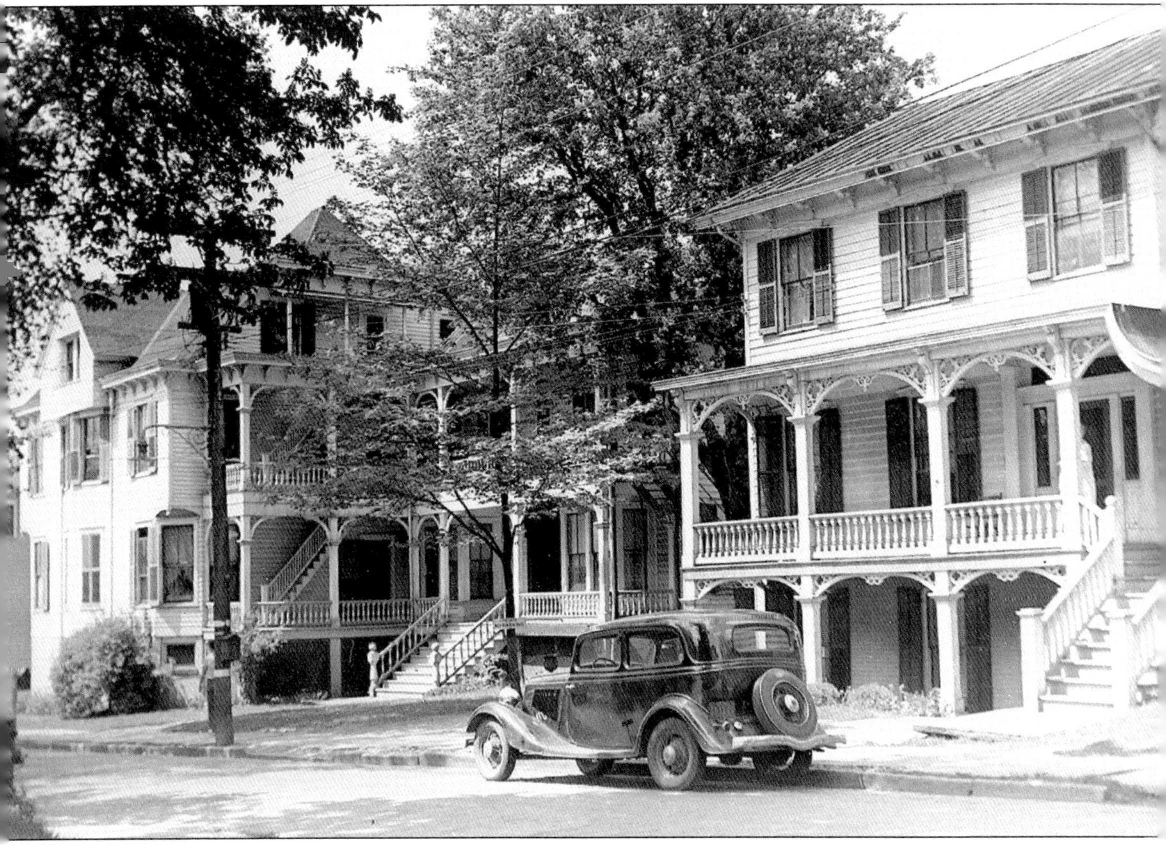

The Orange County Home for Aged Women, known as the Old Ladies Home, was located on South Street for many years. Located in Middletown since 1899, the home was familiar to generations of Middletowners. This scene from 1934 shows the buildings.

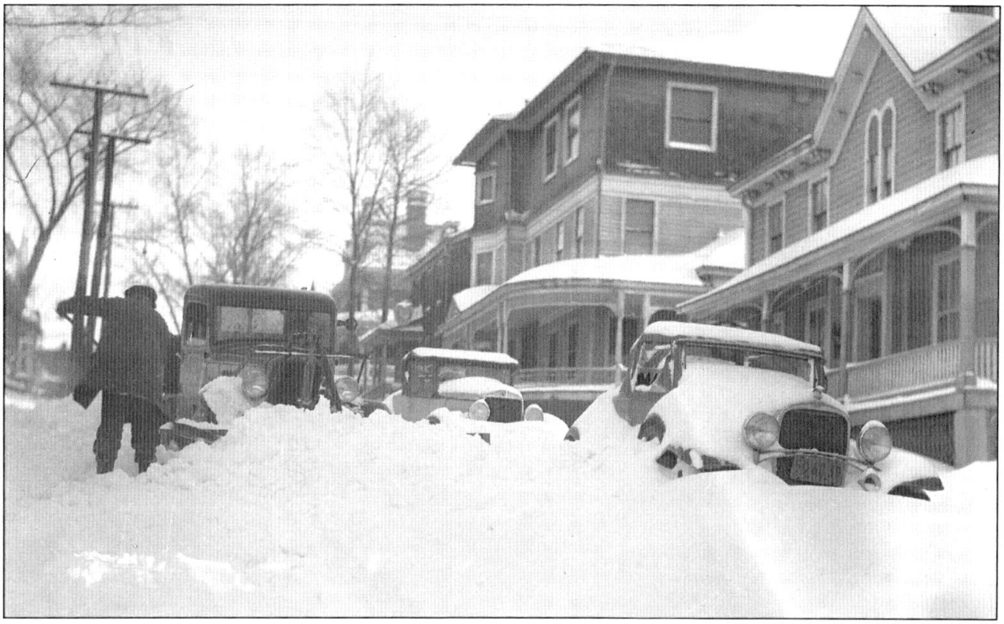

It is January 18, 1936, on Orchard Street, and the city's snowplow looks like it is stuck in a drift. Snow removal in Middletown has changed dramatically since those days.

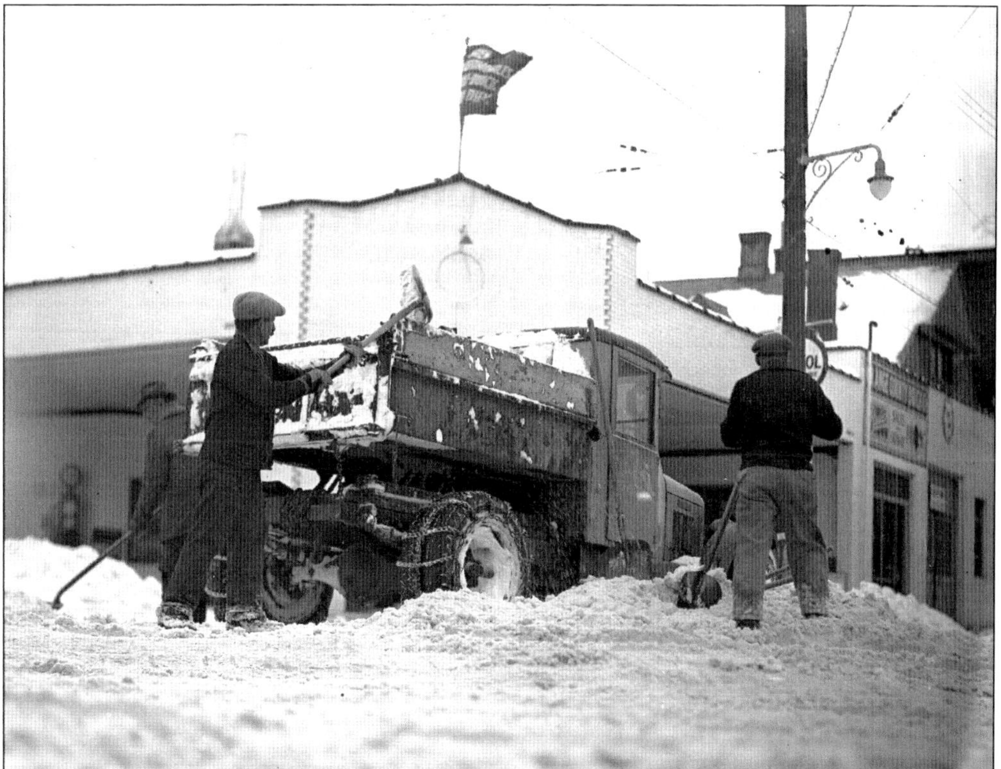

City crews move snow the old fashioned way. Two men are shown loading snow by hand in front of Orange County Buick Company on East Main Street in 1935.

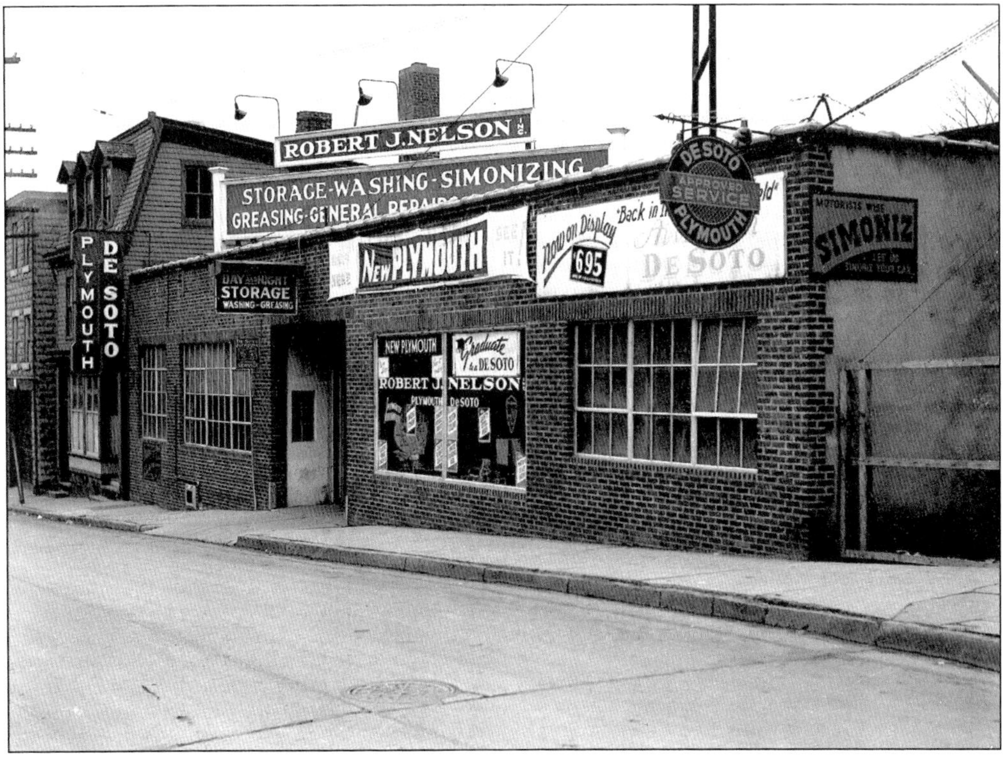

This photograph of Canal Street is before urban renewal. Robert J. Nelson sold Plymouth and DeSoto automobiles in this 1948 view. The location is across from the Borden building and is a parking lot today. George D. Thayer also utilized this site for an automobile dealership.

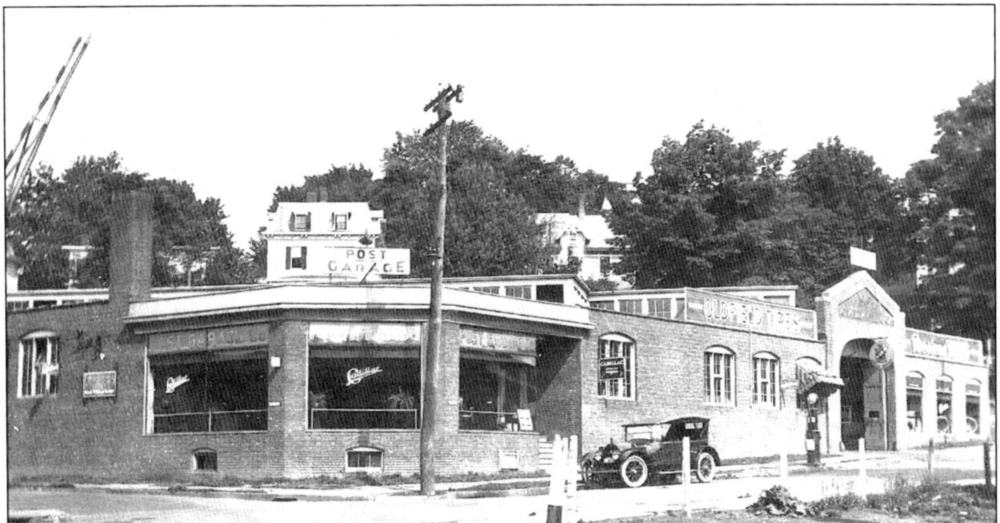

Located at 88 West Main Street, Post Garage was long Middletown's Cadillac dealer. The building is still in use as an automobile body shop today.

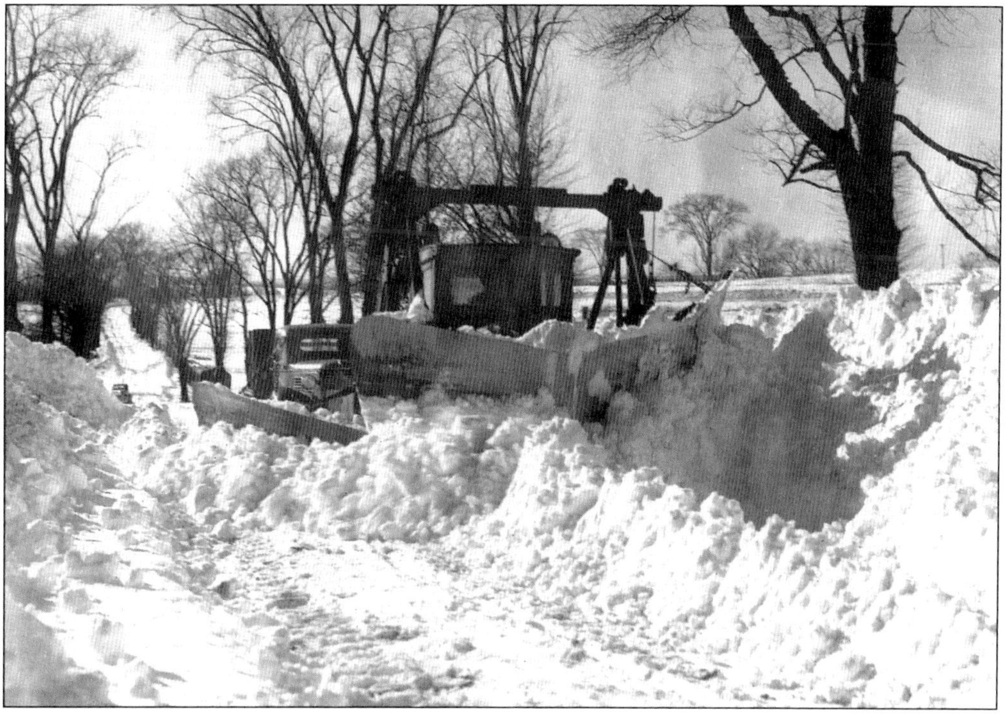

February 14, 1940, was Valentine's Day, but residents awoke to a major snowfall. Here the city's Linn snowplow attempts to clear a roadway with a smaller plow behind. The Linn was a half-track machine and was extremely powerful.

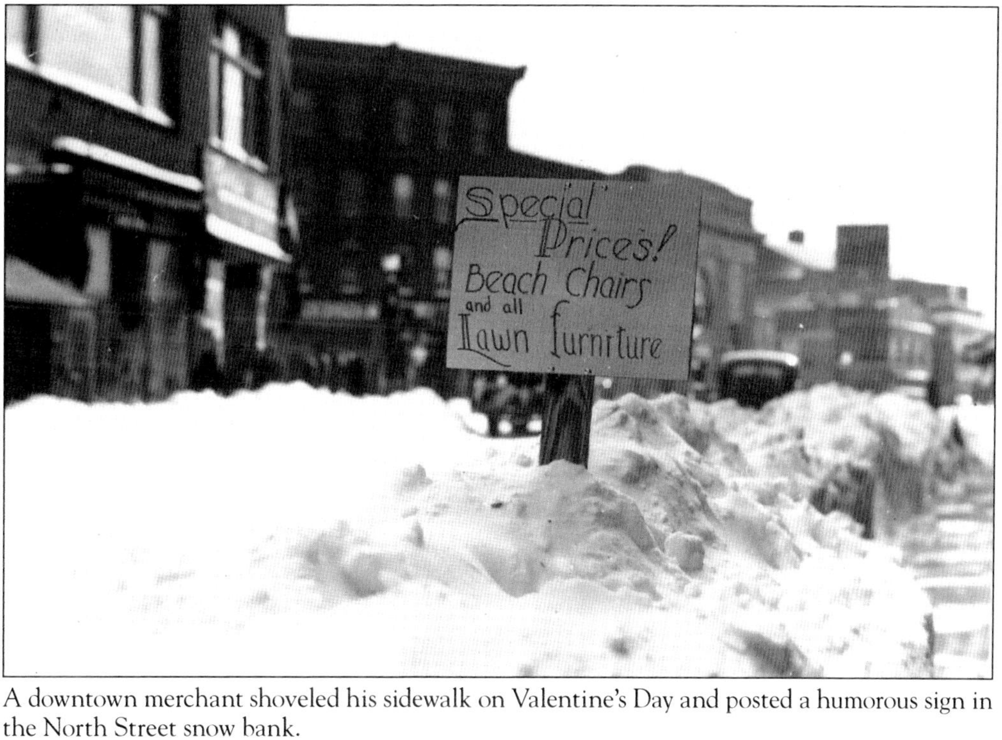

A downtown merchant shoveled his sidewalk on Valentine's Day and posted a humorous sign in the North Street snow bank.

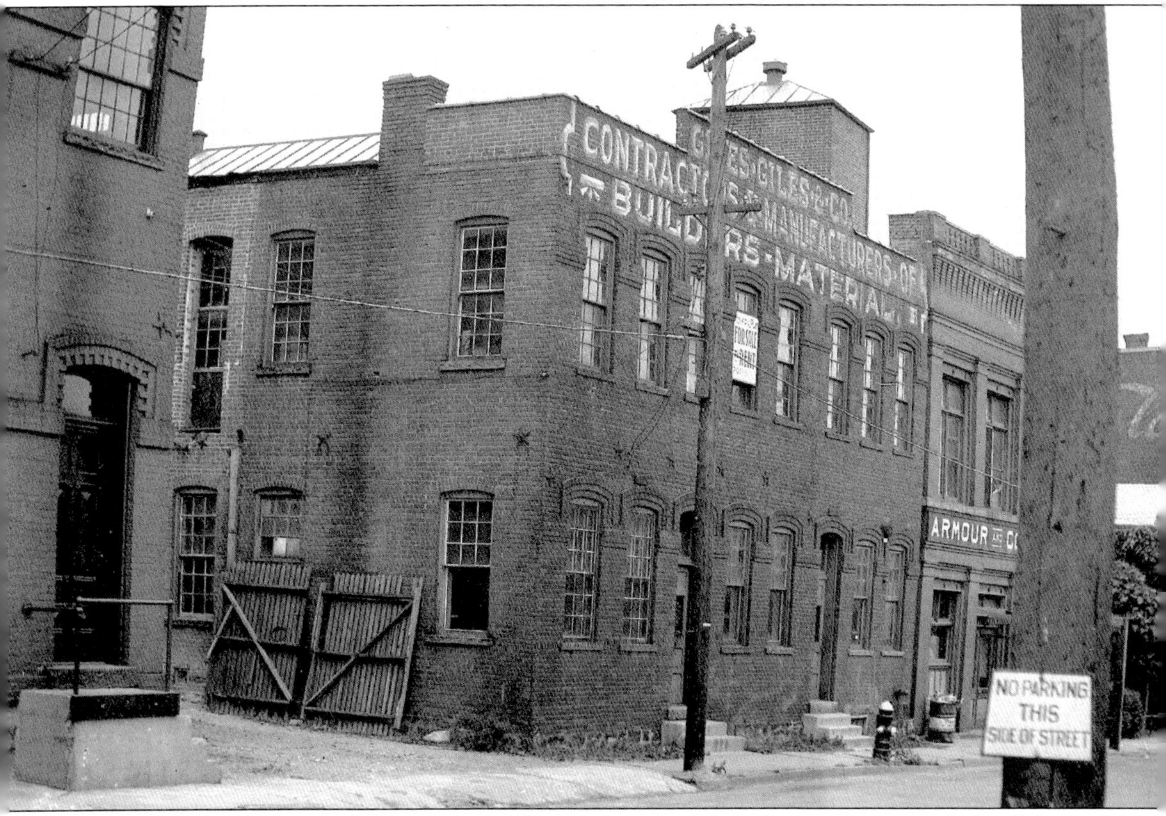

A number of buildings on Union Street have been torn down. Among them was Giles, Giles and Company. Noted local architect Frank J. Lindsey had his office here and worked closely with the Giles brothers. The Armour Beef Company is also shown.

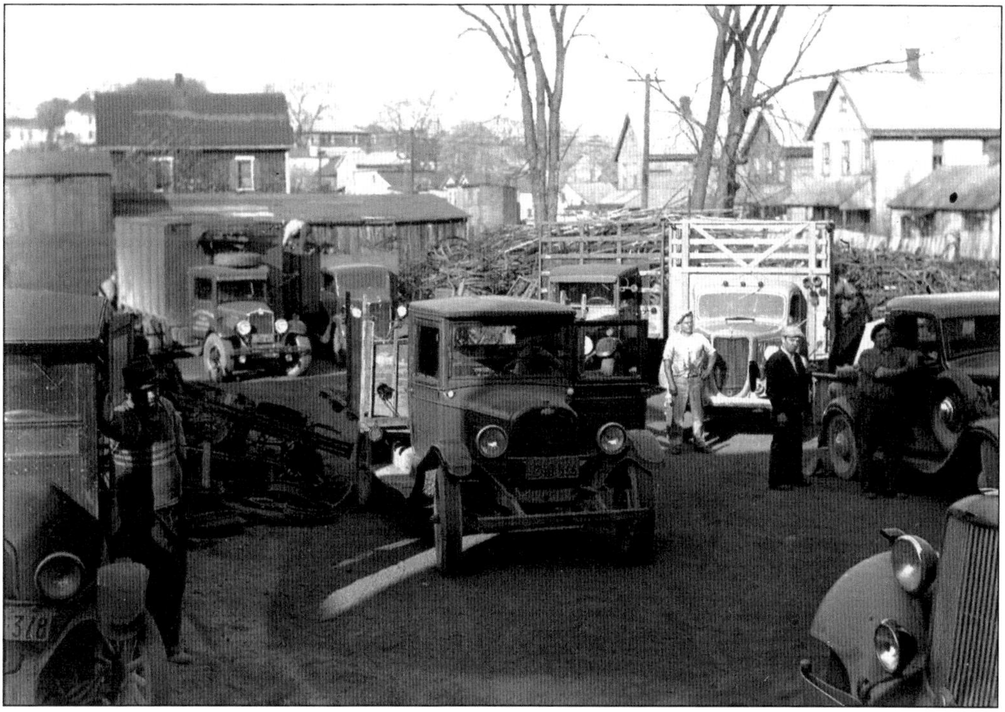

Ralph Salvati's scrap yard is shown here in 1936. The site is Wawayanda Avenue corner of Benjamin Avenue. That looks like Salvati with his arm on the pickup truck at right. The location is now part of the post office's loading dock and rear parking area.

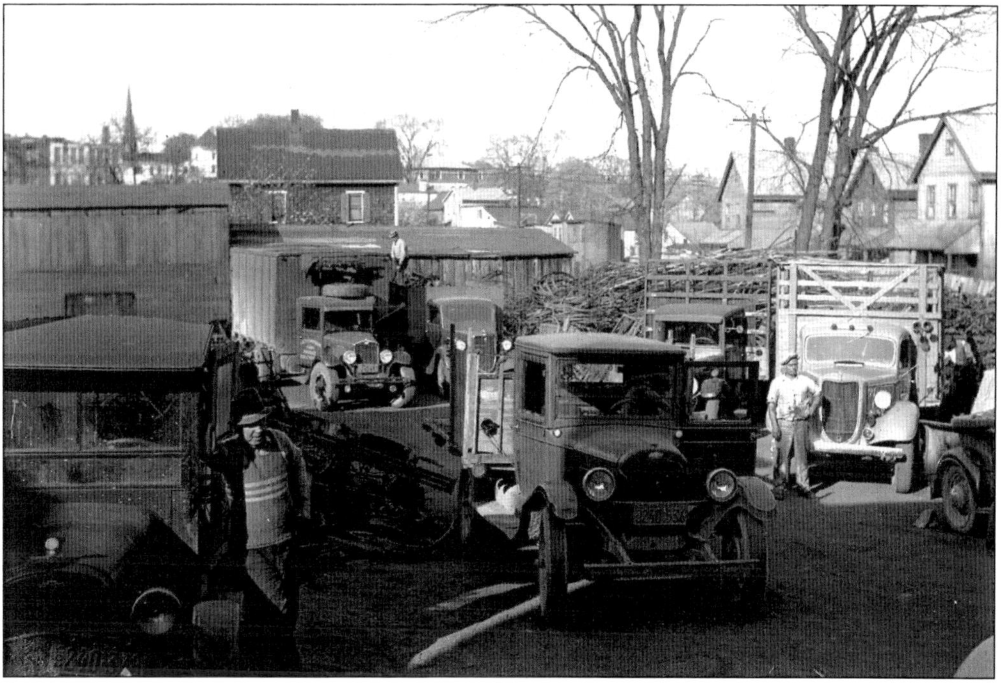

Seen here is another view of Salvati's scrap yard.

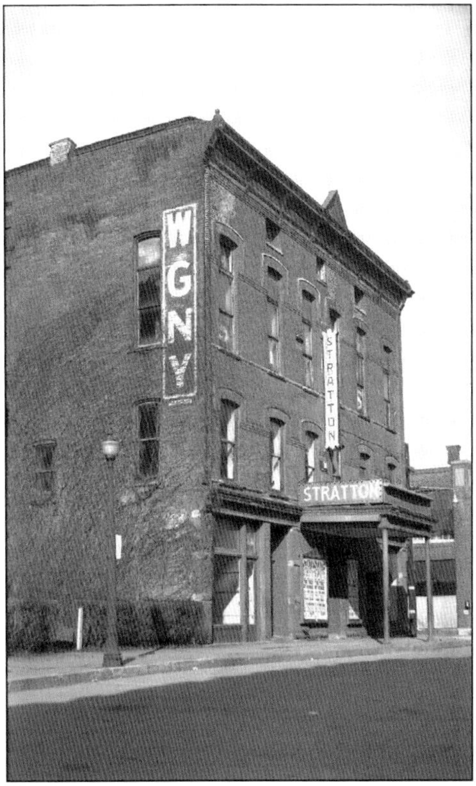

Middletown boasted a number of theaters, among them the Paramount, the State, and the Stratton. The Stratton Theater was located on James Street next to the Avon Building. In this 1940s photograph, radio station WGNY occupied the second floor. The building was demolished in 1951, and the site is now a parking lot.

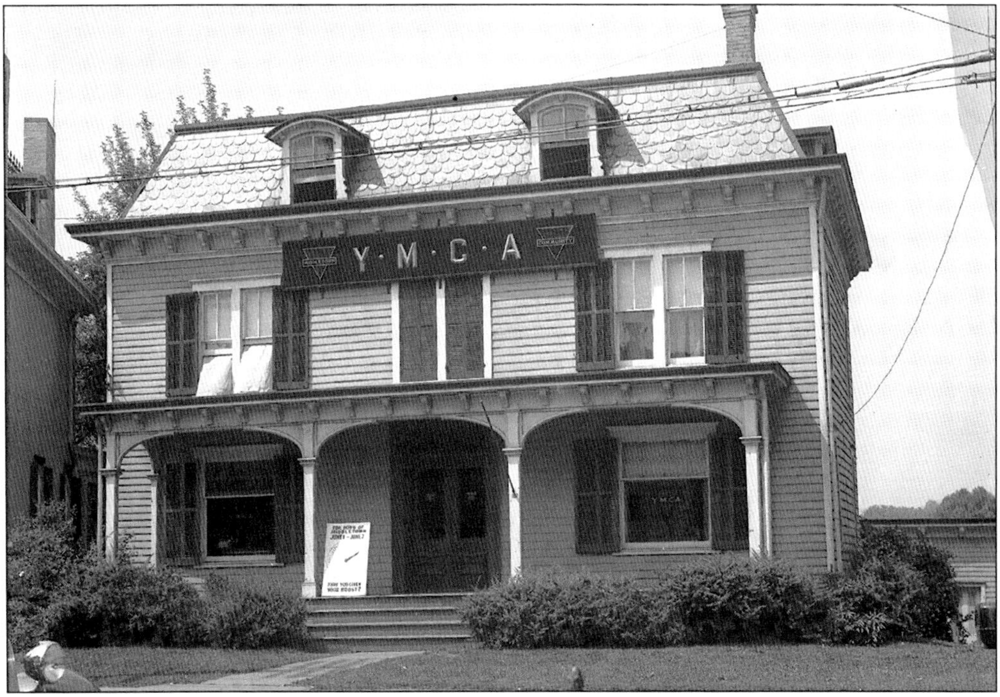

This house on West Main Street housed the YMCA for many years, until its move to Highland Avenue shortly after World War II.

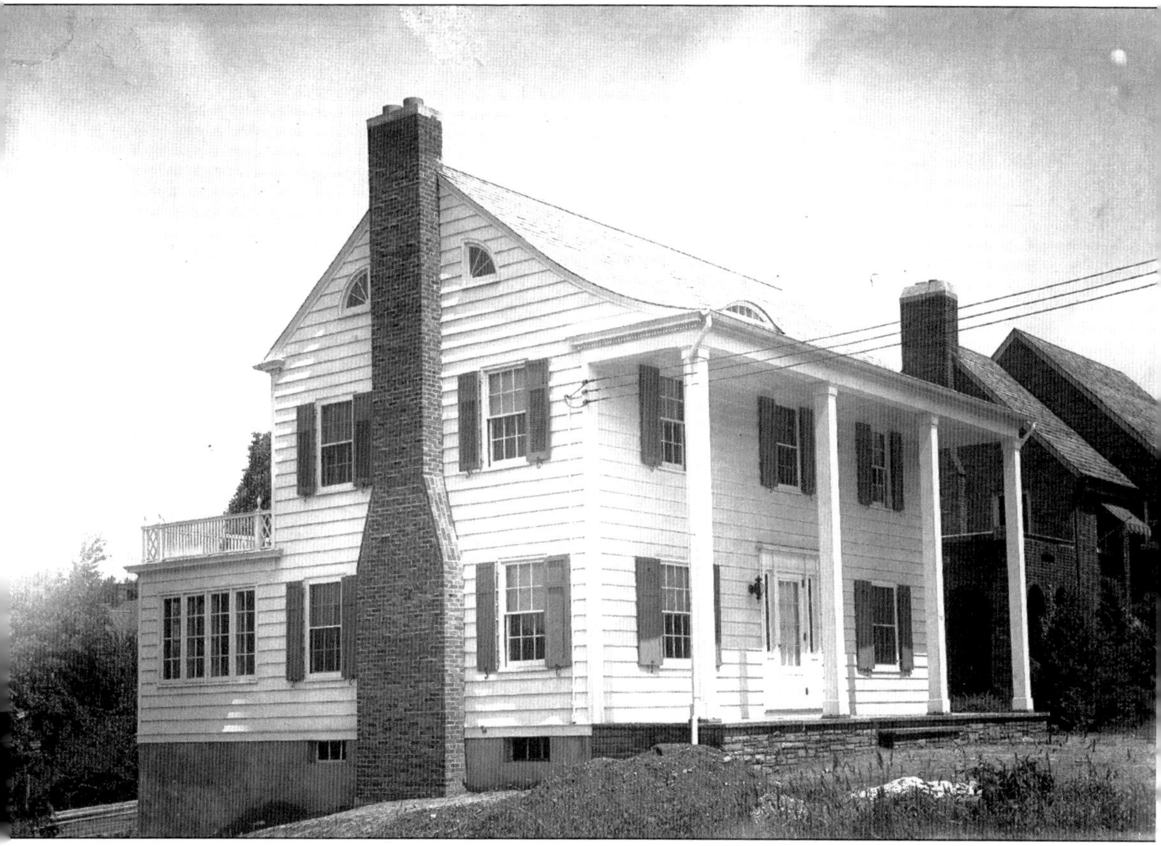

This home at 141 Highland Avenue was built in 1934 for Dr. John McCartney. Martin and Beatrice Rosenblum purchased it and resided there for many years.

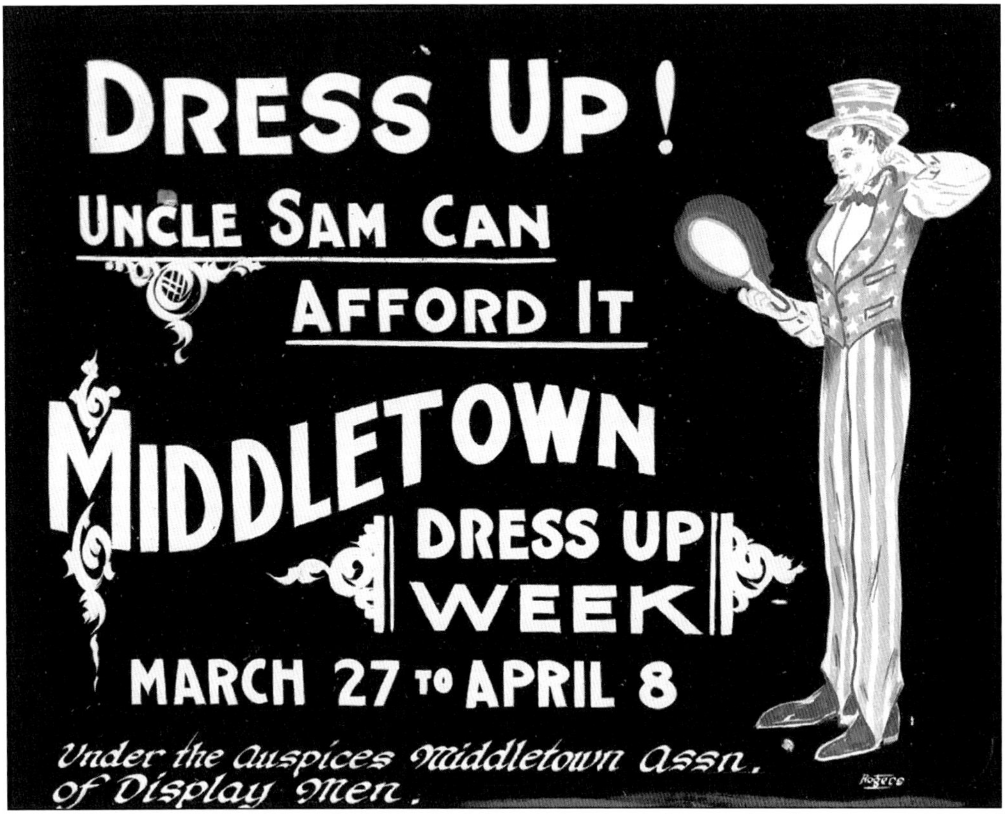

This advertisement might refer to dressing store windows. It is believed to date from the World War I era.

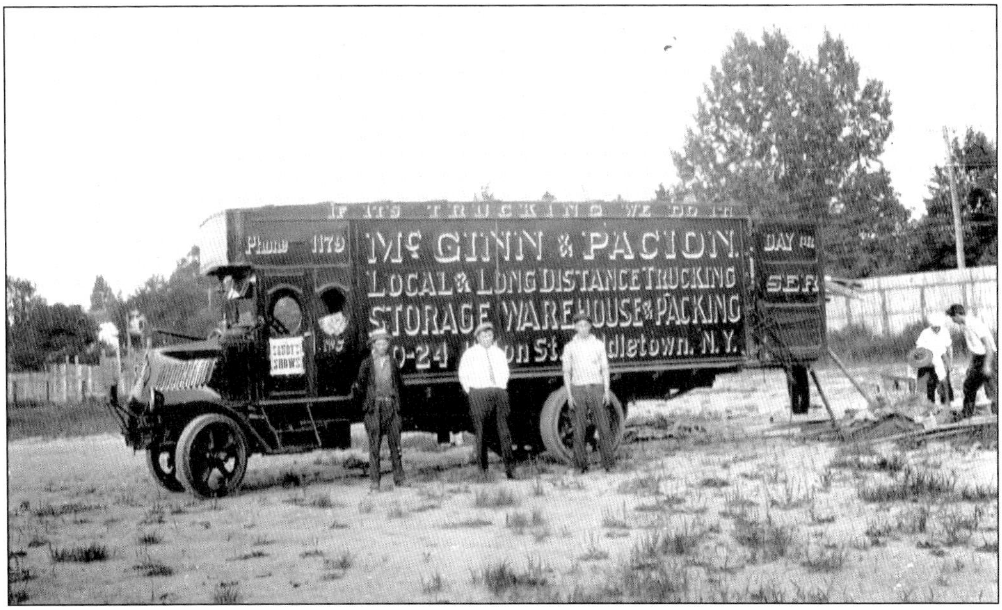

Barney McGinn was an early trucker in Middletown. Here one of his Bulldog Mack trucks is shown hauling for Sandy's Shows. The truck looks almost new.

Four

URBAN RENEWAL

The Urban Renewal Program in the 1950s and 1960s reshaped much of the city of Middletown. A number of sections of the city were perceived to contain substandard housing and these were razed. Portions of the business section were also demolished to widen certain streets and provide much needed parking areas. Downtown, the James Street business district was virtually wiped out. All of the buildings on the east side of the street were removed, the street was widened and a municipal parking lot replaced what was lost. All of the buildings on Fulton Street were torn down and the street made into a four-lane highway. Whatever may be said about urban renewal, it undoubtedly changed the face of Middletown forever.

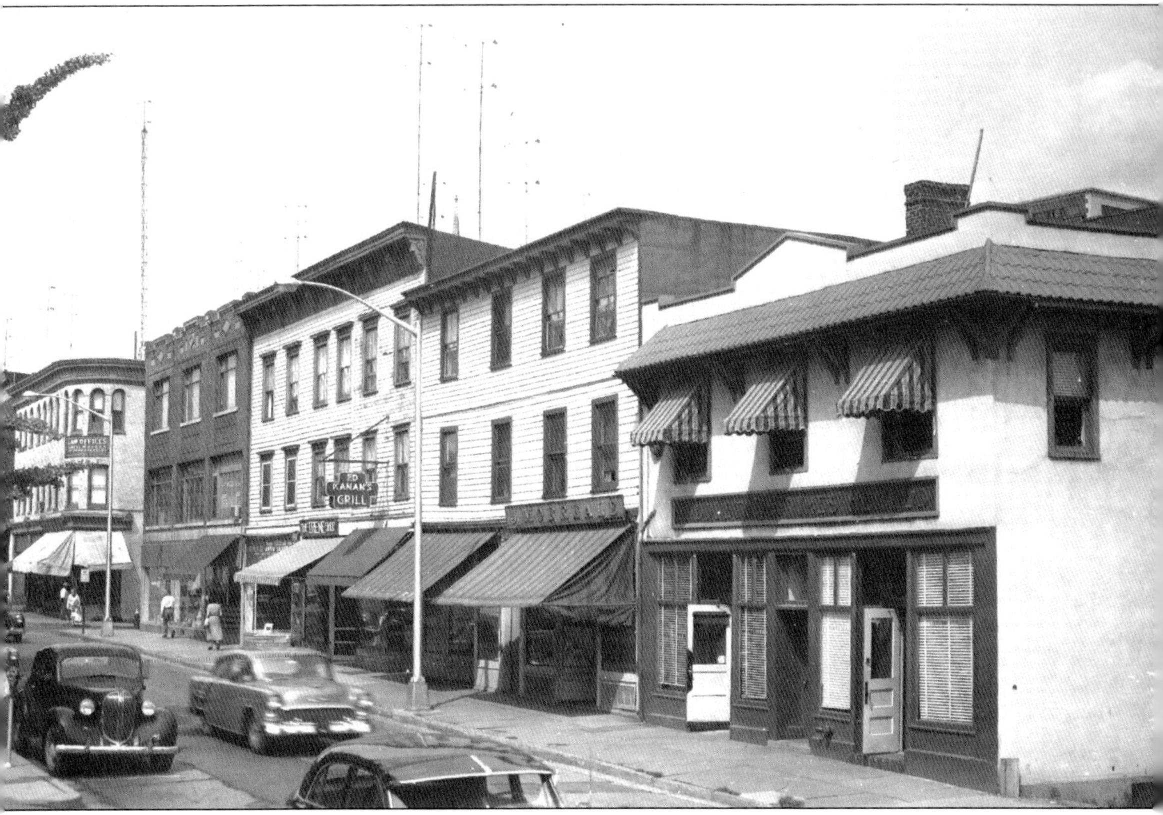

This image is a view of James Street from the steps of city hall. The building with the awnings housed the *Middletown Times-Herald* headquarters. Next to it, J. Morreale's tailor shop can be seen, then Kanan's Grill. All the buildings in view were removed under urban renewal in 1961.

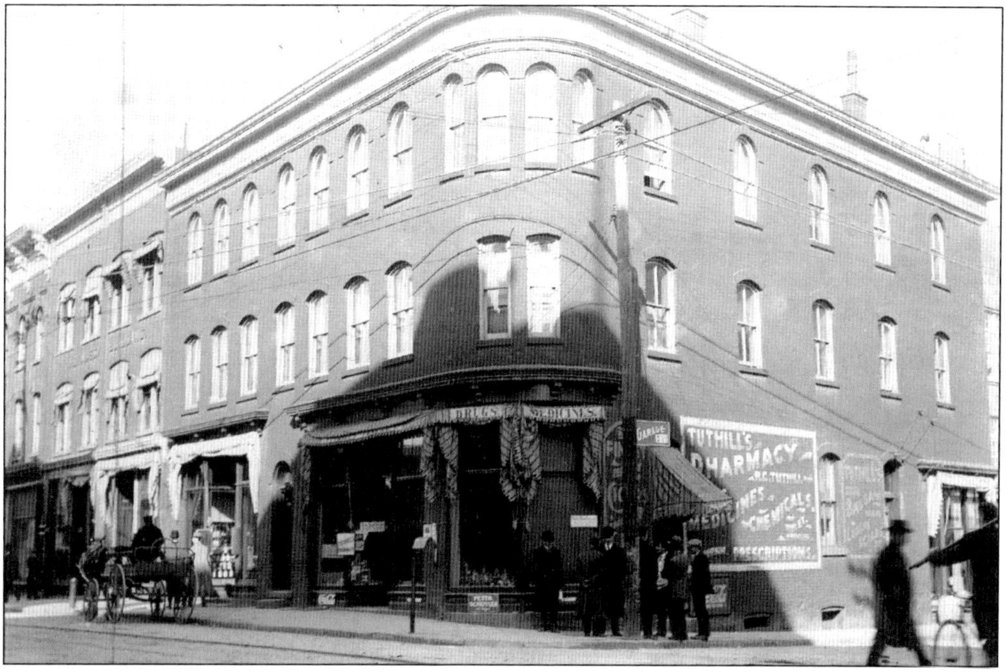

This is an old photograph of Tuthill's Pharmacy, which stood on the corner of James and King Streets.

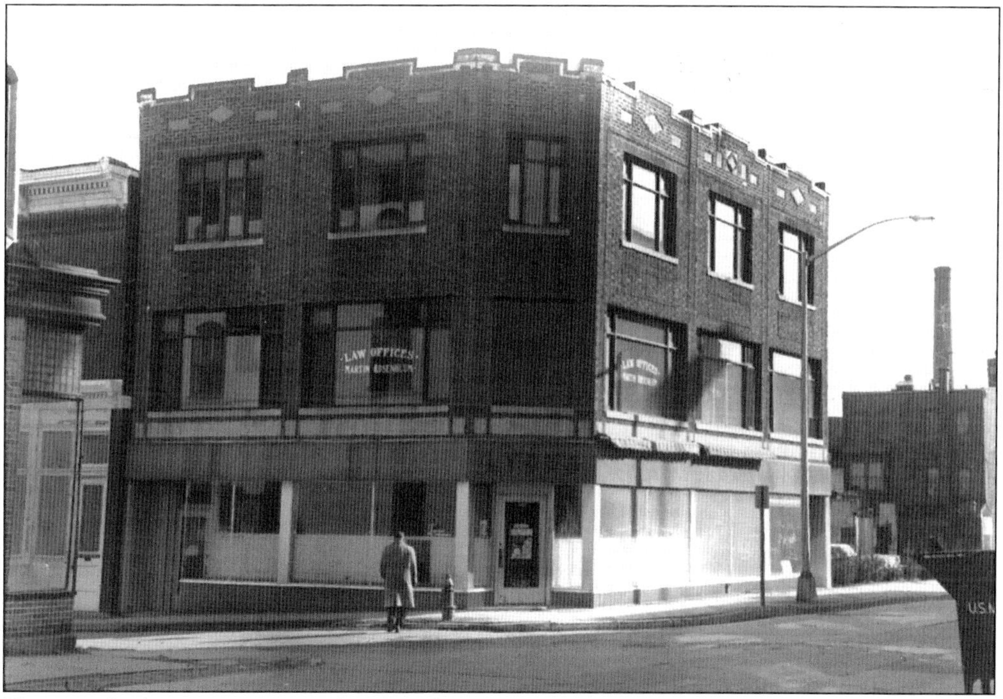

Photographed on June 29, 1961, shortly before being razed under urban renewal, Lyon's Drug Store stood on the corner of James and King Streets. The building was built in 1899 and was known as Everson's Drugs until Allen P. Lyon purchased it in 1941. Situated directly across the street from the Mitchell Inn, the store was a popular meeting place for generations of Middletowners.

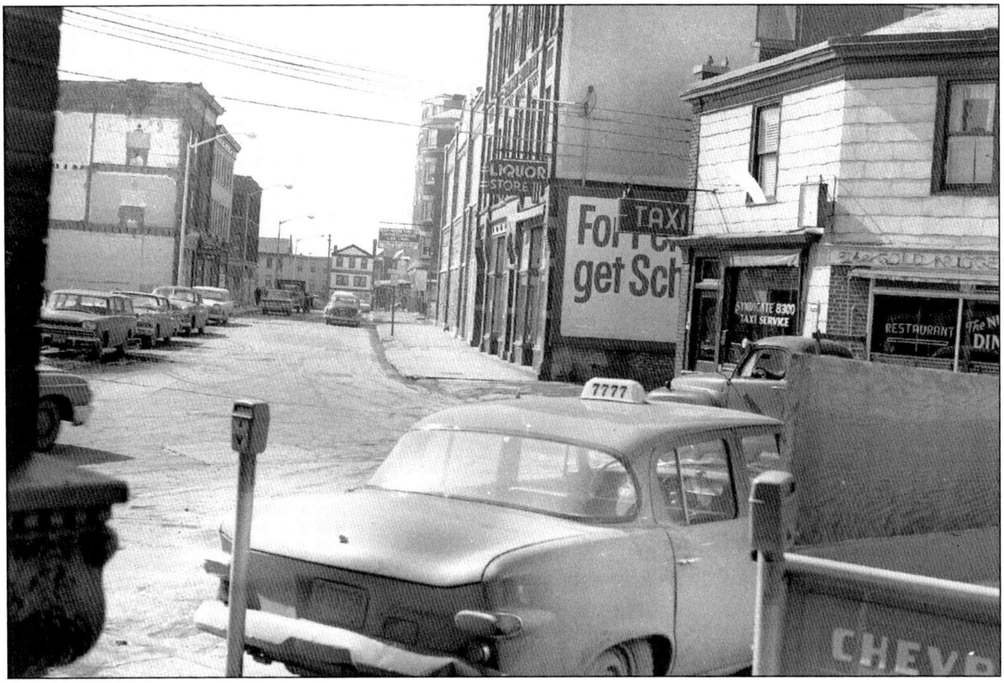

Urban renewal was in progress as this photograph was taken on James Street. The buildings on the left are almost ready to be removed. The Gold Nugget building is also slated for removal. Remember the parking meters?

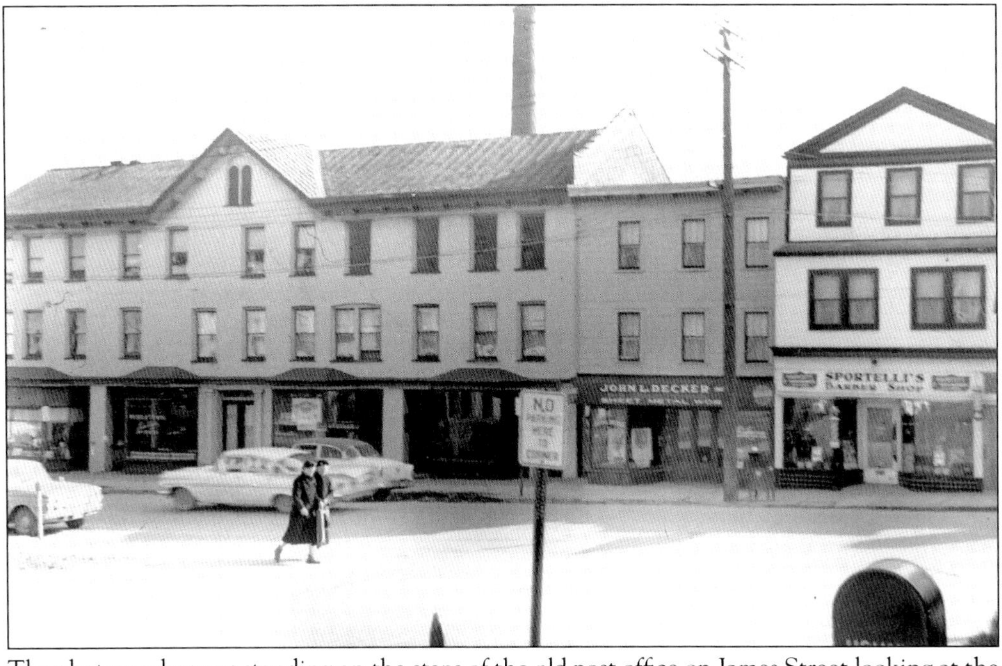

The photographer was standing on the steps of the old post office on James Street looking at the south side of West Main Street. The Sportelli building still stands today, but the other structures were razed during urban renewal. The head of Canal Street is now where those buildings stood. The large building was once Charles Higham's Commercial Hotel.

Five

The CCC

The United States Civilian Conservation Corps, or CCC, was a Depression-era program to provide meaningful work for thousands of unemployed young people. The program operated in every state of the union and was supervised by army officers.

In the Middletown area, the CCC established two camps outside the city near New Hampton, Camp Wallkill and Camp Wawayanda. The young men worked on the Wallkill River, clearing, realigning, and straightening the course of the stream. The enlistees comprised 600 so-called "Negro Juniors," most of whom had never been away from home before. The program was not all hard work. There was ample food, recreation, and educational classes. The men had frequent passes to enable them to visit Middletown.

The CCC spent two years in the area and most people remember it as a highly successful government project. The companies arrived on September 30, 1935, and exactly two years later, all personnel were transferred, and the camps were closed. Today there is little physical evidence that the CCC camps ever existed.

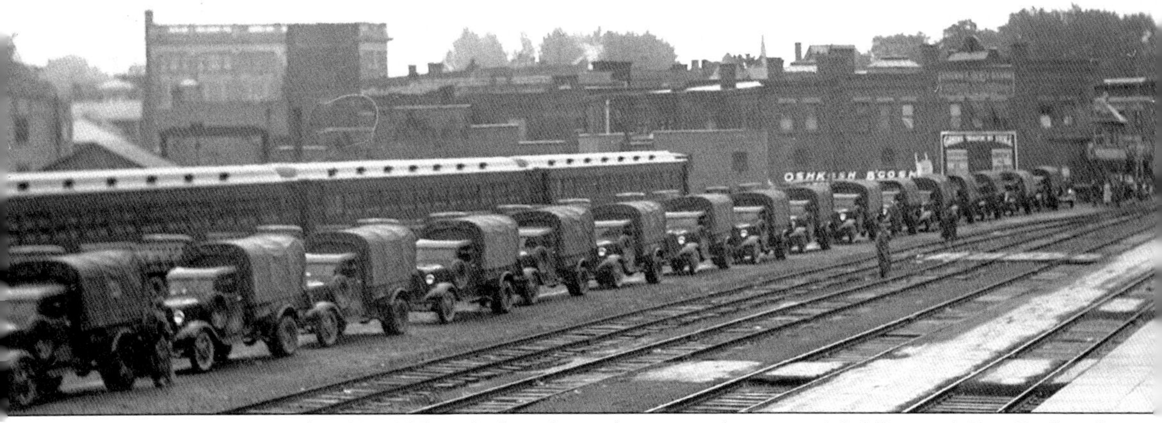

It is a rainy September 30, 1935, and a long line of army trucks wait at Middletown's Erie Railroad yards to transport 600 CCC enlistees to their new camps. A train of 15 coaches and three baggage cars brought the men to their new assignment. A total of 68 army trucks, referred to as "camions" by the local newspaper, were on hand.

A sea of used wheelbarrows awaits disposal at Camp Wallkill. An auction was held to sell the buildings and surplus equipment.

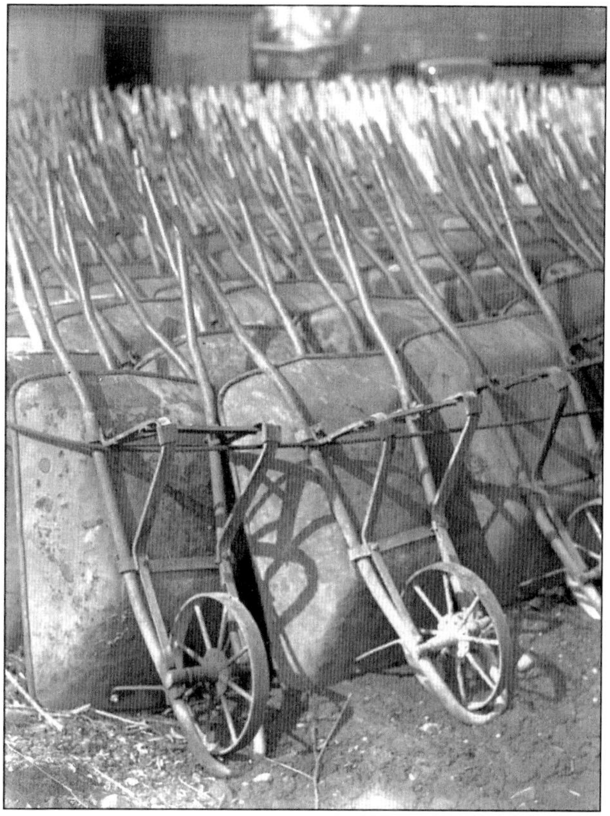

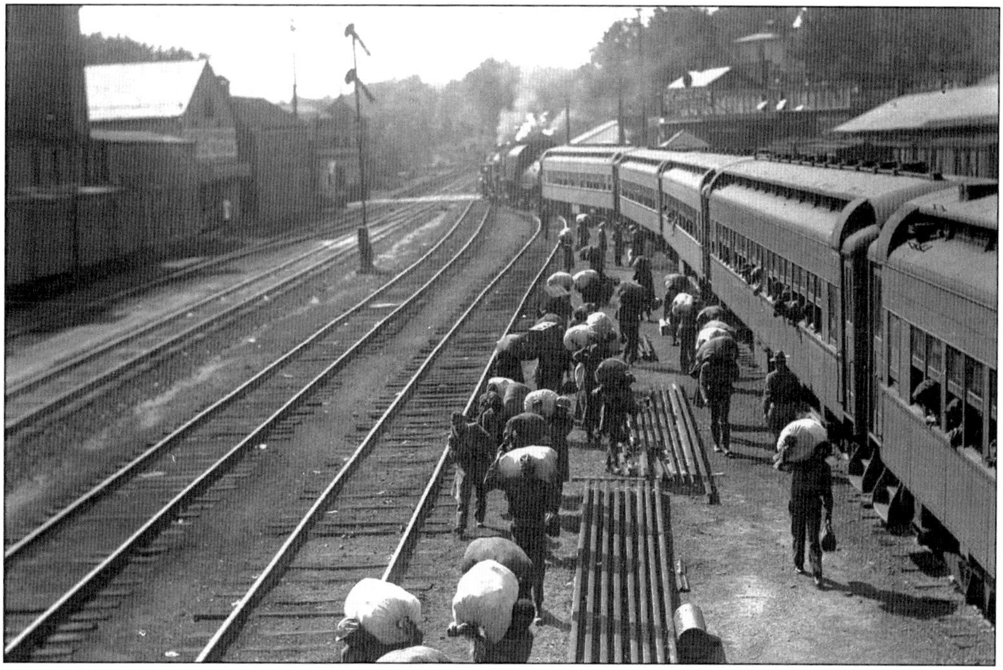

A westbound train loads enlistees in September 1937. These men may be en route to a new assignment. The train is shown in the Middletown yards.

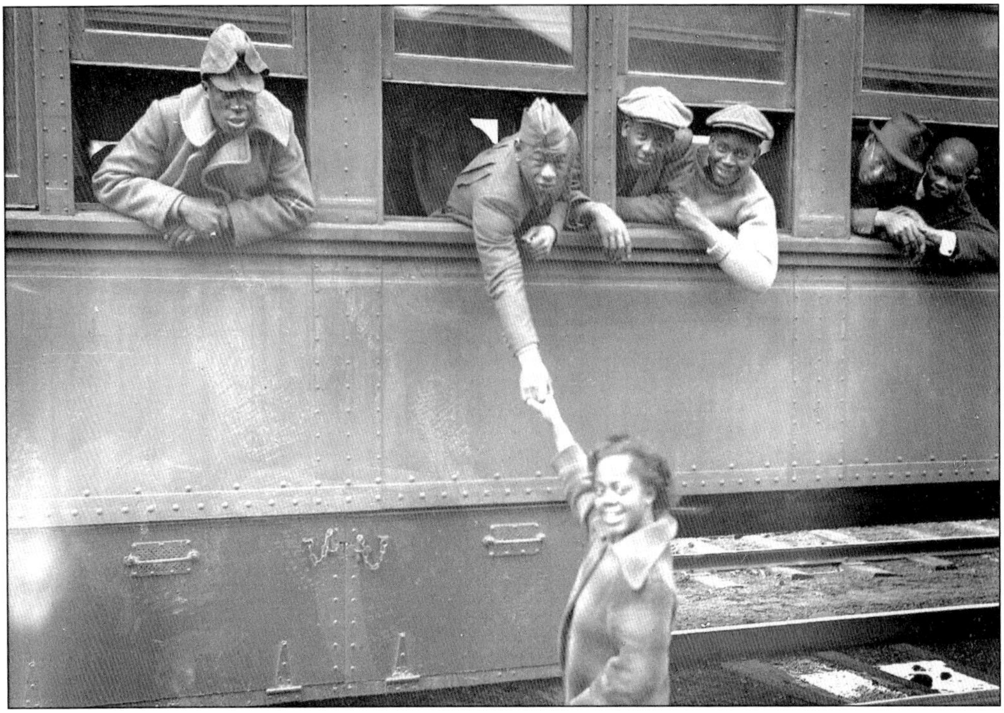

A local girl says goodbye. Her friend in the CCC is on the way to his next assignment.

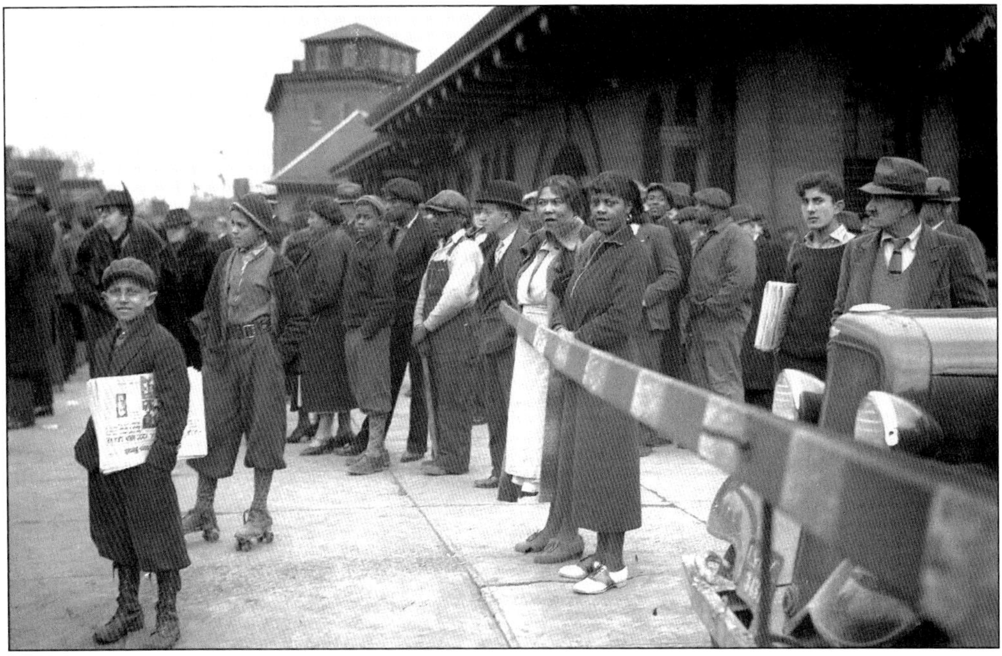

Following a stay of two years in the area, the CCC men board a train for their next assignment. While at New Hampton, the group used equipment ranging from hand tools to large mechanical draglines to straighten and realign the course of the Wallkill River. In this photograph, 12-year-old Joe Candito can be seen selling newspapers. Candito later became a Middletown letter carrier.

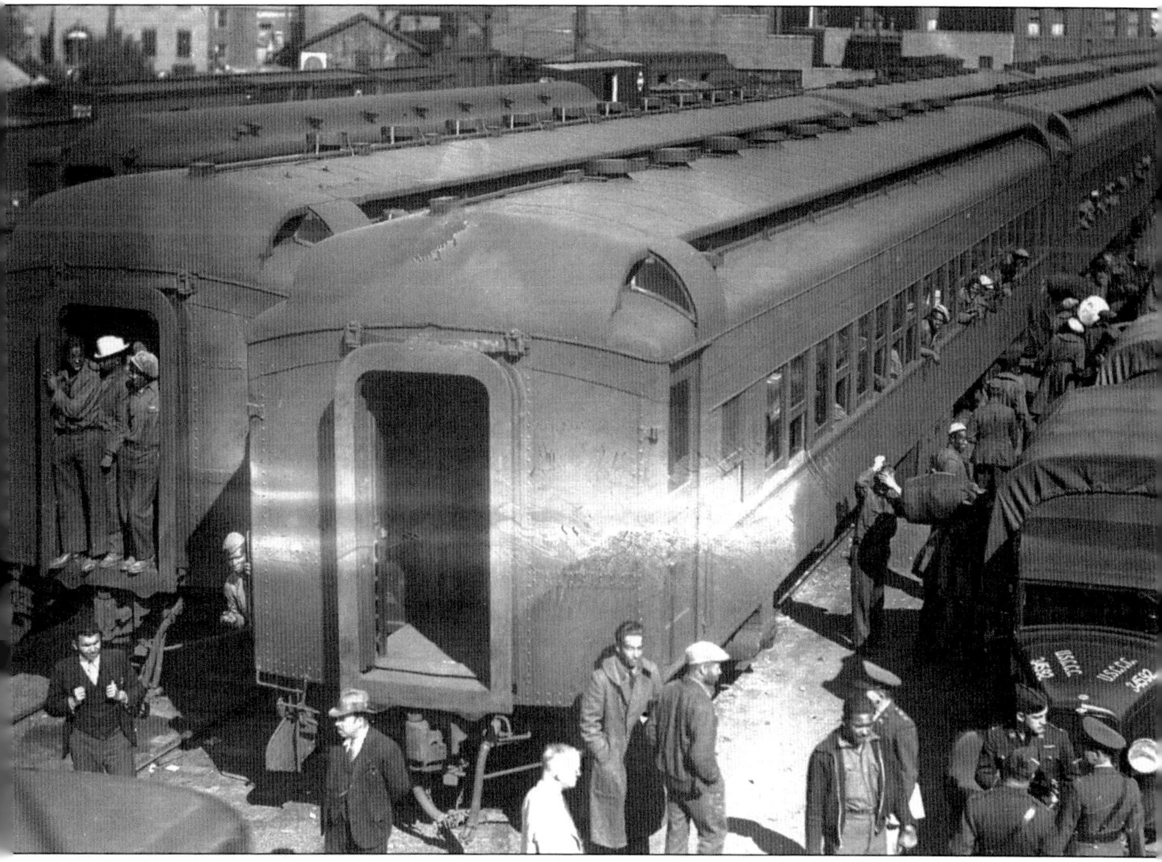

Several tracks of railroad cars are in Middletown's Erie Railroad yards, loading CCC men who have completed their stay in the area. The Chevrolet trucks are stenciled "U.S.C.C.C."

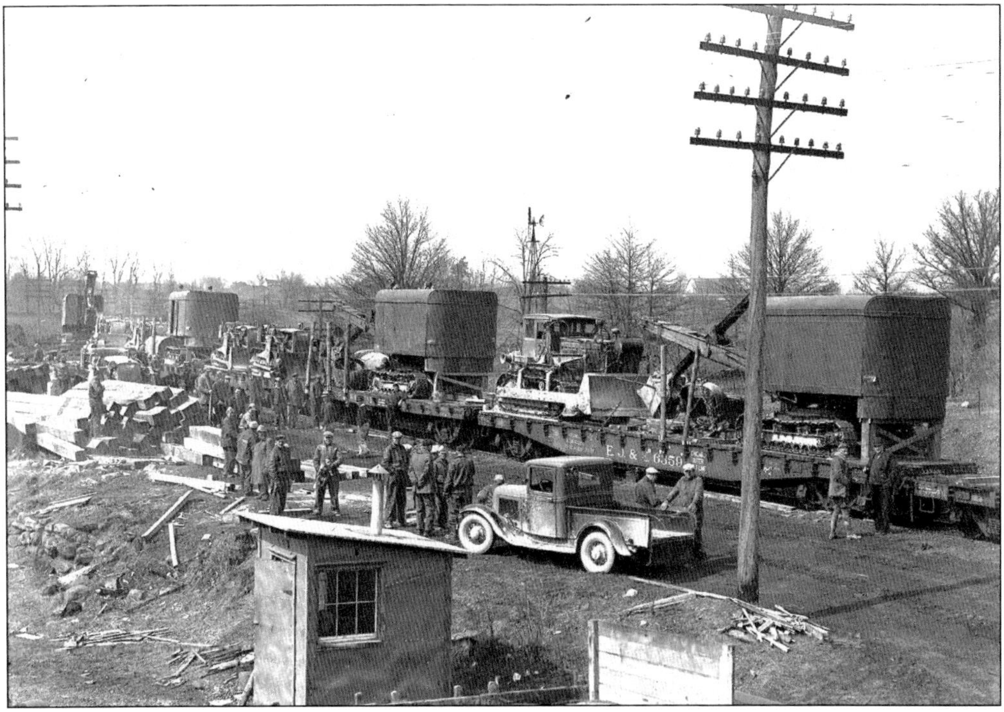

Much of the heavy equipment was loaded onto flatcars at New Hampton for use elsewhere.

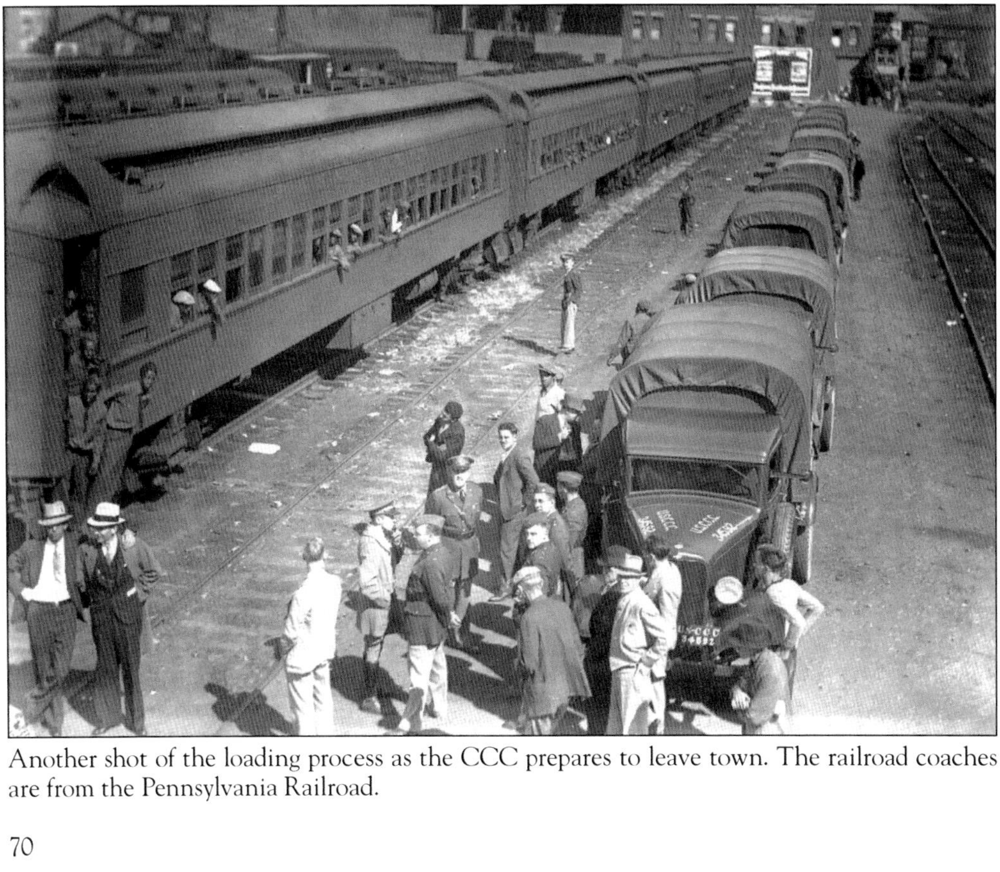

Another shot of the loading process as the CCC prepares to leave town. The railroad coaches are from the Pennsylvania Railroad.

Six

POST OFFICES

Middletown's first post office is preserved at the Historical Society of Middletown on East Avenue. A small, wooden box with a number of pigeon holes, it sat on the counter of Stacy Beakes store on North Street. After being located in several other buildings on North Street, the Post Office Department in 1911 constructed a new Federal Building at the corner of James and West Main Streets. The building featured ornate entrances on both streets.

As mail arriving by railroad began to be replaced by over the road tractor-trailers, the Middletown Post Office was at a disadvantage. There was insufficient room for large trucks to load and unload and in addition, there was very limited customer parking.

When urban renewal leveled large tracts in the Fulton Street area, postal officials decided to relocate the post office to a sizable lot on Fulton Street between South Street and Wawayanda Avenue. The present building was dedicated in 1962 and is leased, not owned, by the U.S. Postal Service.

The 1911 federal building was extensively remodeled and serves today as Middletown's police headquarters.

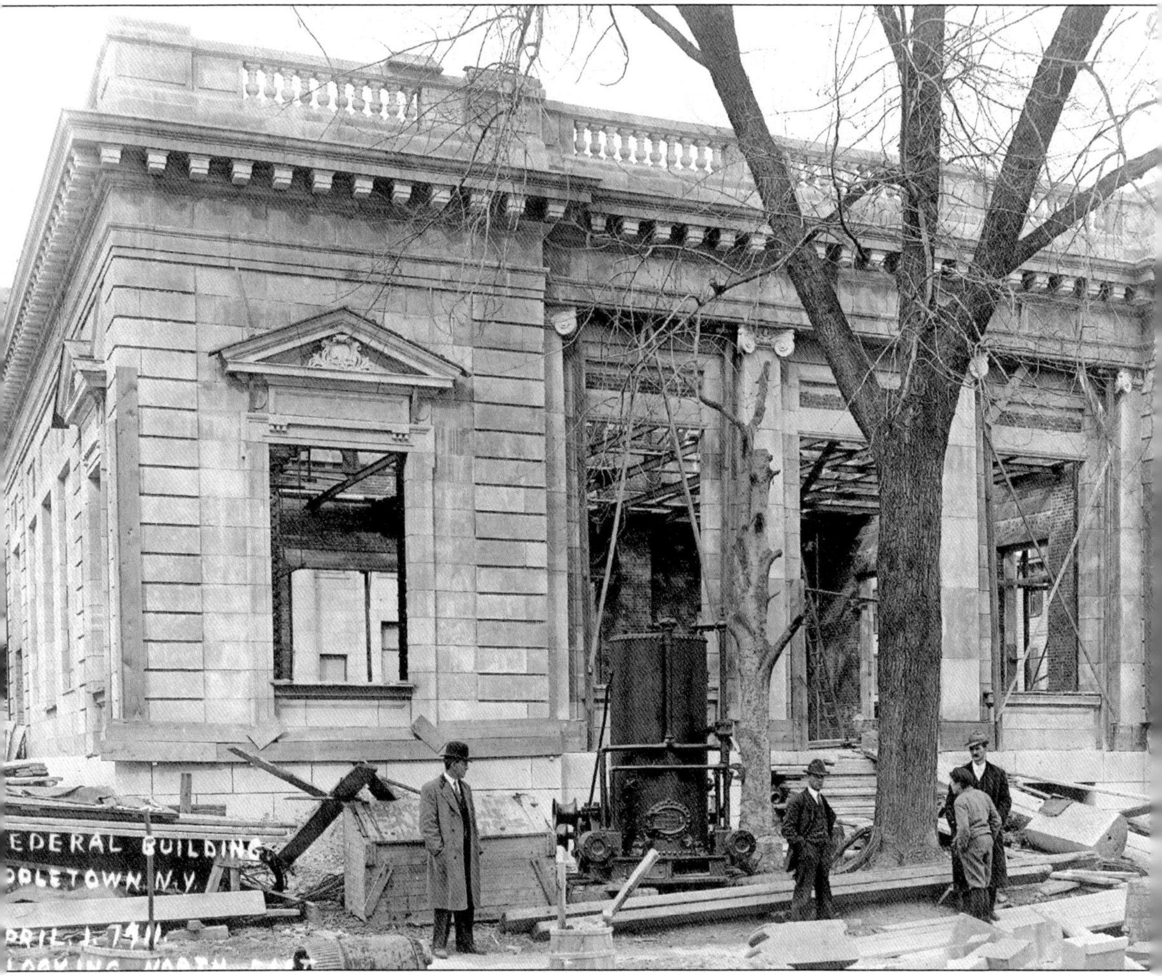

The federal building on James Street is nearing completion in April 1911. The steam-powered boiler in the foreground is a hoist for raising building materials.

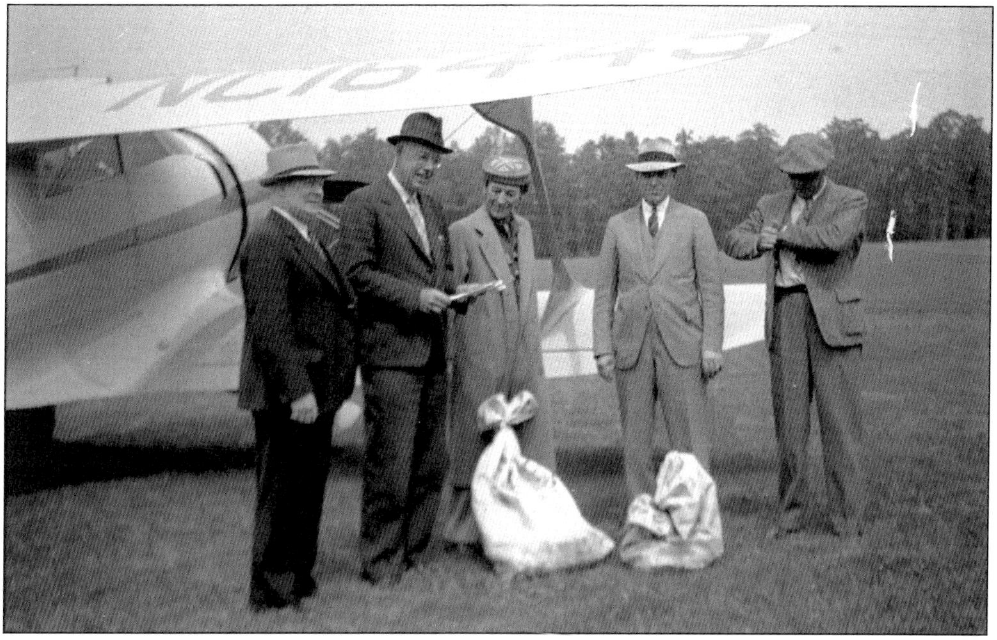

This photograph is taken from Air Mail Week in 1938. This was the scene at Starhaven Airport on May 15, 1938. Seen here are, from left to right, postmaster Fred F. Sheerin, Richard D. Clemson, Mabel Clemson, mayor Robert P. Anderson and pilot Lloyd O. Yost. The mailbags are about to be loaded into Mable's Beech aircraft. Starhaven Airport was located on Randall Heights in Middletown.

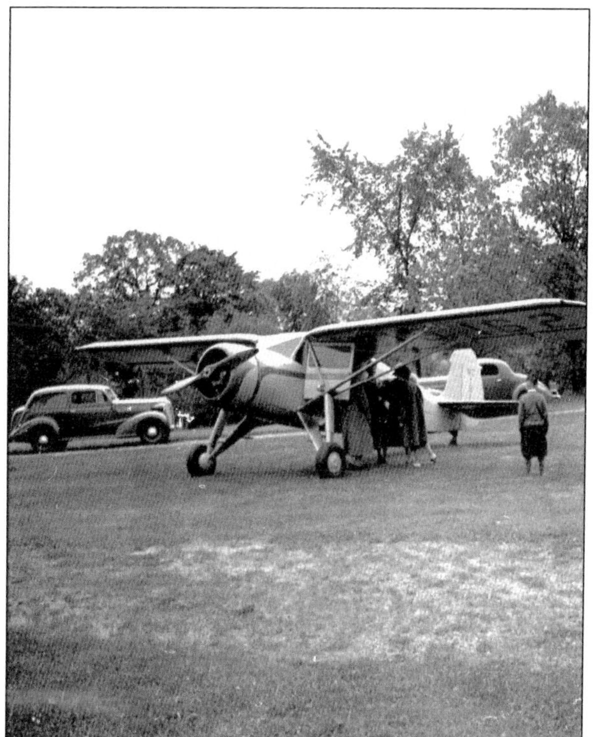

This photograph shows another view of the Starhaven Airport on May 15, 1938.

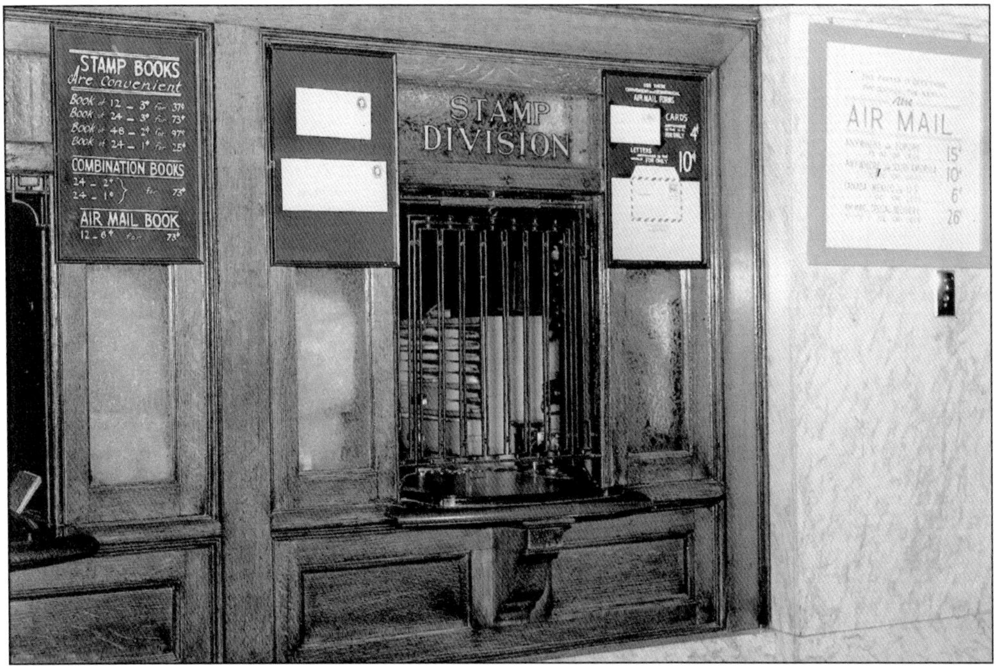

A nostalgic look inside the old post office on James Street is the subject of this photograph. The marble clad walls, the barred stamp window, and, above all, the postage rates hark back to an earlier era. Postage at the time was three cents for a letter or only two cents for local delivery.

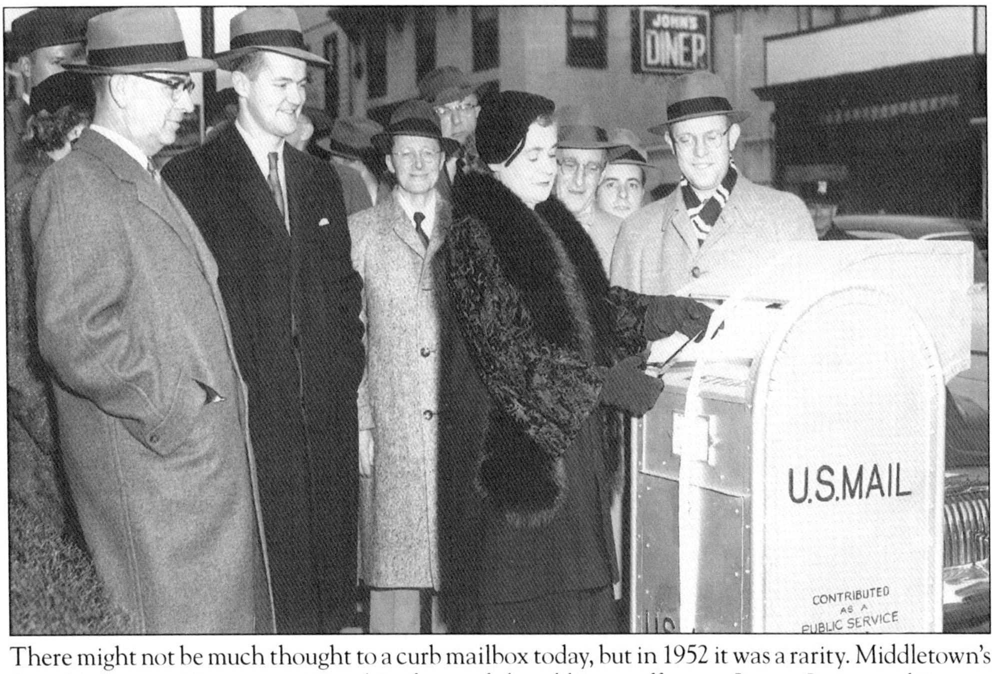

There might not be much thought to a curb mailbox today, but in 1952 it was a rarity. Middletown's first drive-up mailbox was situated in front of the old post office on James Street and is seen here at its dedication. The date is January 5, 1952, and congresswoman Katharine St. George is cutting the ribbon. Looking on, from left to right, are postmaster Robert R. Austell, mayor Louis V. Mills, Vincent Foeller, James Garland, Fred Germain, and Fred Coldwell.

Seven

RAILROADS

Middletown was long noted for its railroads. The Erie Railroad served the city with both passenger and freight trains. Another line, the New York, Ontario and Western Railway (NYO&W), made Middletown the site for its general offices, locomotive and car shops, and principal switching yards. The NYO&W became one of the two largest employers in the city. The NYO&W, a 550-mile line, was finally abandoned in April 1957, the largest railroad in the United States at that time to be completely dissolved. One rail line, however, still exists. The Middletown and New Jersey Railway (M&NJ) operates from a historic depot at 140 East Main Street. From 1960 to 1966, a tourist train with a small steam locomotive operated over the M&NJ. Each weekend between Memorial Day and Labor Day, the steam-powered train ran from Middletown to Slate Hill, a 14-mile round trip.

Plan Now To Attend . . .

ERIE DAY CELEBRATION

In MIDDLETOWN

WEDNESDAY MAY 26

FREE! — $150 in War Bonds — FREE!

$50	FIRST PRIZE!	To the Person Wearing the Oldest Costume in the Parade!
$25	SECOND PRIZE!	To the Person Wearing the Next Oldest Costume in the Parade!
$50	FIRST PRIZE!	For the Oldest Horse-drawn Vehicle in the Parade!
$25	SECOND PRIZE!	For the Next Oldest Horse-Drawn Vehicle in the Parade!

SEE THE EVOLUTION OF TRANSPORTATION!

PARADE! MUSIC! PRIZES! CELEBRETIES!

COSTUMES OF "DAYS GONE BY!"

HORSE-DRAWN VEHICLES! OLD TRAINS!

HISTORIC STORE — WINDOW DISPLAYS!

And Many Other Attractions Wednesday, May 26

The Erie Railroad Company and the City of Middletown jointly sponsored the Erie Day Celebration. This rare handbill survived in pristine condition.

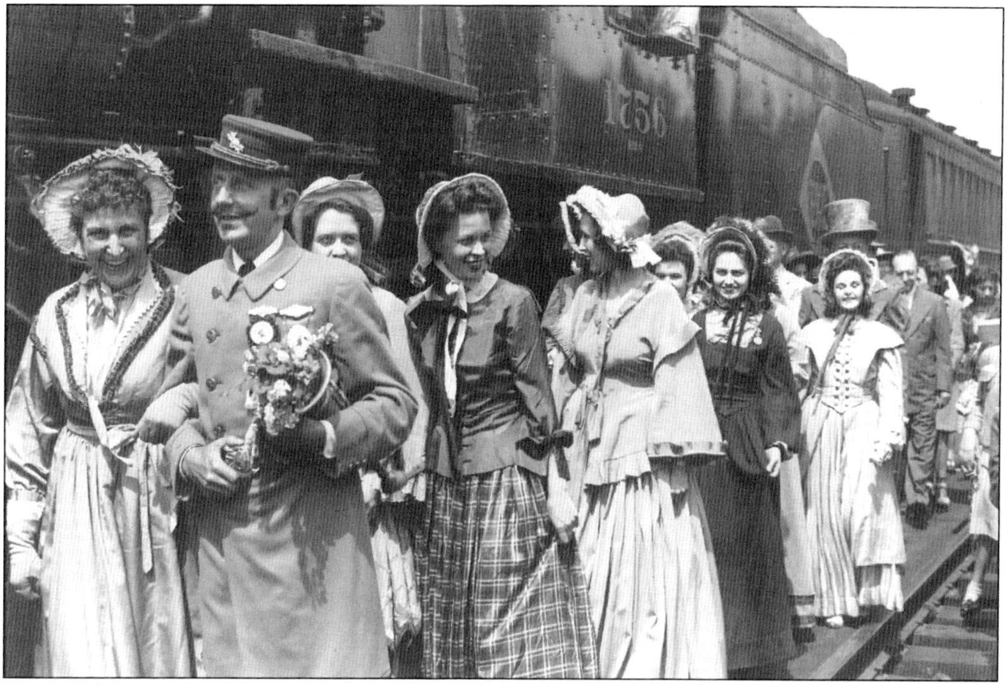

Wednesday, May 26, 1943, was Erie Centennial Day in Middletown. On that date in 1843, the first train entered the city. Here the scene is recreated, and the passengers disembark. Dan Frolin and Betty Schuerholz lead the colorful procession.

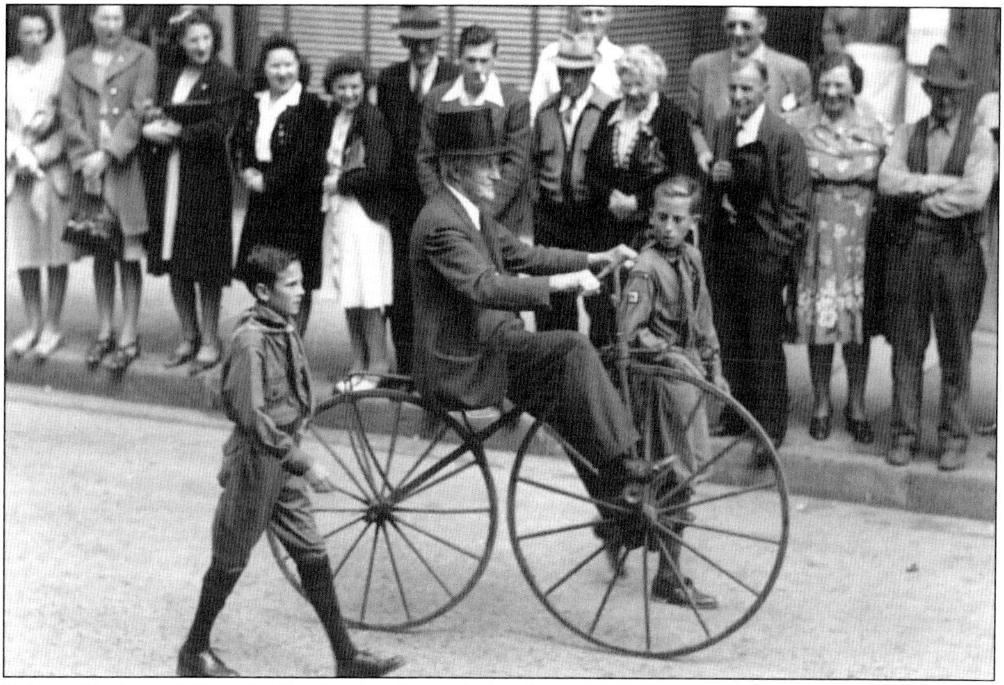

Egbert Tooker of Slate Hill rides his boneshaker bicycle on Erie Centennial Day. Tooker was then 82 years of age. The wooden bicycle, long in the possession of the Historical Society of Middletown, was transferred to the Wawayanda Historical Society a few years ago.

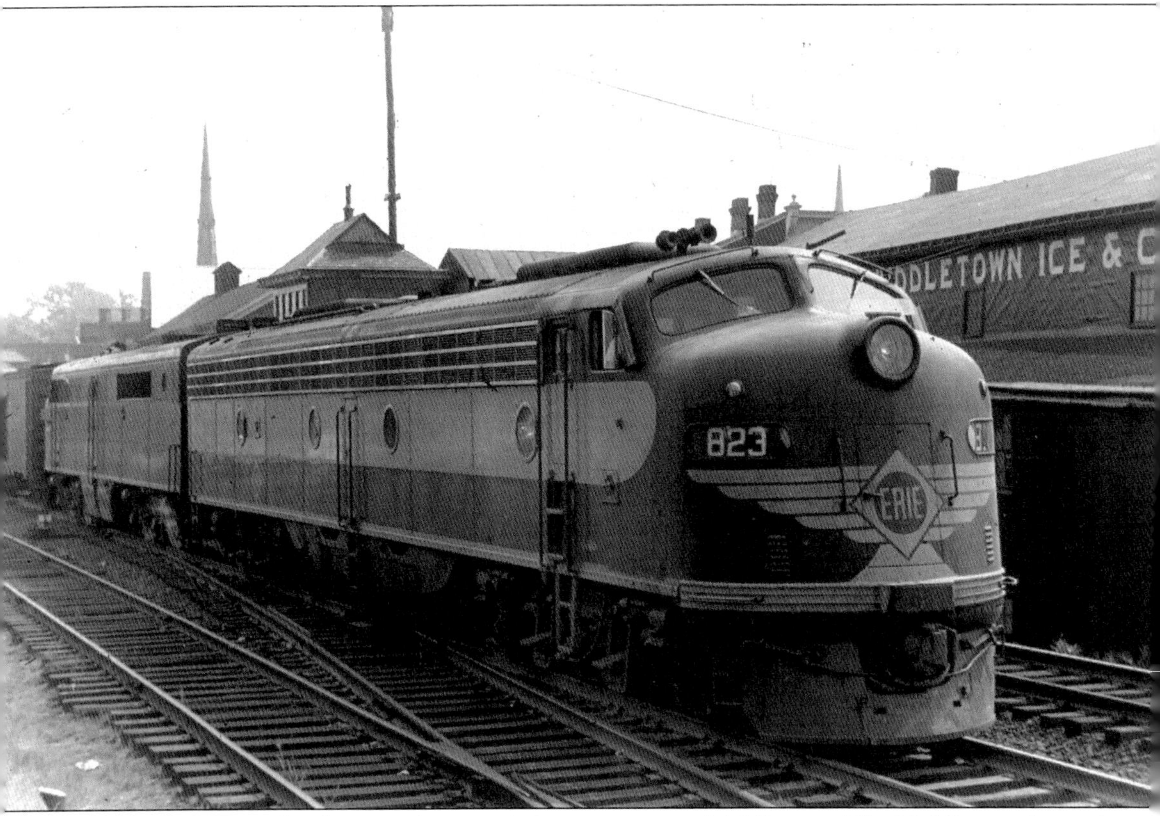

The Erie Limited is shown making its daily station stop at Middletown. The Middletown Ice and Coal Company building is now the site of the Salvation Army.

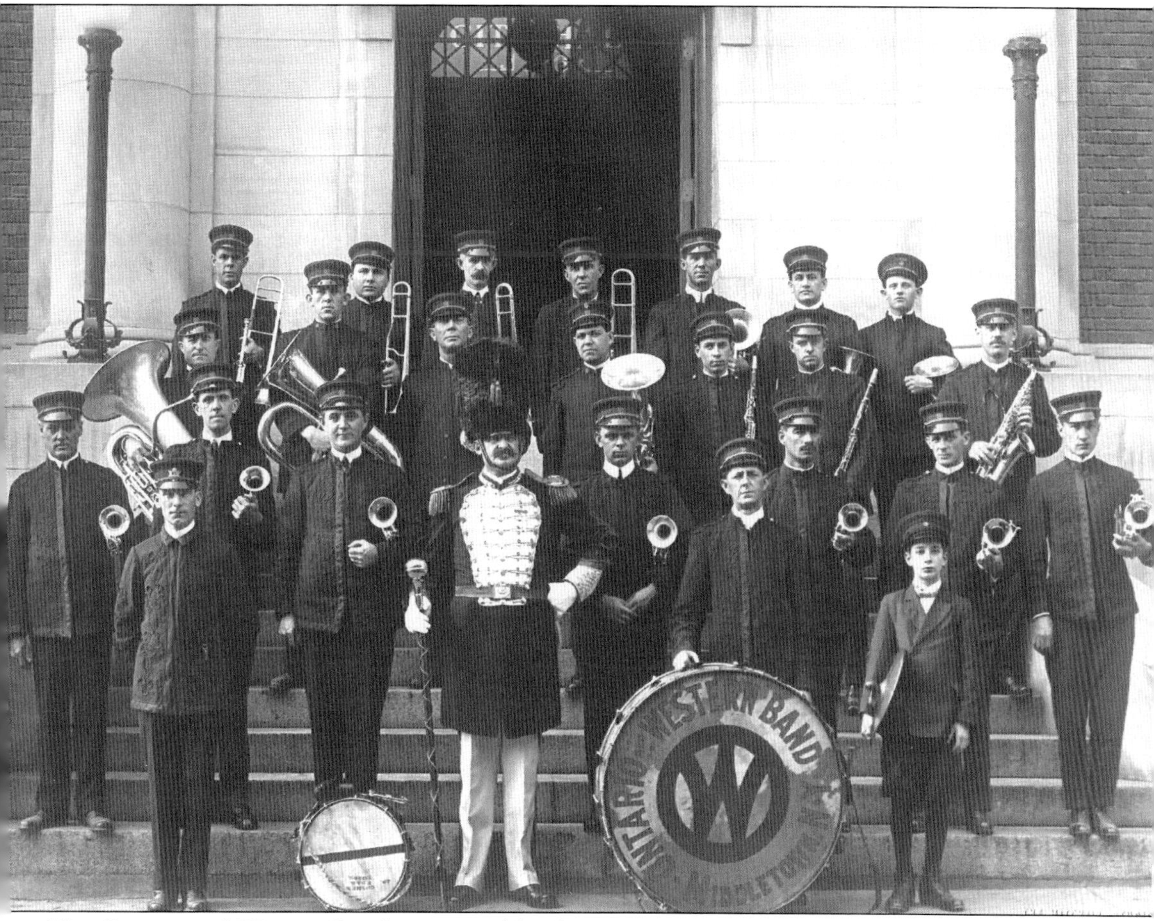

The Ontario and Western Band, sponsored by the NYO&W, poses on the steps of city hall in this undated photograph. John M. Wilson is drum major. The NYO&W was one of the largest employers in the city.

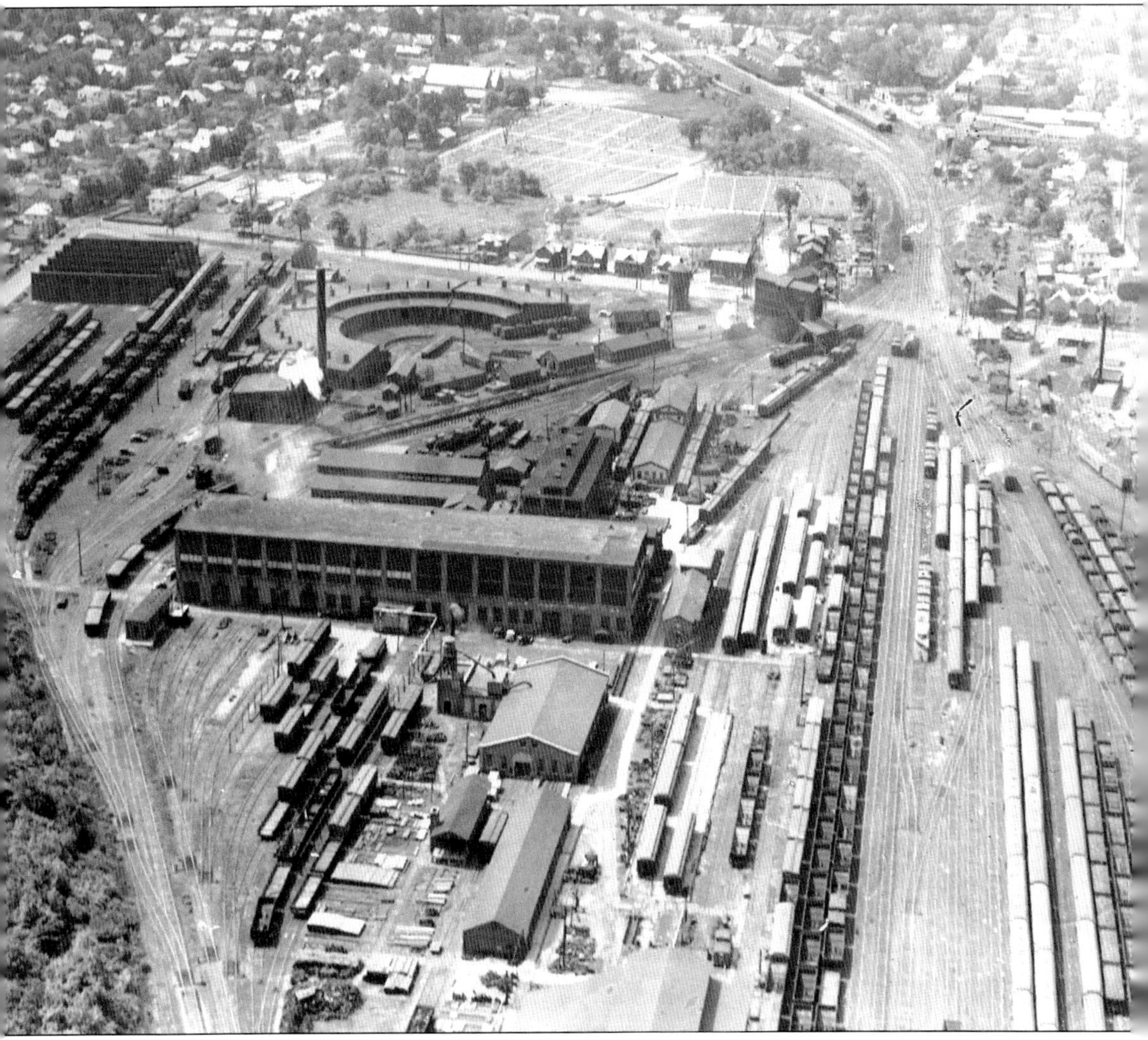

This photograph will give some idea of the NYO&W's presence in Middletown. This aerial view shows Wisner Avenue at the top of the picture. The open space in the top center is St. Joseph's Cemetery. The large building in the foreground is the locomotive shop, which still stands. The roundhouse is evident with its turntable. On the left with the saw tooth roof was the paint shop, which also remains. The multitudes of yard tracks are gone, save for one line of rails which remain in place today.

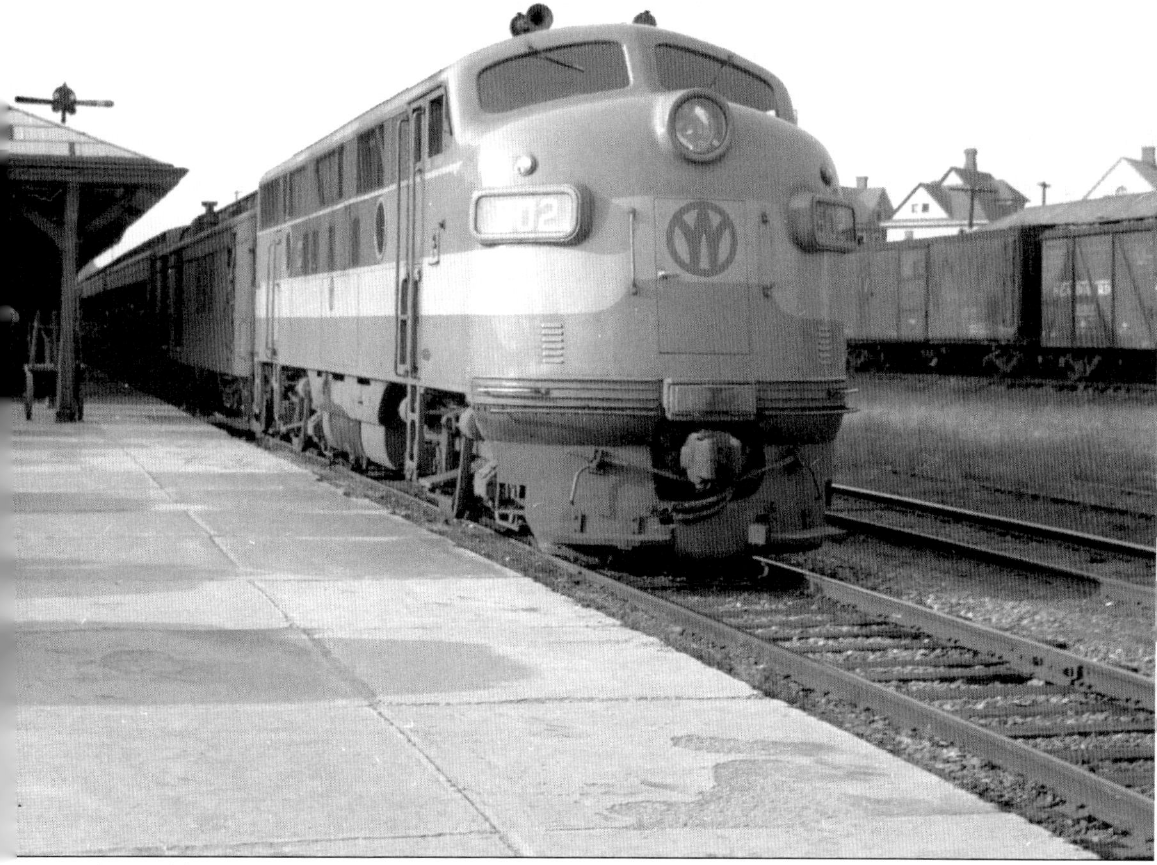

At the Wickham Avenue station of the NYO&W locomotive 502 waits for departure time. It is almost the end of passenger service on the line, but today the 502, a mail and express car, and several coaches are ready to make the run to Weehawken, New Jersey.

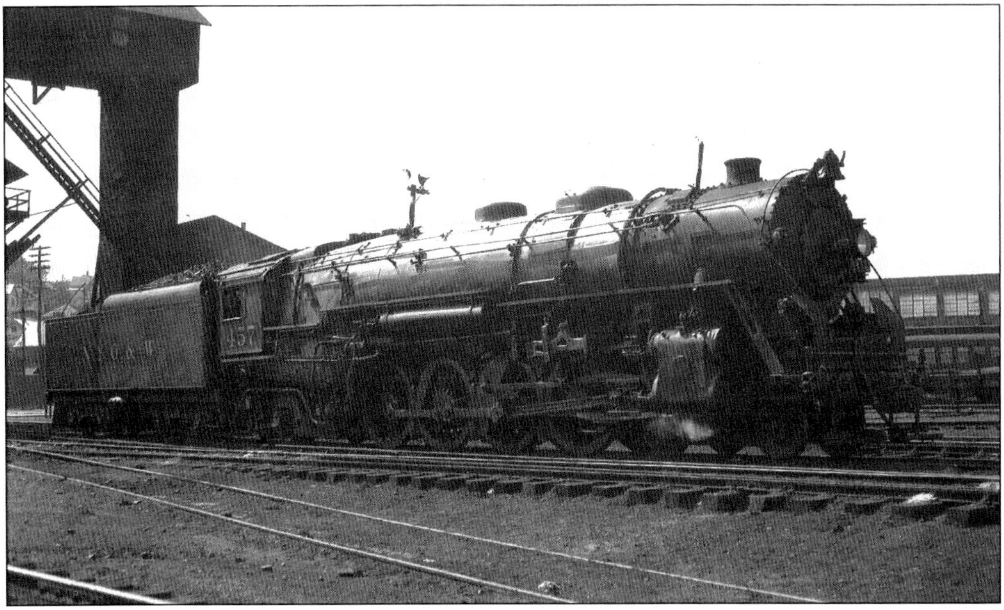

NYO&W locomotive 457 was known as a heavy Mountain type and powered the roads through freight trains. It is shown here at Middletown yards in the 1930s

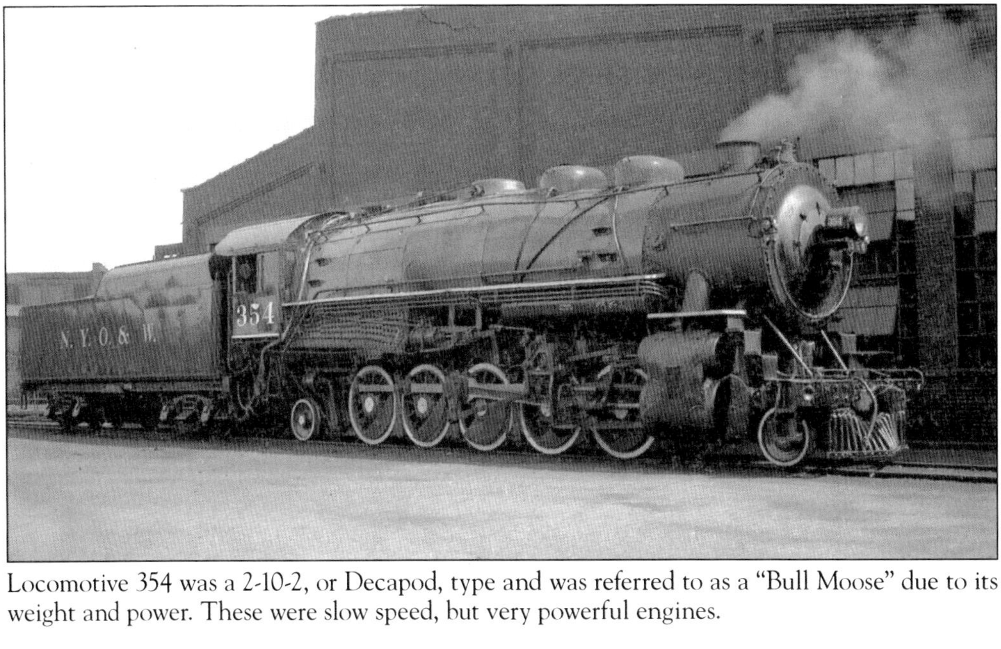

Locomotive 354 was a 2-10-2, or Decapod, type and was referred to as a "Bull Moose" due to its weight and power. These were slow speed, but very powerful engines.

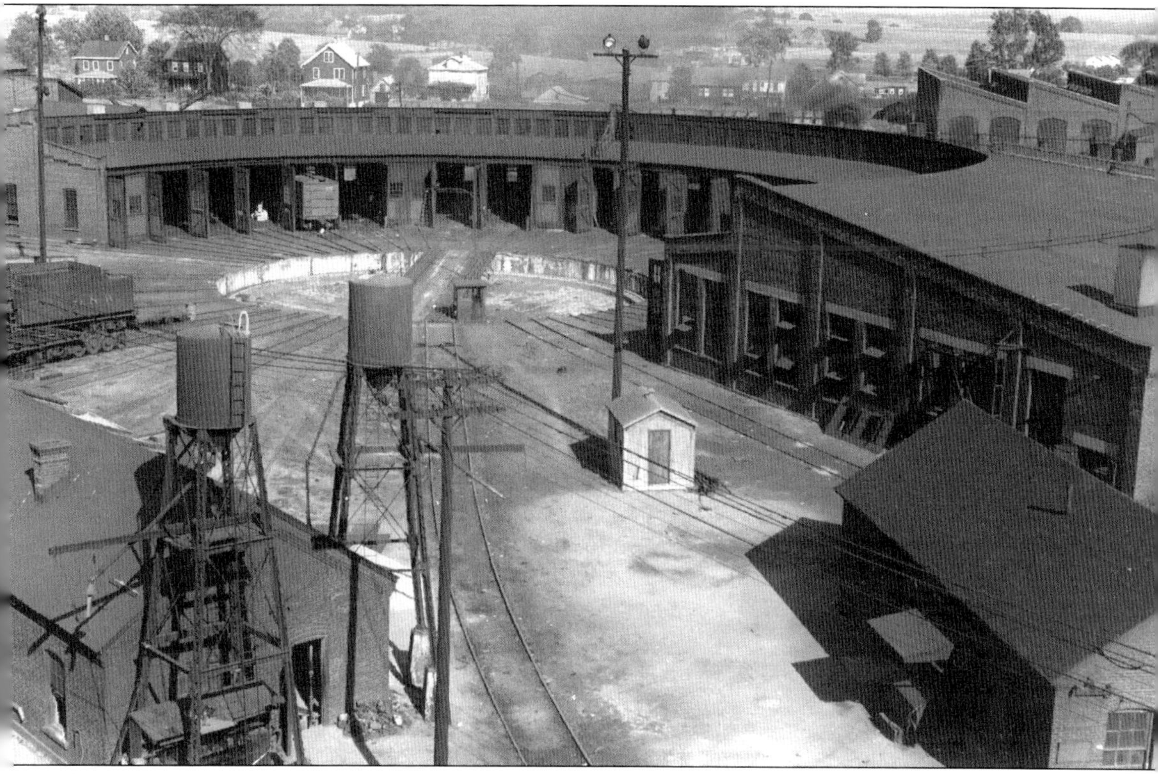

This close-up shows a view of the roundhouse. A locomotive would run onto the turntable, which would transfer it to one of the stalls. The roundhouse staff made running repairs to the engines and prepared them for their next duty. Also shown here are two sand towers and the sand house. Locomotives require clean, dry sand to help with adhesion.

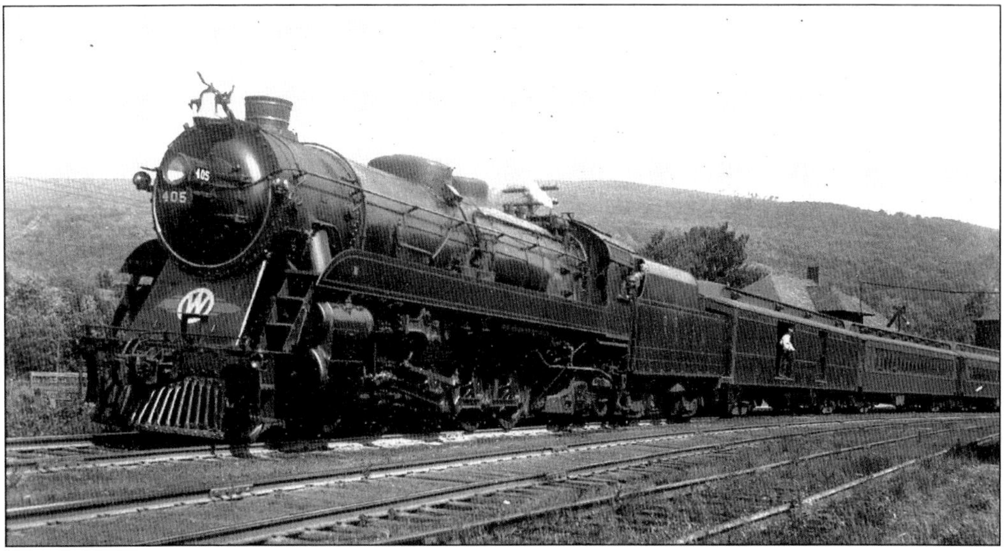

Mountaineer locomotive 405 makes a station stop with a northbound passenger train.

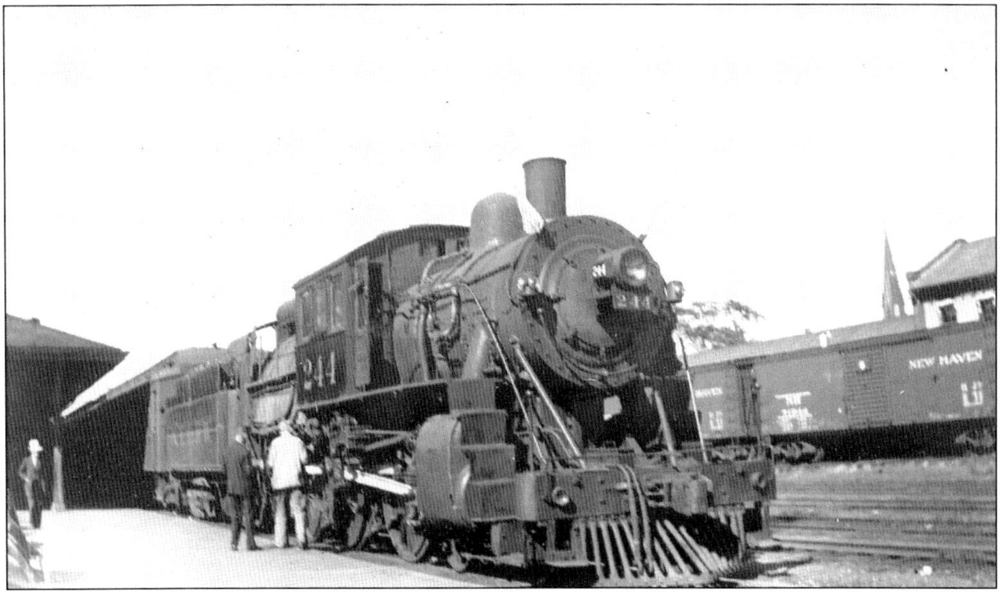

NYO&W engine 244 prepares to leave with an eastbound extra passenger train in the mid-1930s. No. 244 was a camelback type locomotive with the cab placed over the boiler. The Middletown freight station can be seen in the background. The white flags on the front of the engine denote an extra train.

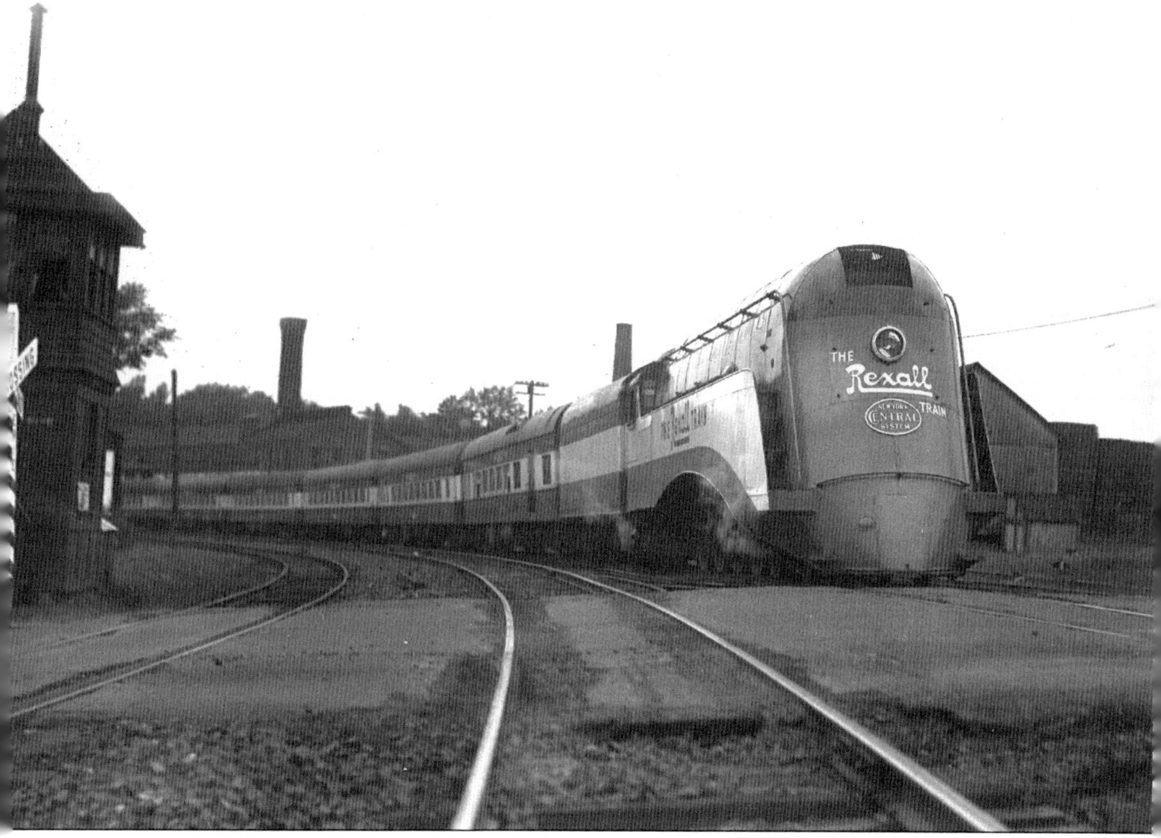

The Rexall Train visited Middletown on August 28, 1936. Sponsored by the Rexall Drug Company, the special train toured the United States and Canada. The streamlined New York Central locomotive is seen here crossing East Main Street.

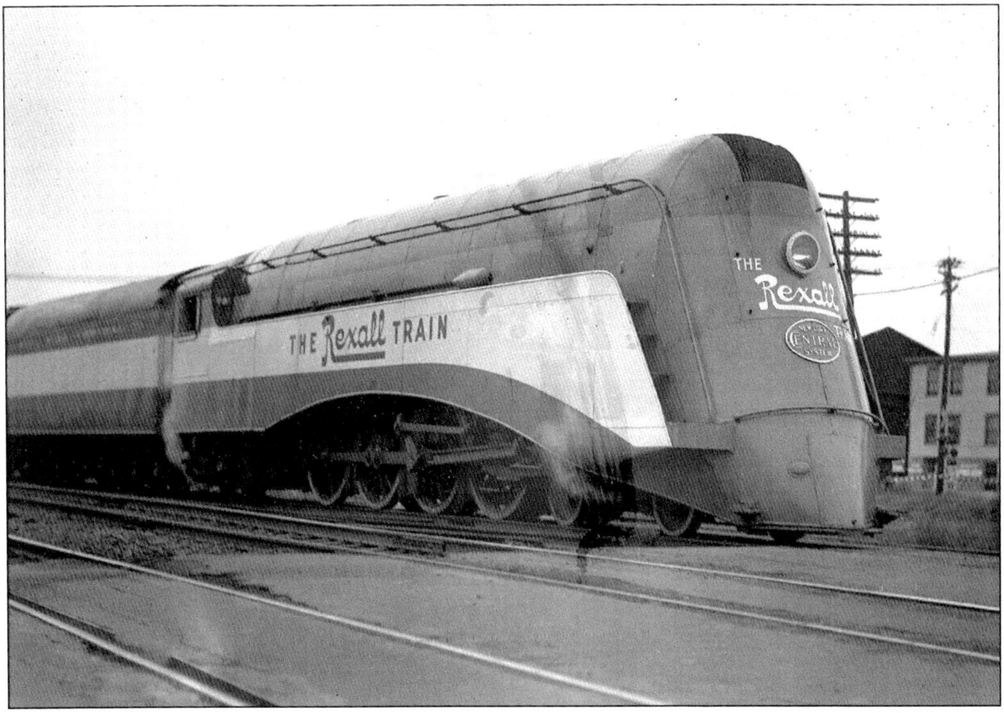

A picture of the Rexall Train's locomotive is seen here. The drug company leased this engine from the New York Central Railroad.

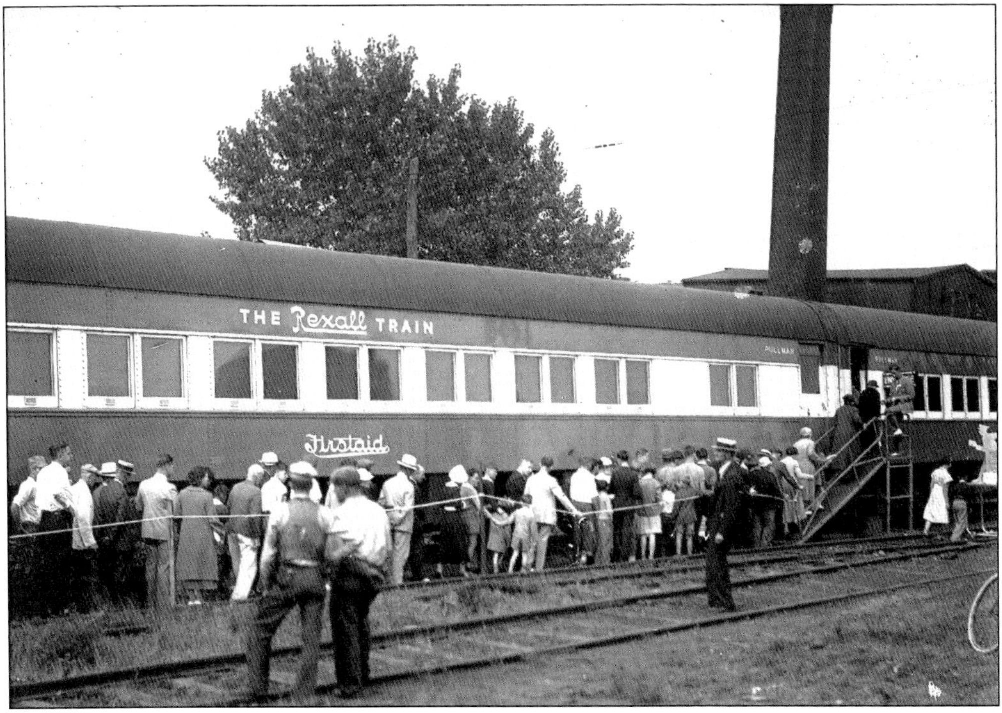

This view of the Rexall Train shows how the display cars were positioned on Railroad Avenue for public viewing.

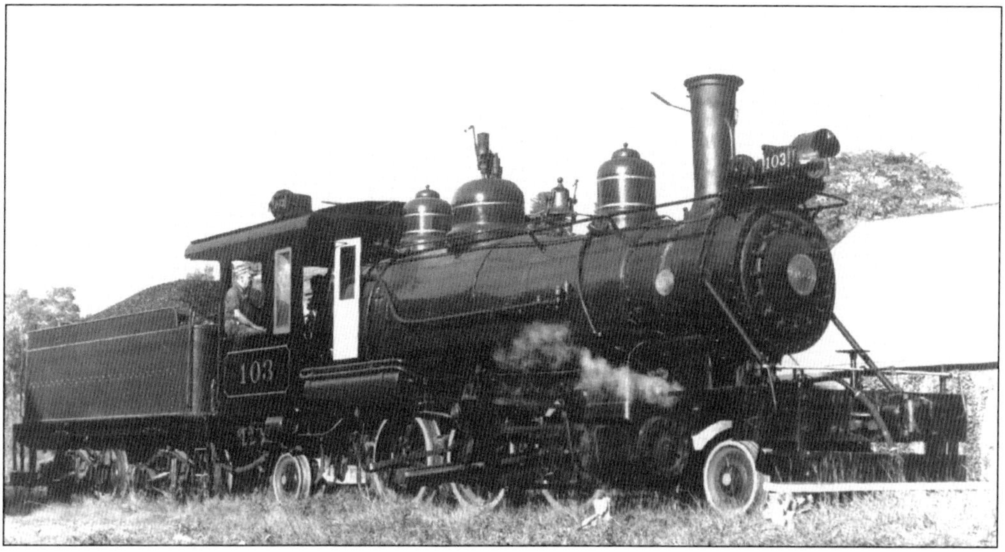

In 1960, the Empire State Railway Museum purchased and restored this steam locomotive for excursion service. No. 103 came from the Sumter and Choctaw Railway and operated from 1960 to 1966 over the Middletown and New Jersey Railway between Middletown and Slate Hill.

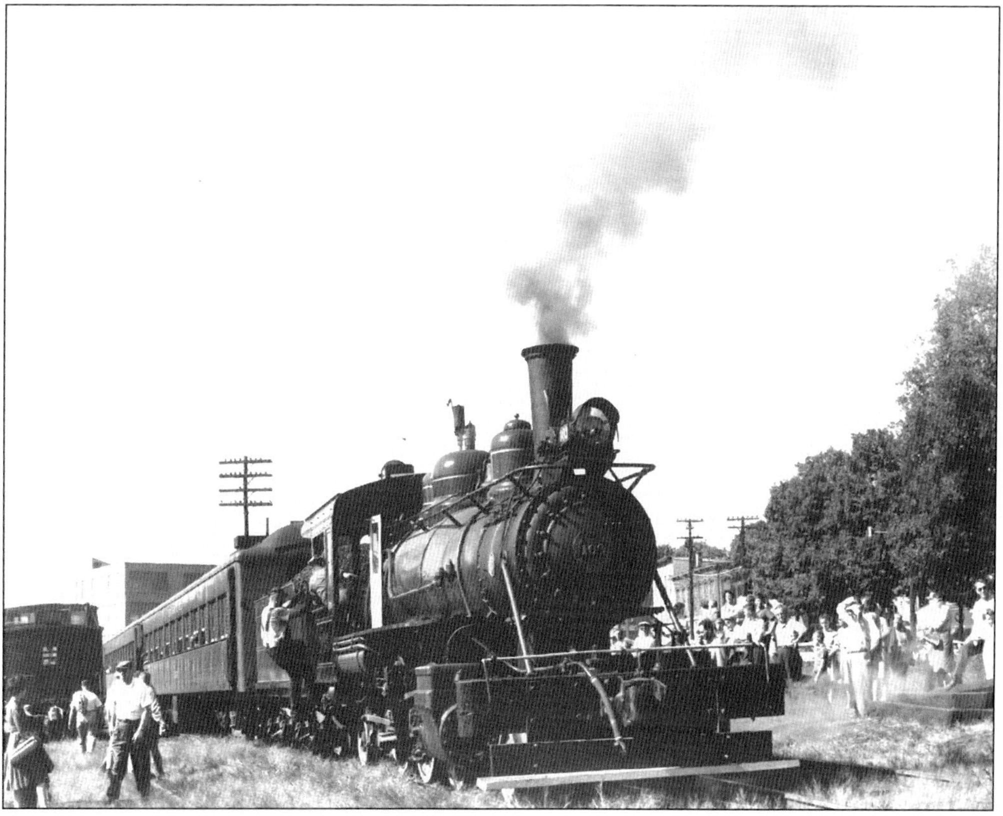

The train is seen at Middletown on an early excursion. Engineer Pete Rasmussen climbs into the cab.

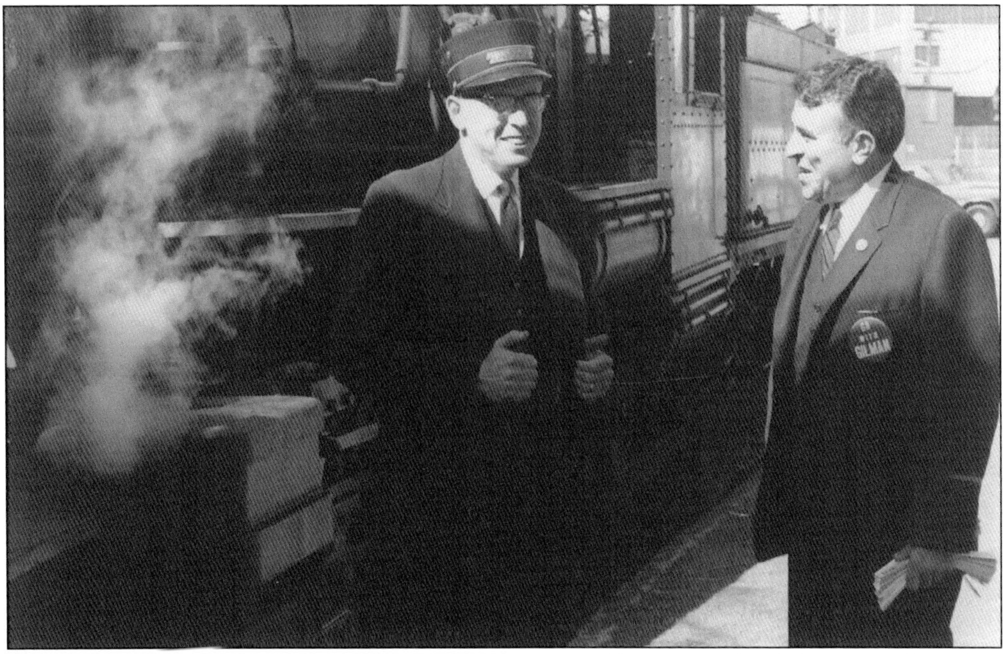

The author, Marvin Cohen, talks with congressman Benjamin A. Gilman in this 1964 photograph. Cohen was a volunteer conductor on the tourist train.

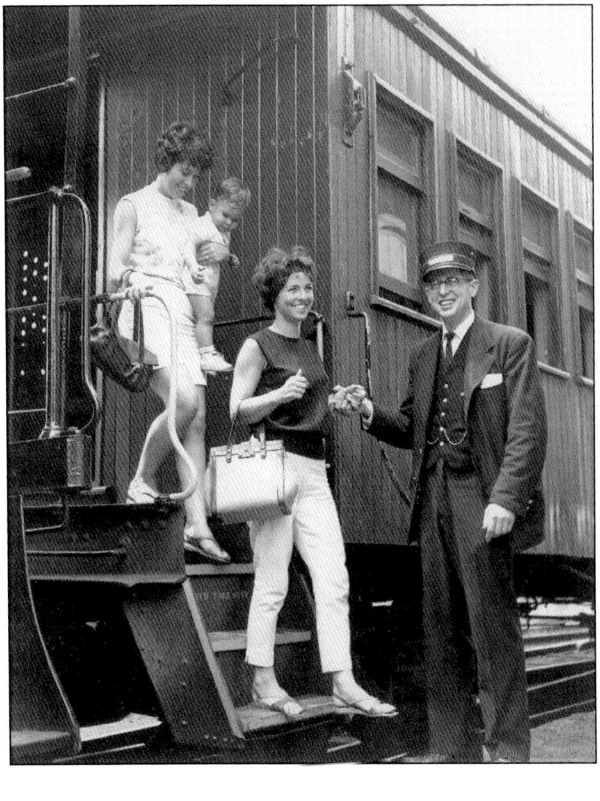

Conductor Cohen helps a passenger alight from the caboose at the end of a journey over the Middletown and New Jersey Railway. The train ran from Middletown to Slate Hill.

Eight

Education and Institutions

During the days when all children walked to school, neighborhood, or ward, schools were a necessity. Middletown had eight such buildings, a few of which are still being used today. With the consolidation of Middletown and Town of Wallkill school districts, new buildings were gradually constructed.

"The City on the Hill" was the title applied to the Middletown State Hospital. For many years the city's largest employer, the Middletown State Hospital boasted over 100 buildings at one time and housed a patient population of several thousand people. In 1954, for instance, there were 3,809 patients in the institution. Originally known as the Middletown State Homeopathic Hospital, it was one of a number of such institutions in New York State. Today while many buildings remain, the Middletown State Hospital is but a shell of its former self.

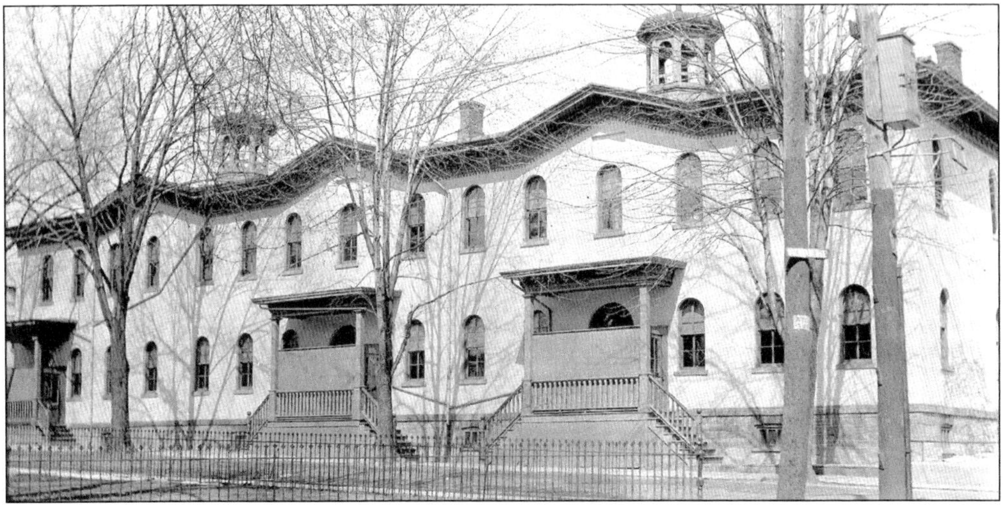

The old Liberty Street School bore no resemblance to the present building. This view was taken in June 1927, shortly before the structure was razed. The new school building opened in 1928 and still stands.

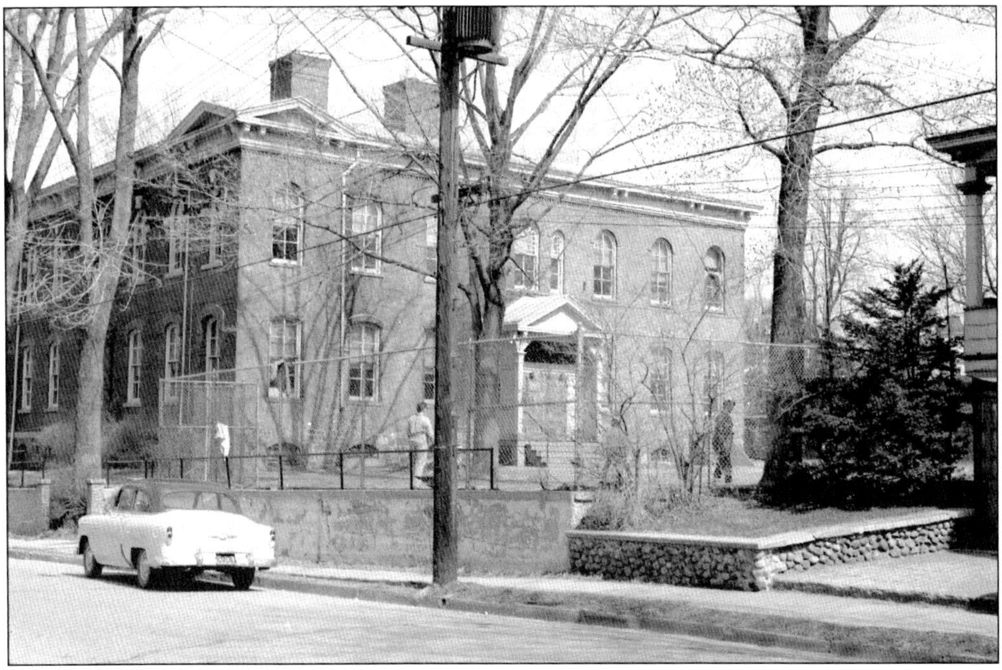

This is a view of Benton Avenue School from the Benton Avenue side. The school was closed in 1963 and suffered a disastrous fire in 1980, which caused the structure to be razed.

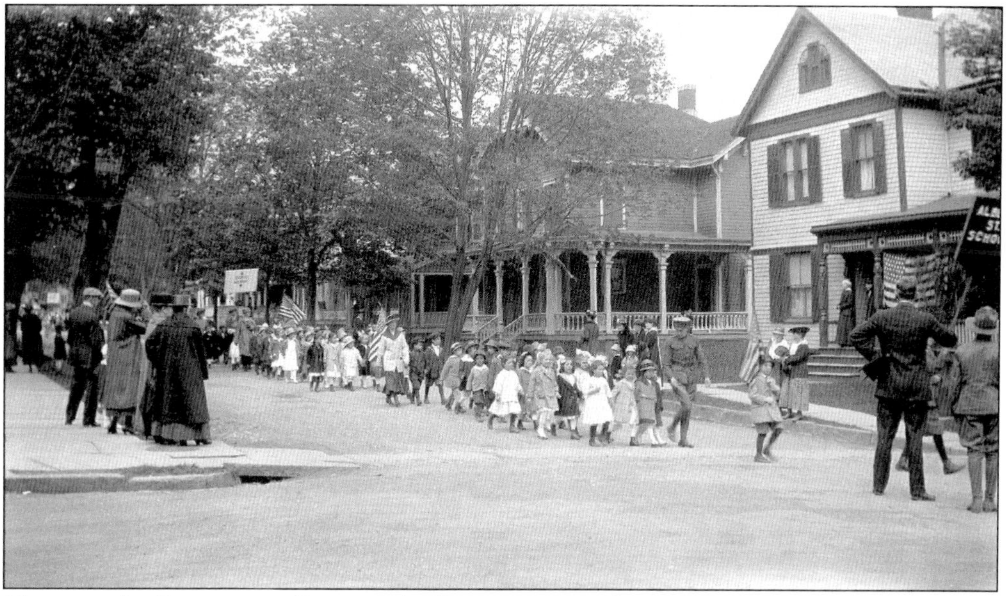

This was the Registration Day parade, June 5, 1917. All men between the ages of 21 and 31 years were required to register for the draft on this date. Children from Albert Street School are shown on Highland Avenue preparing to march down West Main Street. Patriotic parades like this were held throughout the country on this date.

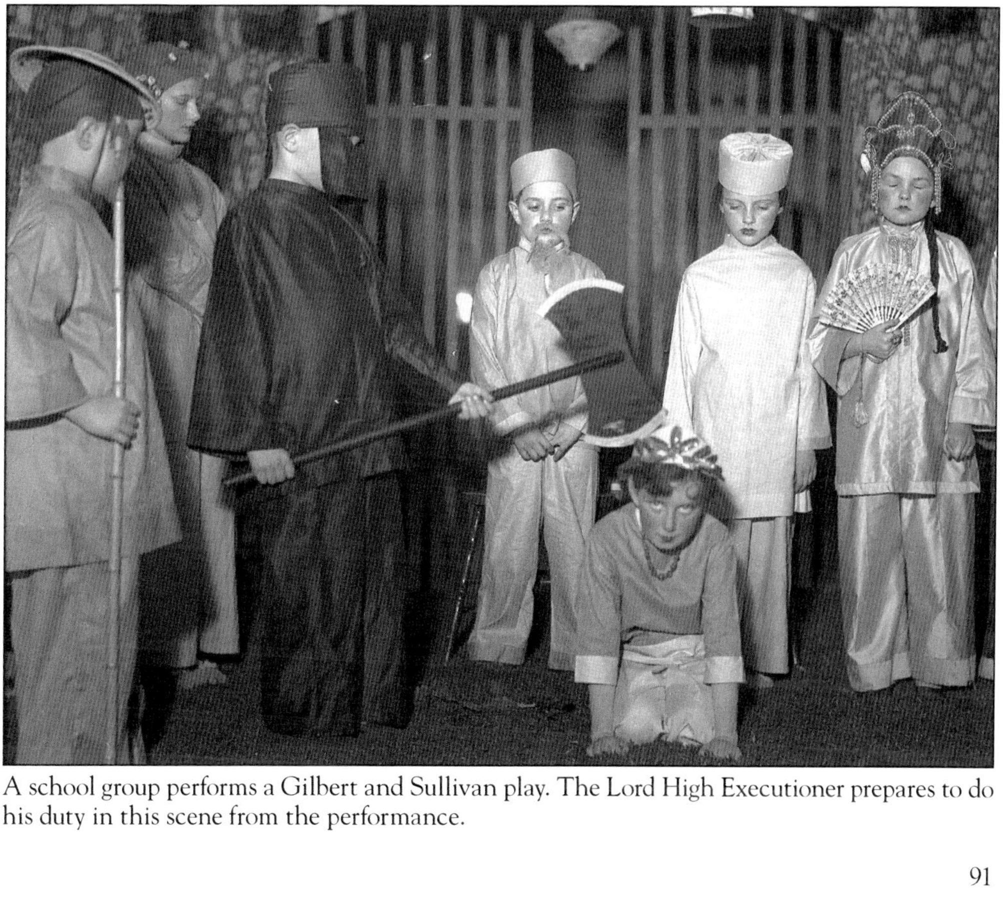

A school group performs a Gilbert and Sullivan play. The Lord High Executioner prepares to do his duty in this scene from the performance.

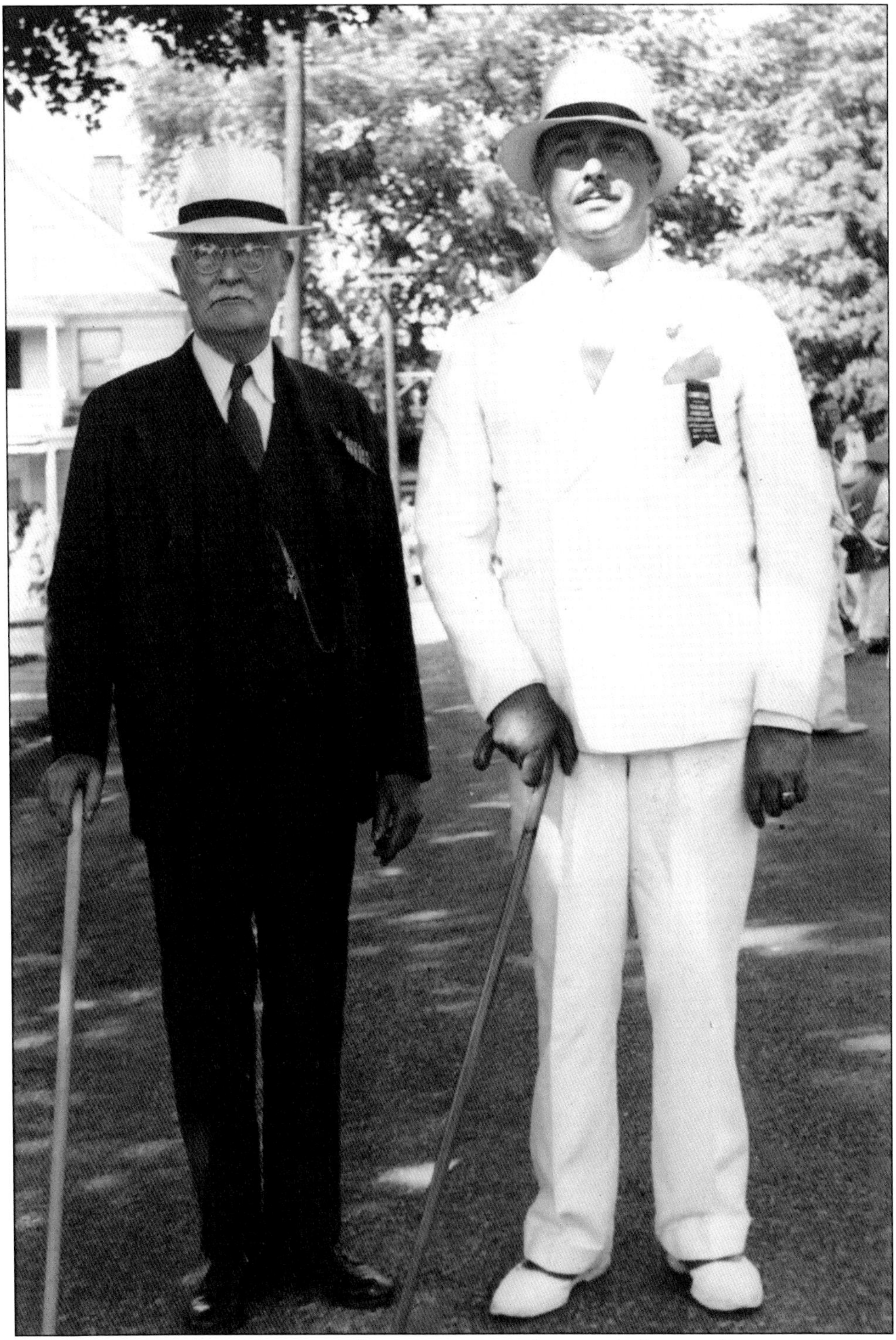

Two well-known educators pose with their Panama hats and their walking sticks during Middletown's Golden Jubilee parade in 1938. On the left is William Wilson, principal of Middletown High School, with Frederic P. Singer, vice principal.

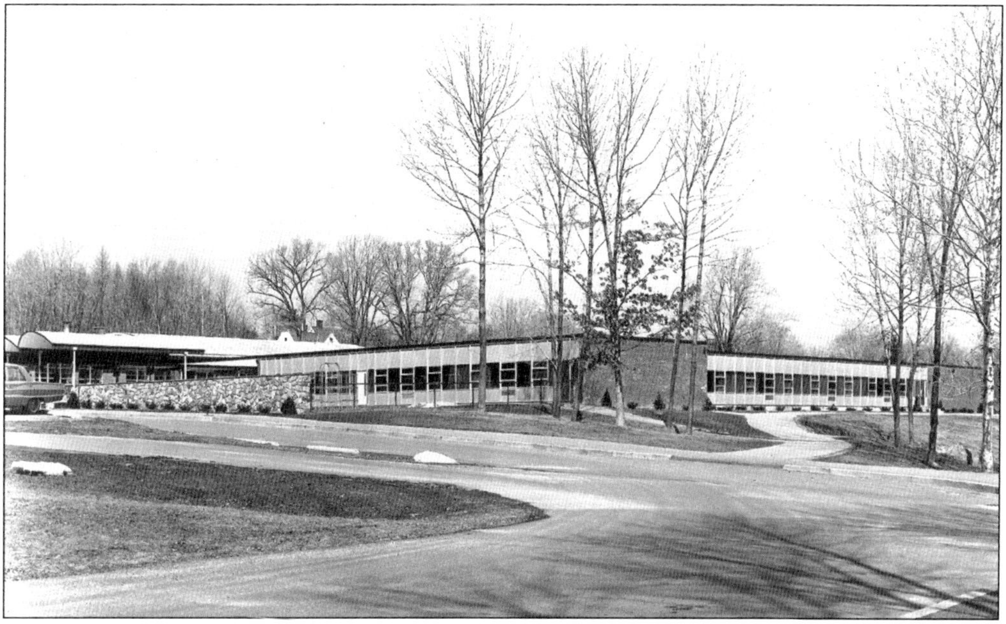

In 1955, a new elementary school was opened on Bedford Avenue. The school was named in honor of longtime educator Truman Jesse Moon, who taught in Middletown from 1907 to 1937.

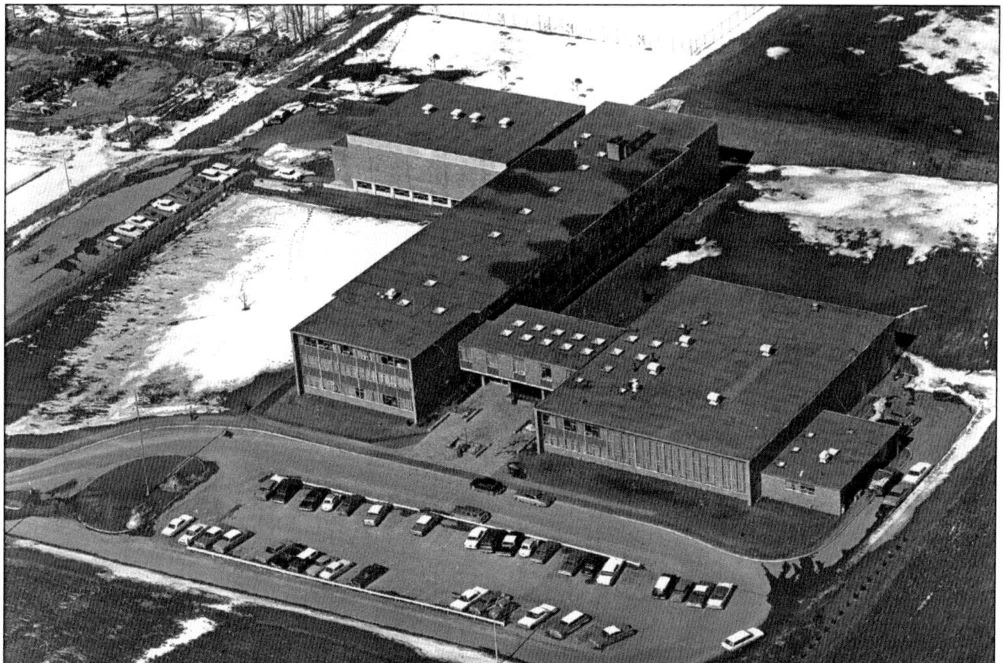

Anthony J. Veraldi Junior High School looked like this when first built. This school on Gardner Avenue replaced Memorial Junior High School. Later in an exchange of buildings, the junior high moved to Grand Avenue and was renamed Twin Towers Middle School. The newer structure became Middletown High School. Anthony J. Veraldi Junior High School was named for a Middletown attorney who served many terms as president of the board of education.

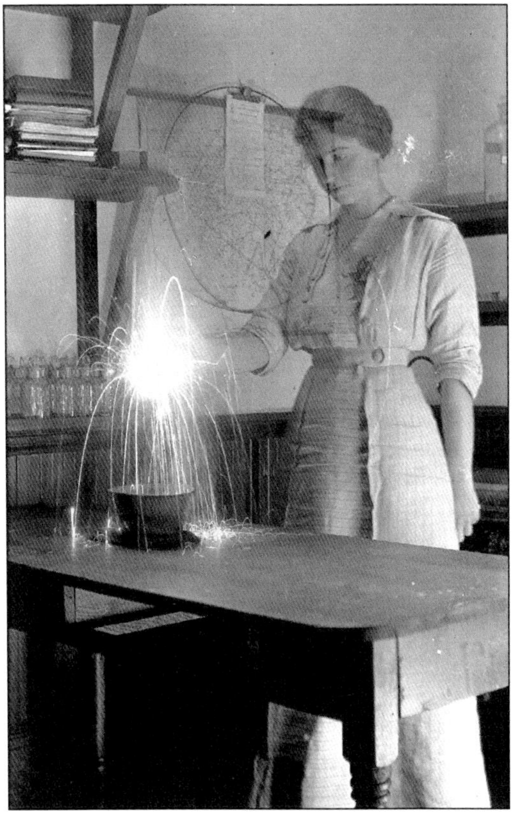

Eudora Horton performs an experiment in Truman Moon's chemistry class in Middletown High School. The year was 1914.

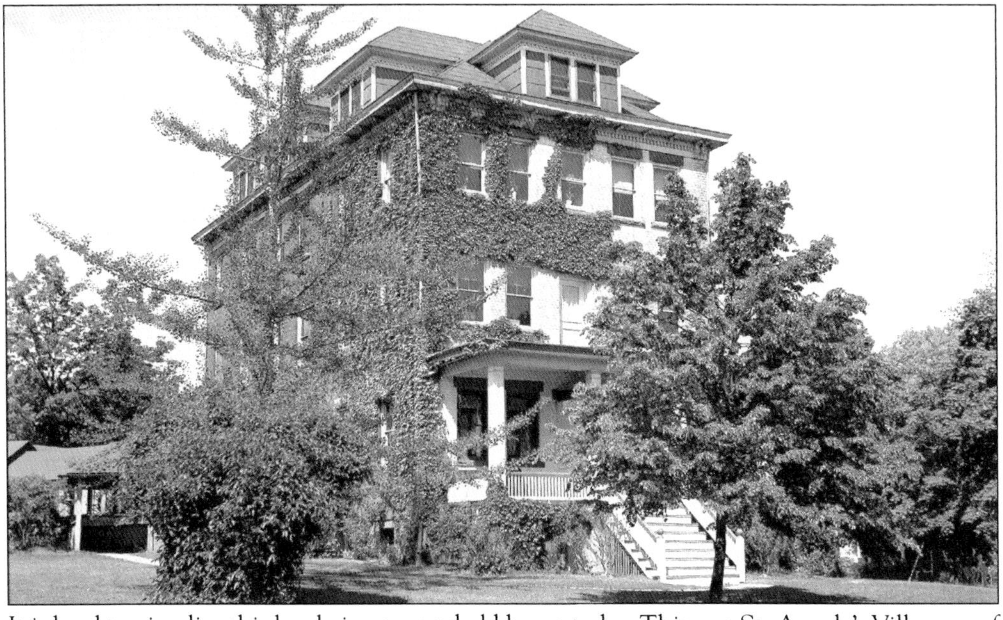

It is hard to visualize this lovely ivy-covered old home today. This was St. Angela's Villa, one of two houses of the Ursuline Academy at the corner of East Main Street and Grand Avenue. The academy graduated its last class of female students in 1952. Shortly after the school closed the main building was destroyed by fire. A drug store and strip mall occupy the site today.

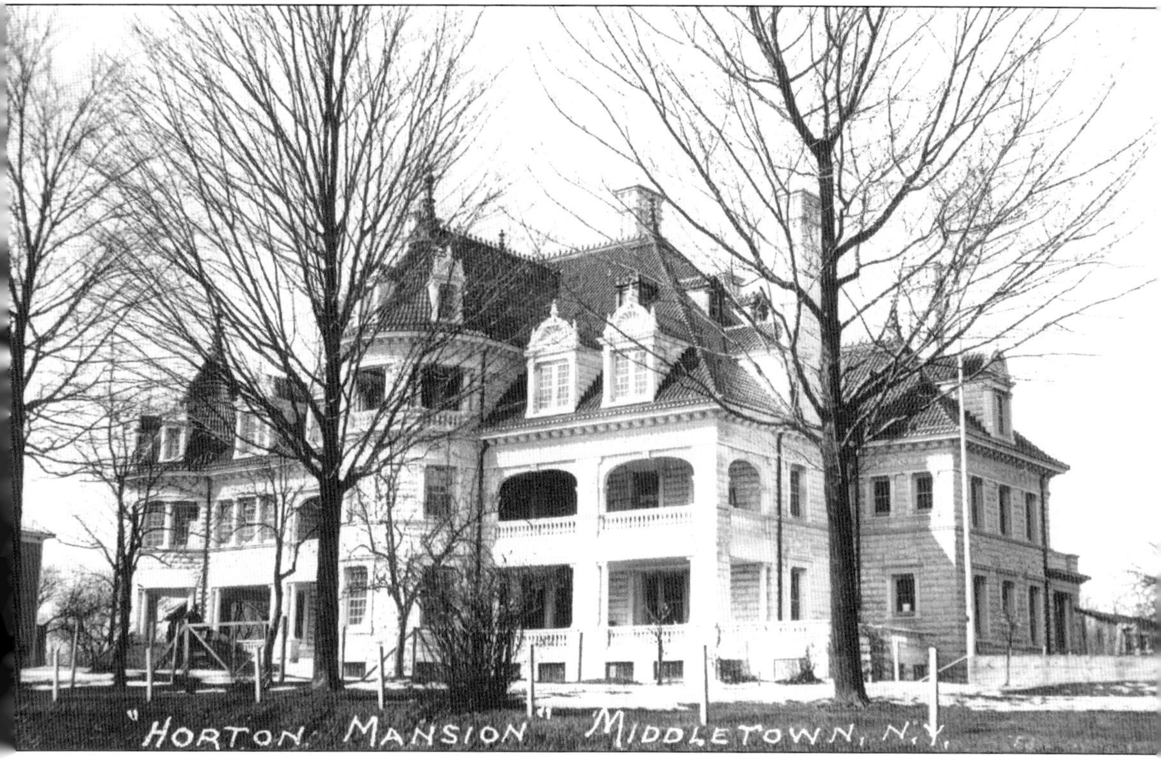

One of the gems of the city is Morrison Hall. The former home of Webb Horton and later the Morrison family, the building is now the centerpiece of the local college. Originally Orange County Community College, the institution is now known as State University of New York (SUNY) Orange.

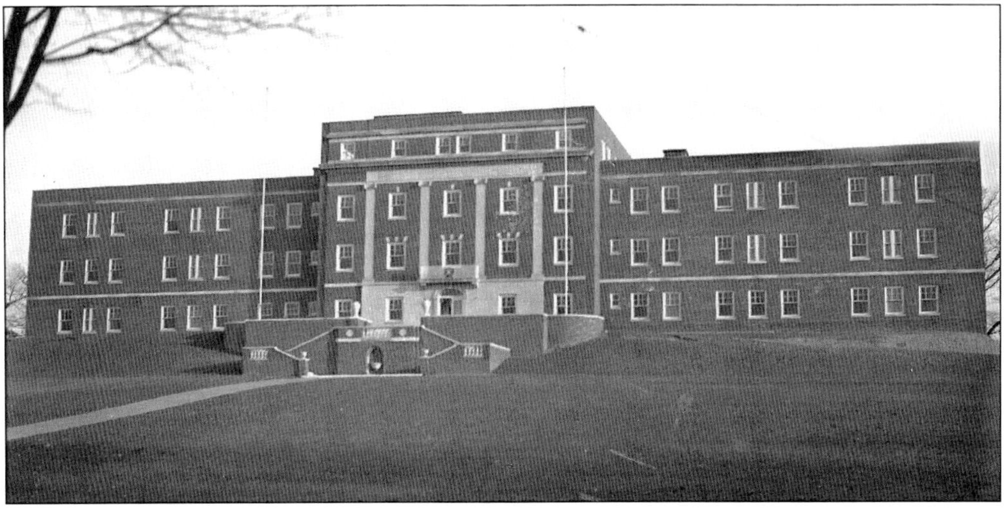

Elizabeth A. Horton Memorial Hospital is shown shortly after its construction in 1928.

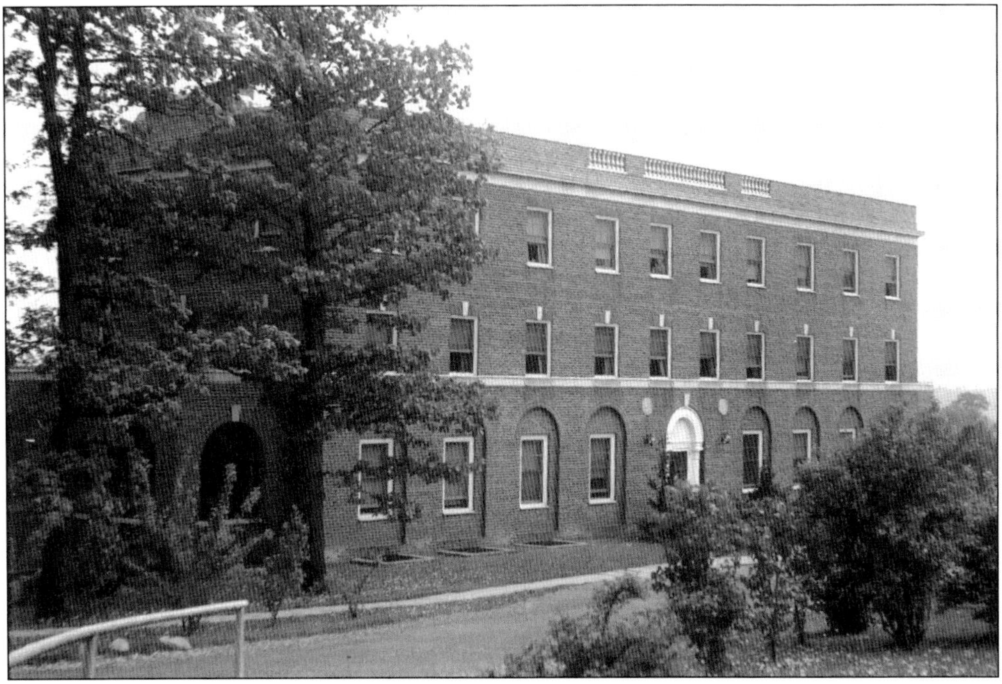

The Nurses' Home was a part of Horton Hospital and was situated on Jackson Avenue.

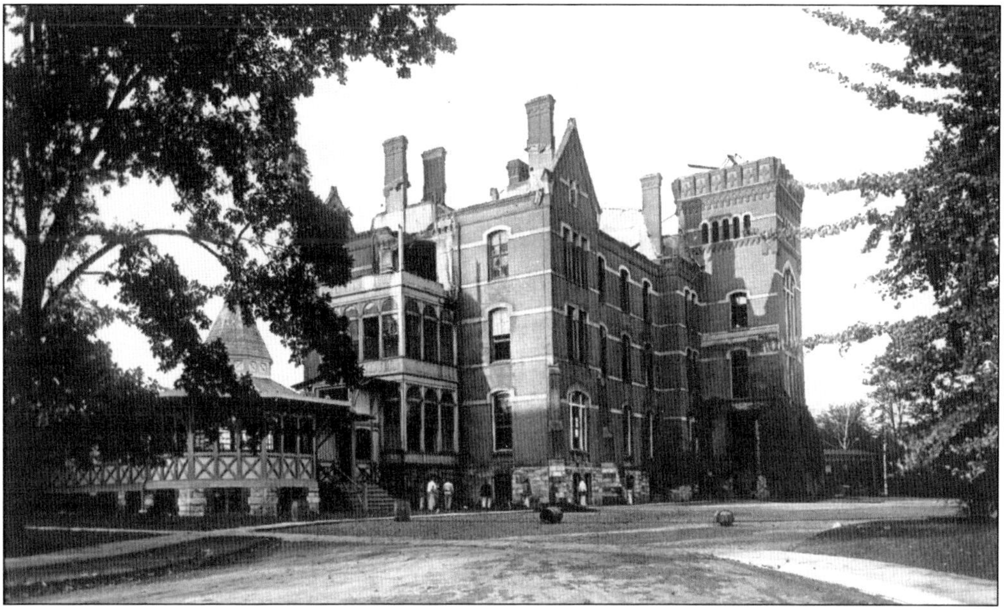

The main building of the Middletown State Hospital is pictured here after the fire of October 18, 1921.

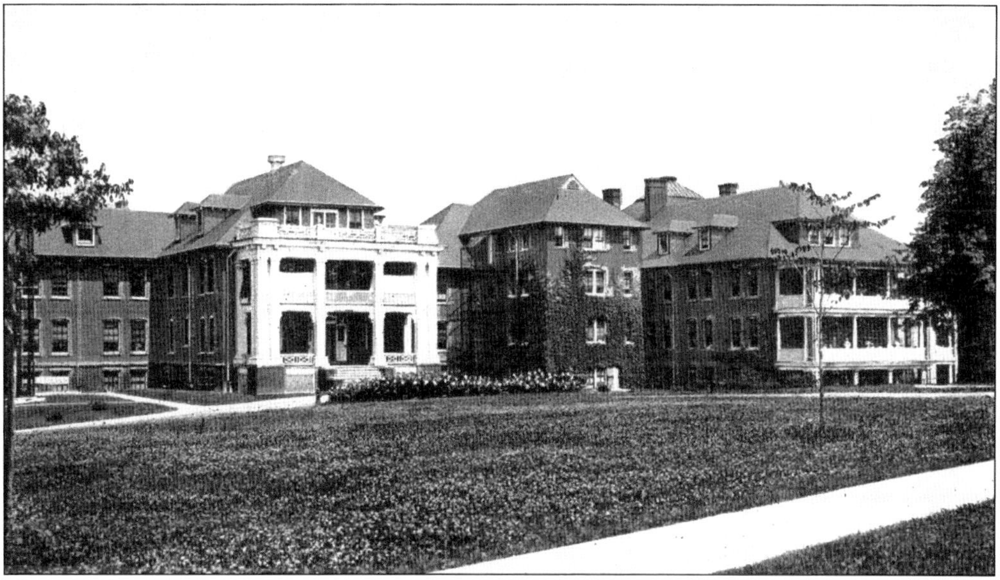

These buildings were known as the West Group and accommodated patient housing.

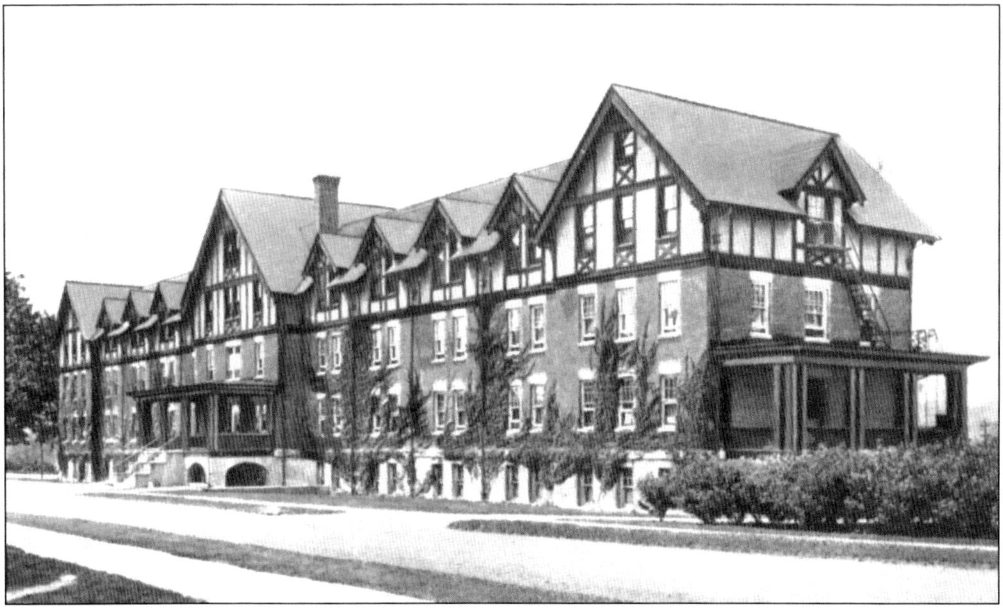
Shown in an old postcard, the Nurses' Home at the Middletown State Hospital still stands today.

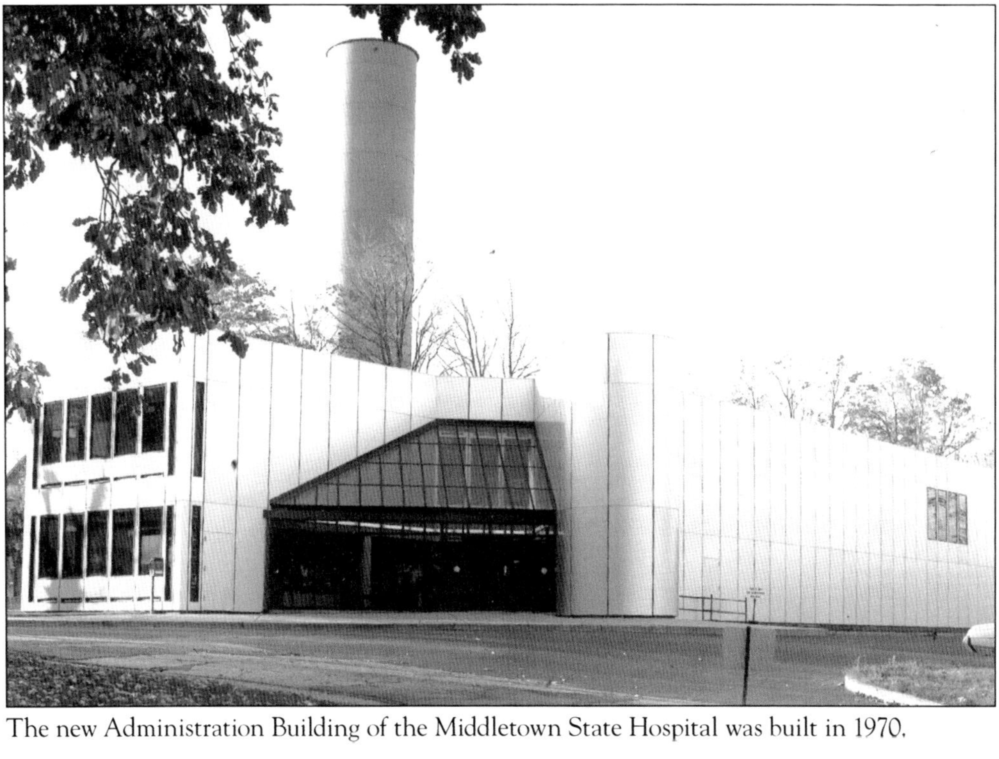
The new Administration Building of the Middletown State Hospital was built in 1970.

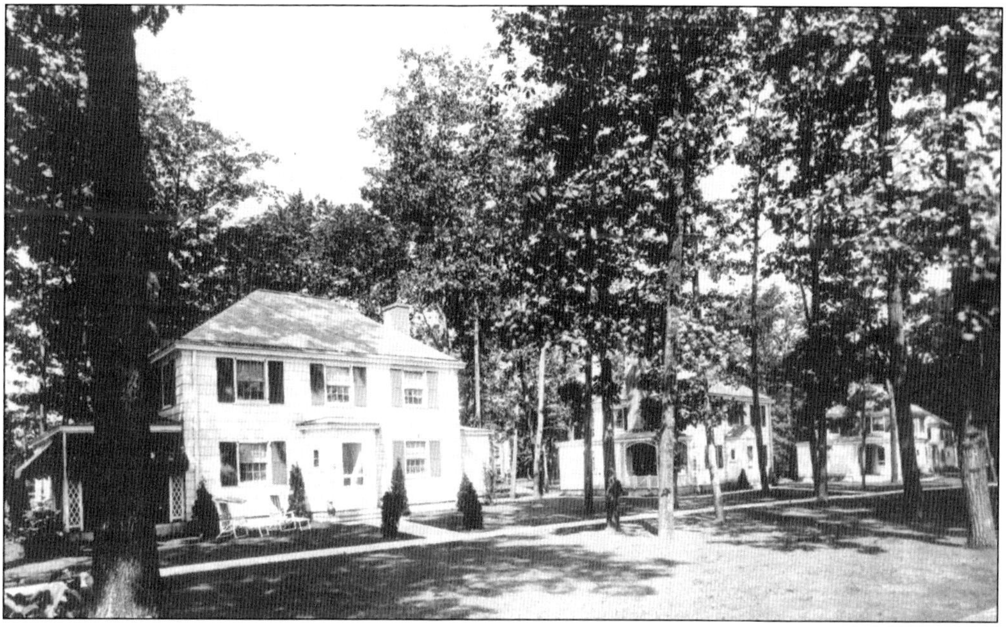

Some of the homes on Monhagen Avenue were built for hospital doctors.

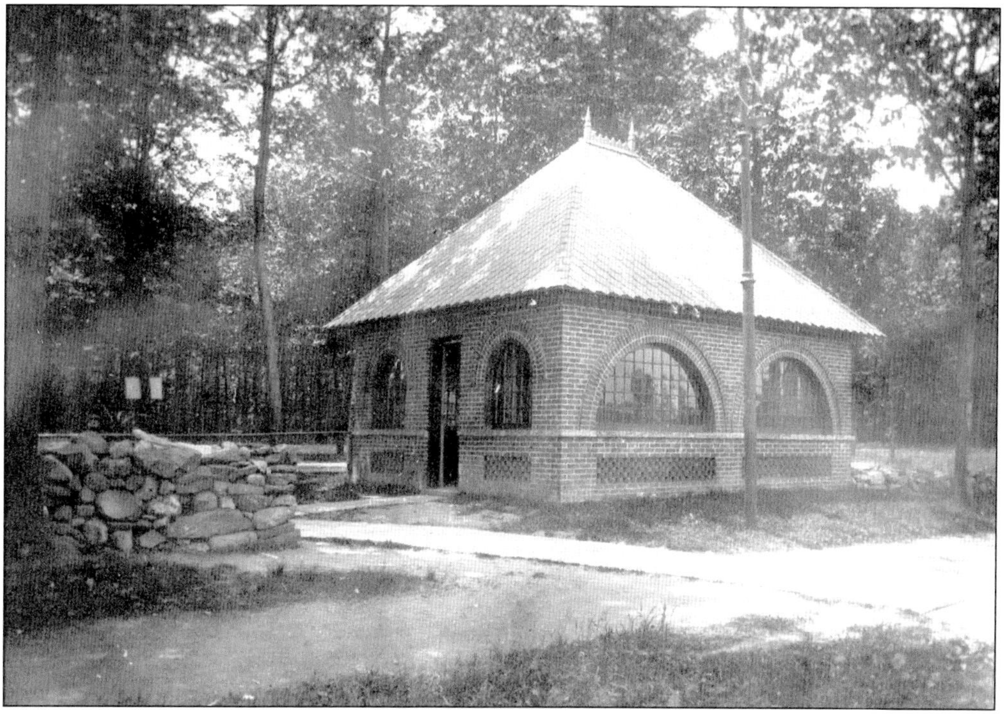

This attractive little building was the trolley station, located on Monhagen Avenue near the upper gate of the hospital. The Wallkill Transit Company's Middletown State Hospital line served this station until the end of street railway operations.

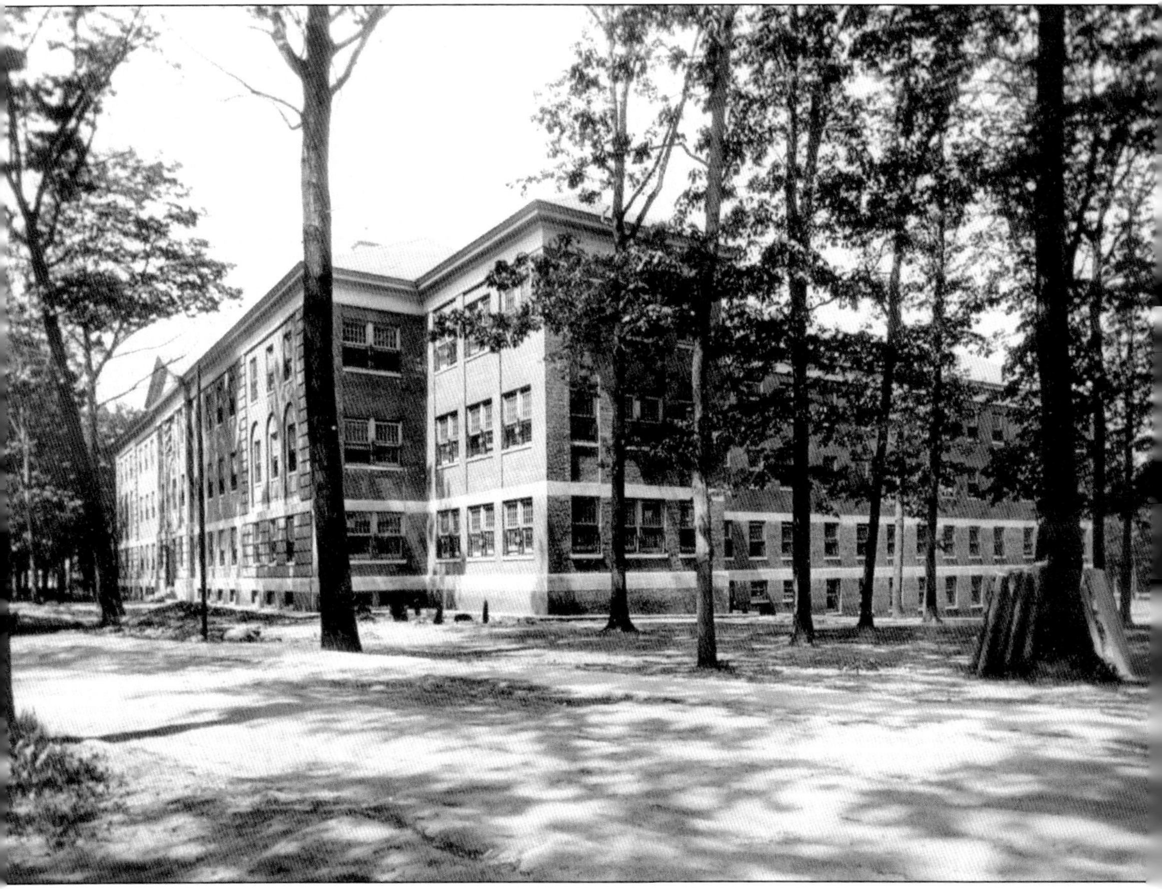

Woodman Hall, also known as the infirmary building, was a prominent structure on the Middletown State Hospital grounds.

Nine

Fire Department

Middletown's Fire Department will celebrate its 150th anniversary in 2009. Fire protection in Middletown dates back to 1821 but it was not until 1859 that the present fire department was organized. The department's seven fire companies are housed in three stations, Central Fire Station on East Main Street, North Street Fire Station on Wisner Avenue ,and the Waalkill Fire House on Wallkill Avenue. The organization is a combination department with professional drivers and volunteer firefighters. The department responds to well over a thousand calls for service each year.

In addition to fire suppression the department responds to numerous medical calls, alarms for automobile accidents, and other rescue related dispatches. Fire prevention and education is also a priority. The city can justifiably be proud of its fire department.

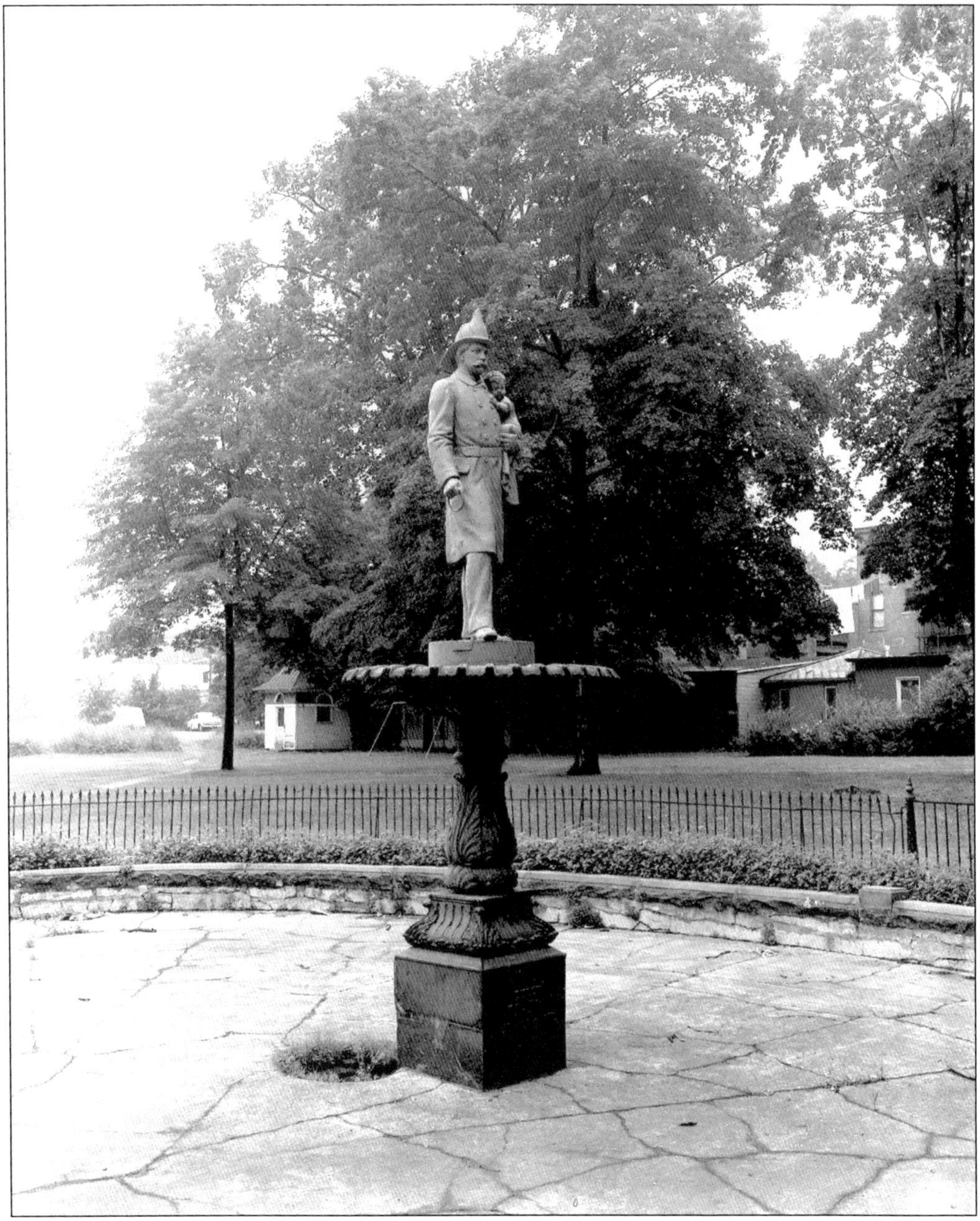

The Firemen's Statue stood in Thrall Park for many years. Originally it incorporated a fountain in its base. After being vandalized in 1999, the figure was restored and rededicated in Wallace Park in 2002. Known as "Old Joel" after Joel B. Wheeler, who spearheaded its purchase, the statue commemorates the city's force of volunteer firemen.

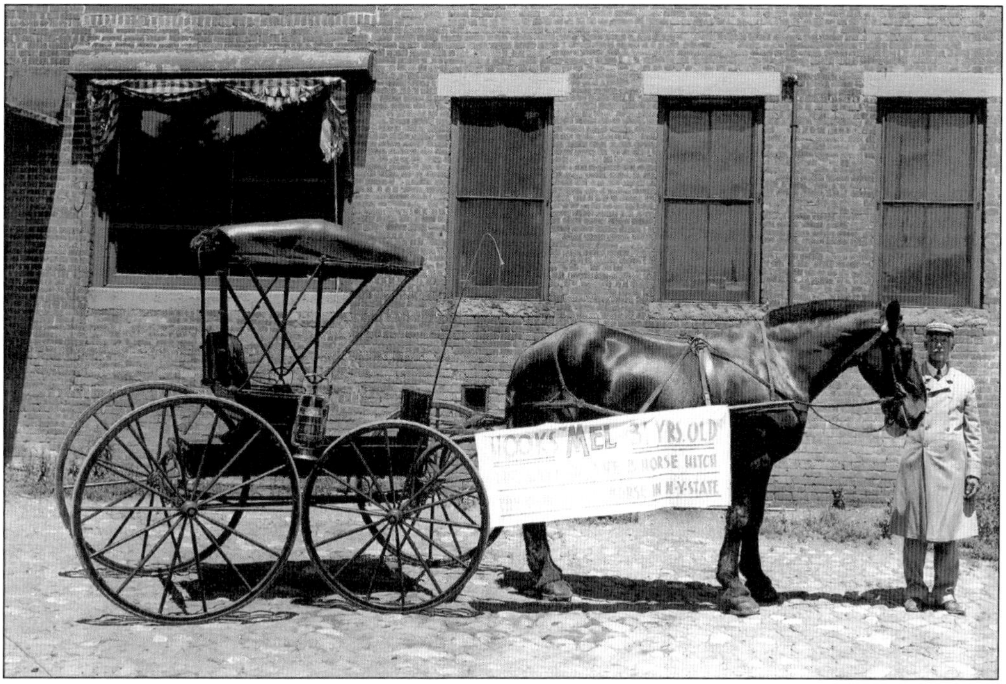

"Old Mel" is seen here, the last of the three-horse hitch. Mel was a fire horse assigned to pull the Excelsior Hook and Ladder Company's apparatus. When the company motorized in 1927, Mel was transferred to the street department to pull a wagon. Here he is shown in the Golden Jubilee parade in 1938, reputed to be the oldest fire horse in the state.

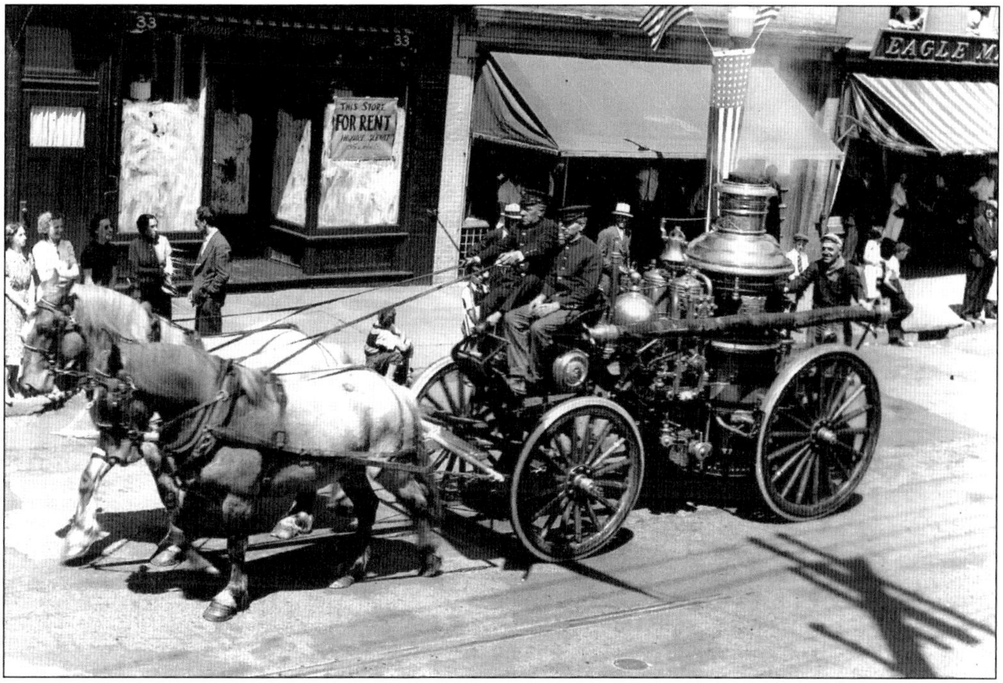

Middletown's only fire steamer is also shown in the Golden Jubilee parade driving down West Main Street. The historic apparatus is preserved in poor condition at Museum Village in Monroe.

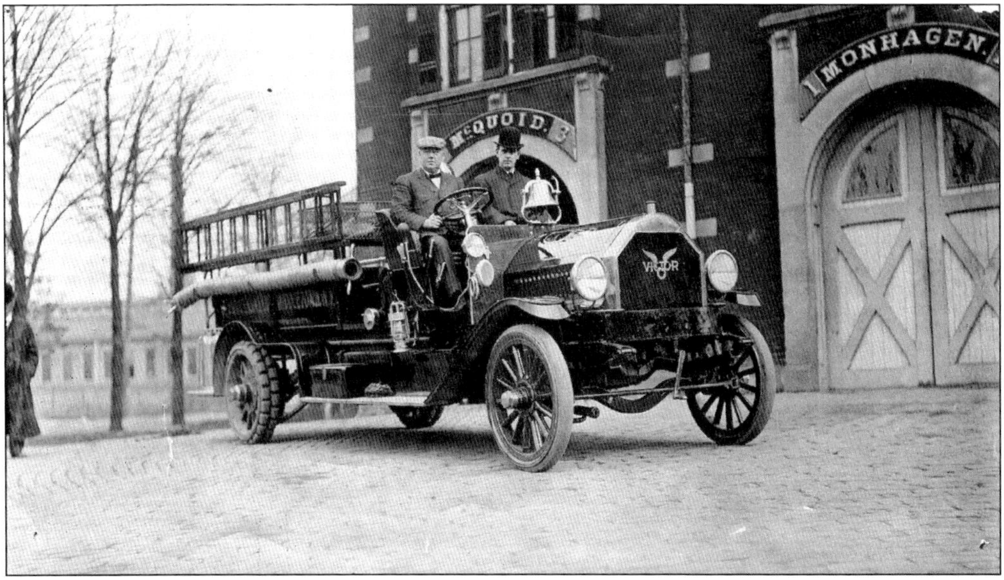

McQuoid's placed this Victor apparatus in service in 1911. Victor trucks were manufactured in Buffalo. Behind the steering wheel is fire chief Charles Higham.

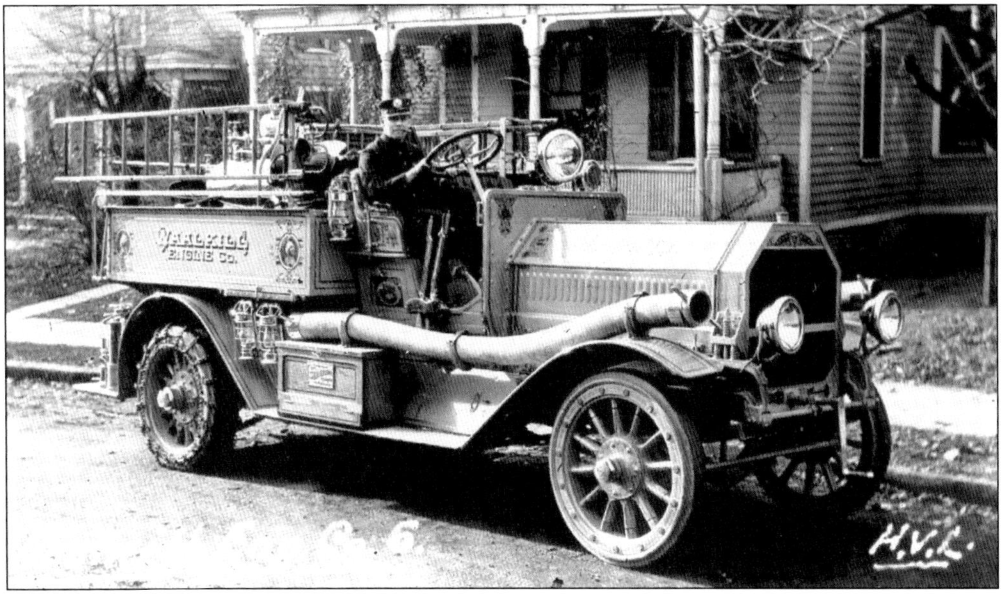

In 1914, the Waalkill Engine Company No. 6 received this massive Seagrave pumper. Painted a mustard brown color, this apparatus featured a rear mounted centrifugal pump, unusual for the time, as well as chemical tanks in the hose bed.

The home of Waalkill Engine Company No. 6, this is the city's oldest fire station still in use. The bell tower shown was demolished after ringing out its last alarm in December 1949. The bell itself was apparently scrapped.

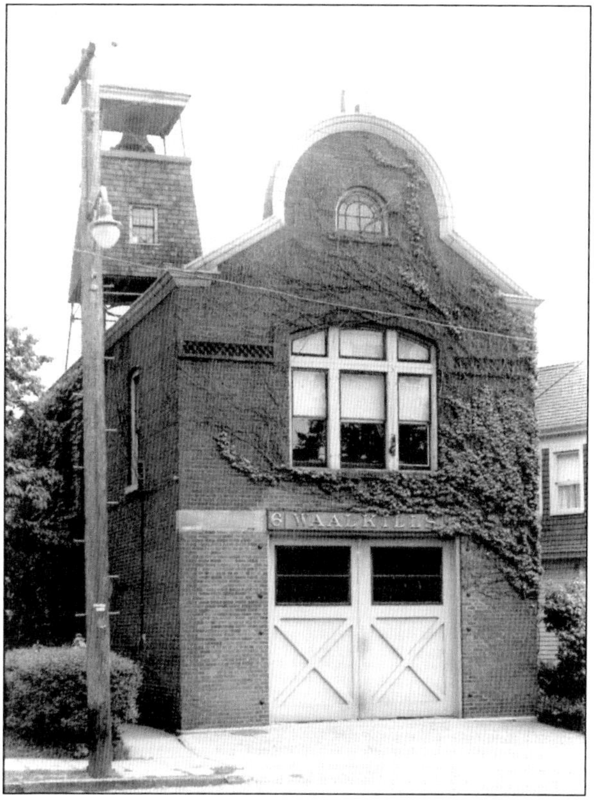

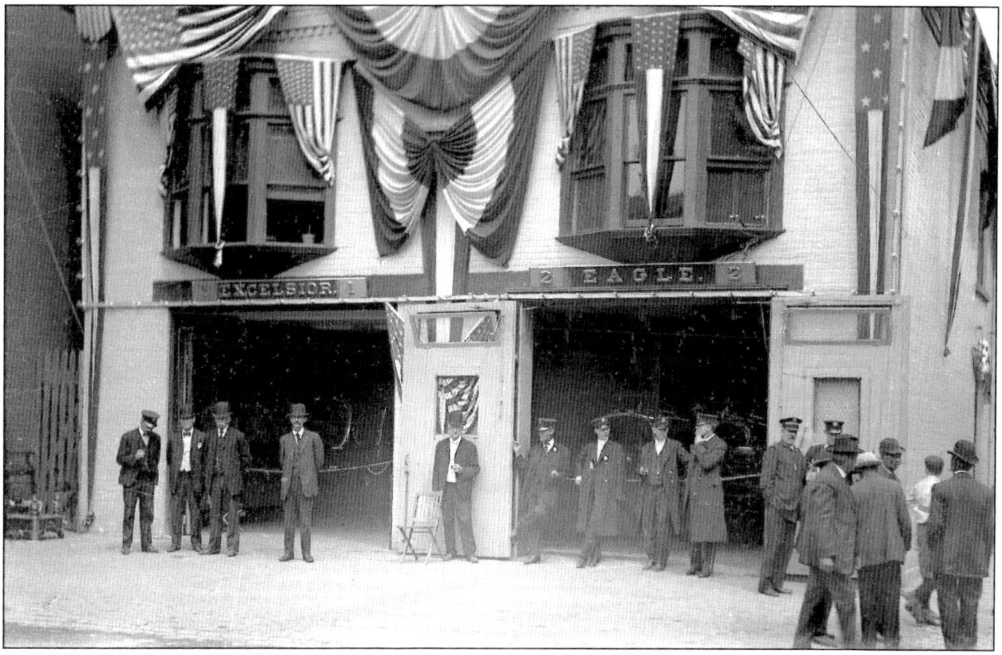

The King Street firehouse is shown on a parade day. Excelsiors and Eagles were both horse-drawn at that time and the hanging harness can be seen through the doors. Firehouses always had chains across the doors to prevent the horses from getting out.

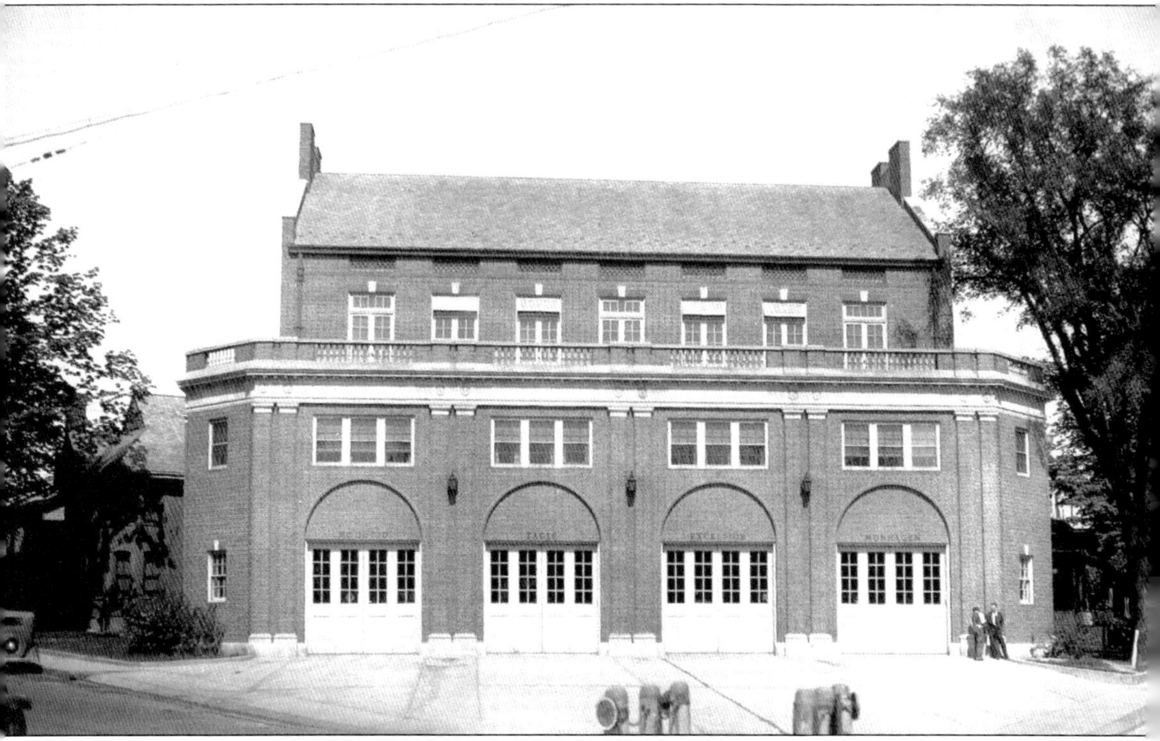

Central Fire Station as it looked when built in 1928 is seen here. Today the folding doors have been changed to overhead doors, radio antennas have been placed on the roof, and the stanchions in the foreground have been removed.

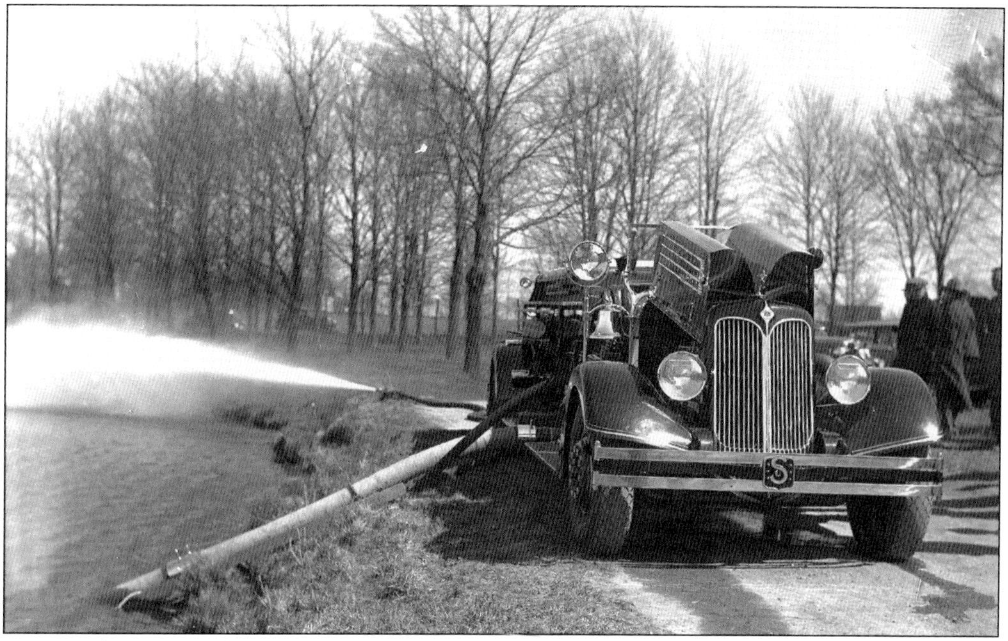

In 1936, the McQuoid Engine and Ladder Company No. 3 received a new Seagrave fire apparatus. This long ladder truck also had a pump, a booster tank, and a hose bed. Here it undergoes its underwriters test prior to acceptance by the city.

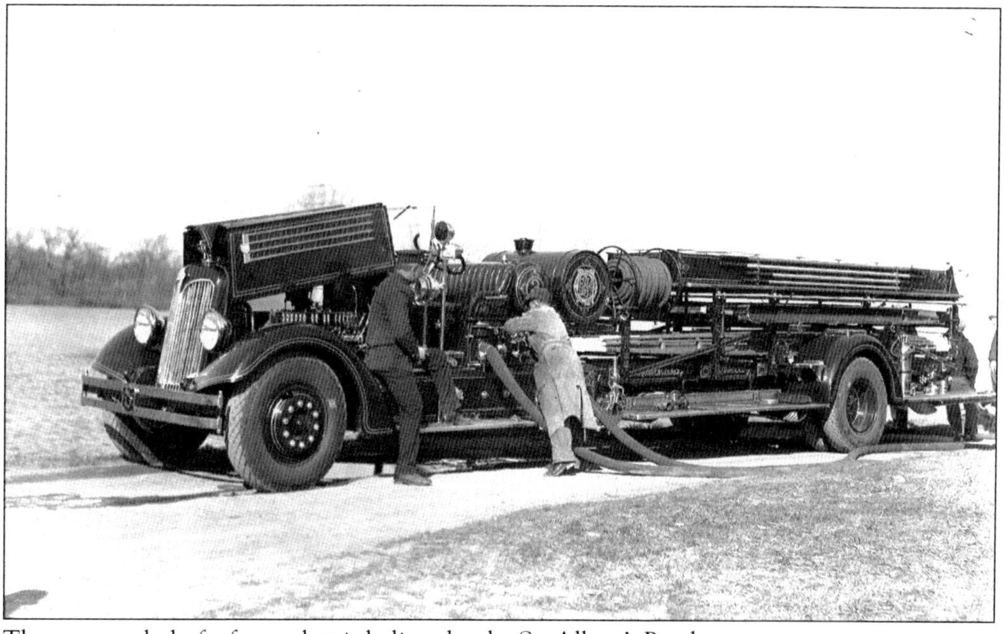

The new truck drafts from what is believed to be St. Albert's Pond.

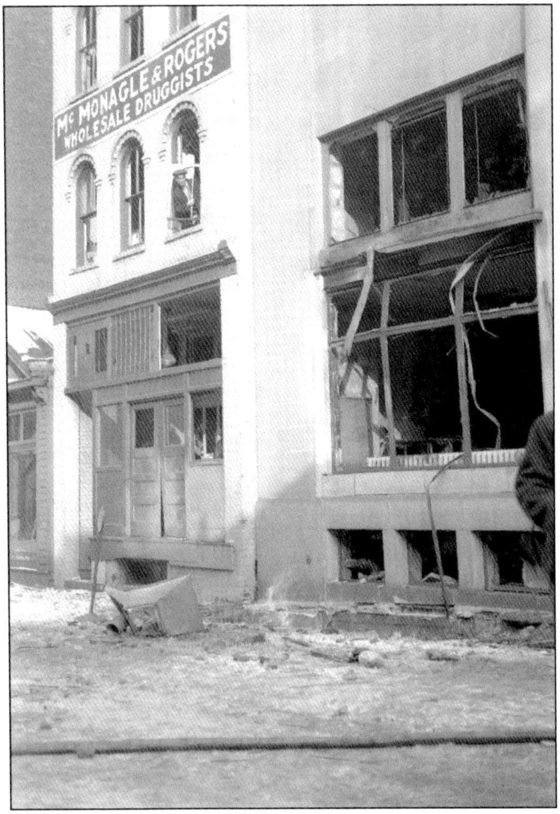

On the morning of February 5, 1945, the downtown area was rocked by a loud blast. It was not an air raid as first thought, but a gas explosion in the Merchants Bank building at North and King Streets. Numerous windows were broken throughout the business district. The photograph shows the King Street side of the bank building.

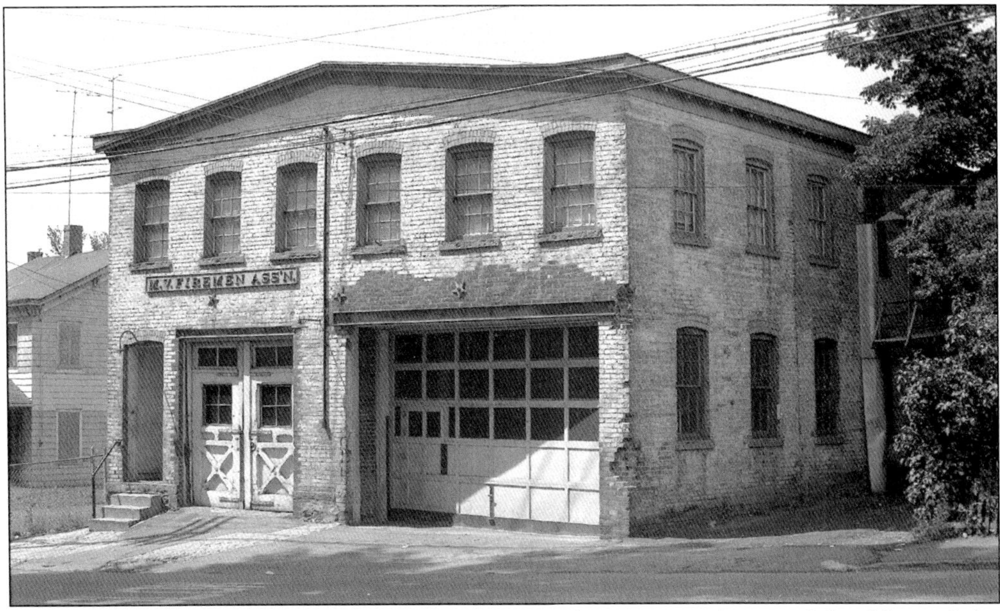

The municipal building on Academy Avenue across from Benton Avenue School housed the Middletown Veteran Firemen Association in this 1940s view. The veterans' rooms were on the second floor while the city's water department was below. The building has now been remodeled and contains offices.

Ten

PEOPLE AND EVENTS

From time to time, there occurred special events in Middletown that deserve to be remembered. Middletown's Golden Jubilee in 1938 commemorated 50 years as a city, while the Diamond Jubilee in 1963 recognized the city at 75 years. Other celebrations, almost forgotten, also took place, such as Registration Day in 1918, when every eligible man had to register for the draft, followed by the Armistice on November 11, 1918. The National Recovery Administration parade in 1934 during the Great Depression brought renewed hope to the area. The Erie Centennial Day in 1943 celebrated the coming of the railroad to Middletown with a giant parade.

Some of the people of the community must also be recognized. Some little known photographs of people and events are included in this chapter of *Middletown Revisited*.

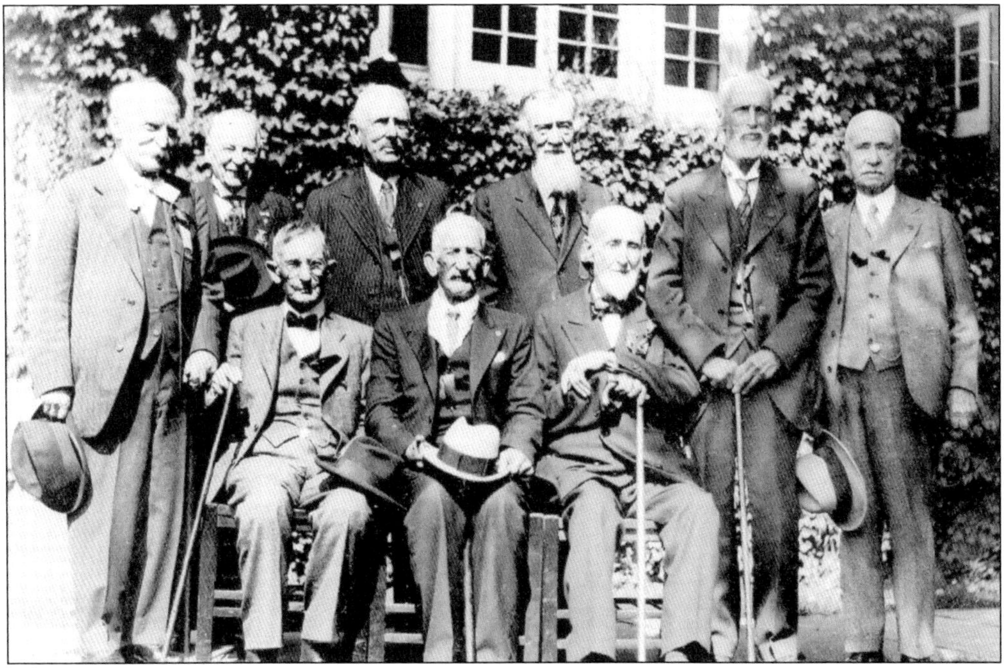

Their individual names are not known, but here are Middletown's remaining Civil War veterans awaiting the Grand Army of the Republic (GAR) parade in 1931.

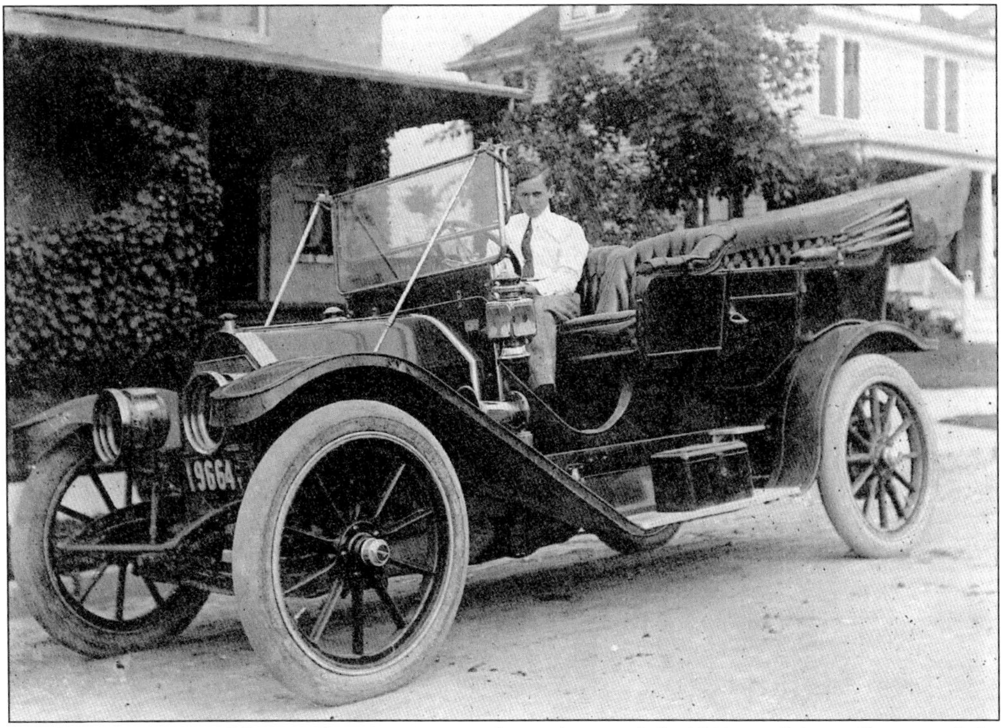

Ralph B. Towner, Middletown businessman, is shown here in July 1910 in a Maxwell automobile. The location is 10 Lenox Place. Towner was the long-time head of Carson and Towner Dry Goods Company.

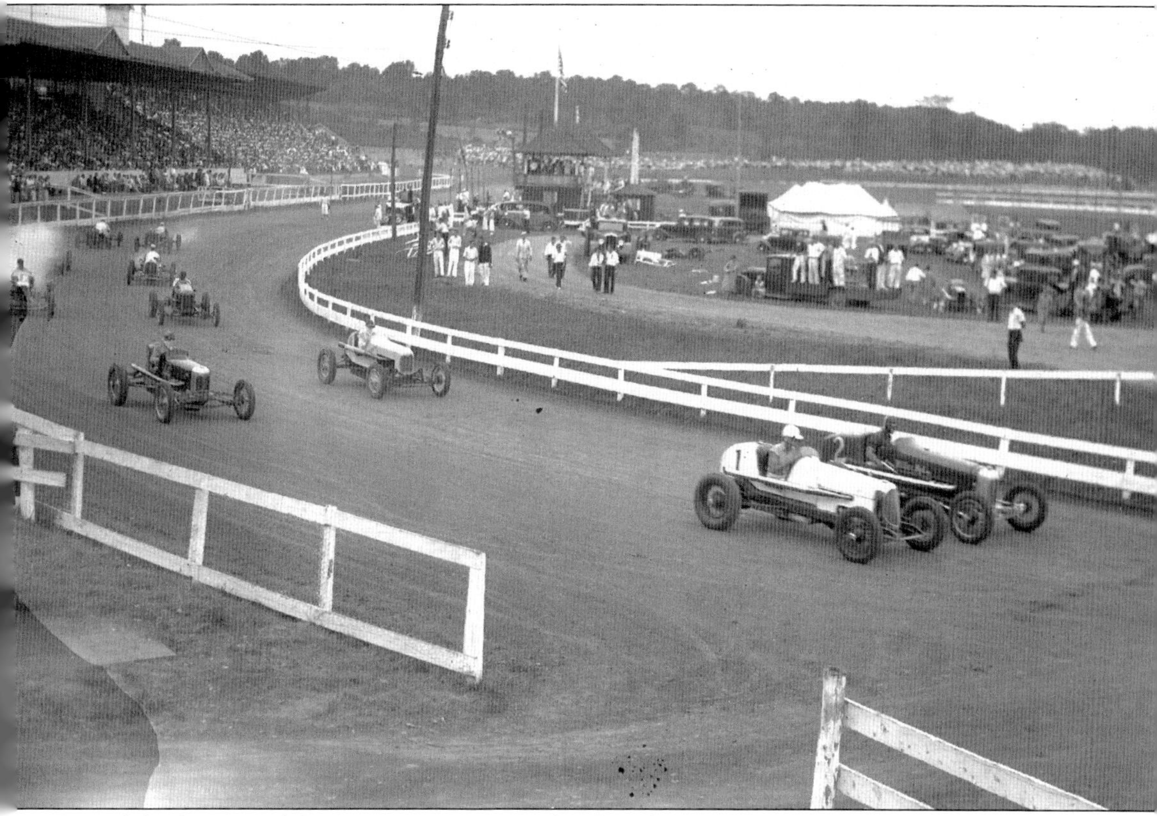

One of the features of the Orange County Fair has long been automobile racing. The first such race on the Harry Clay Oval was in 1919. Here the 1934 race is seen, with driver Bob Sall in midget car No. 1.

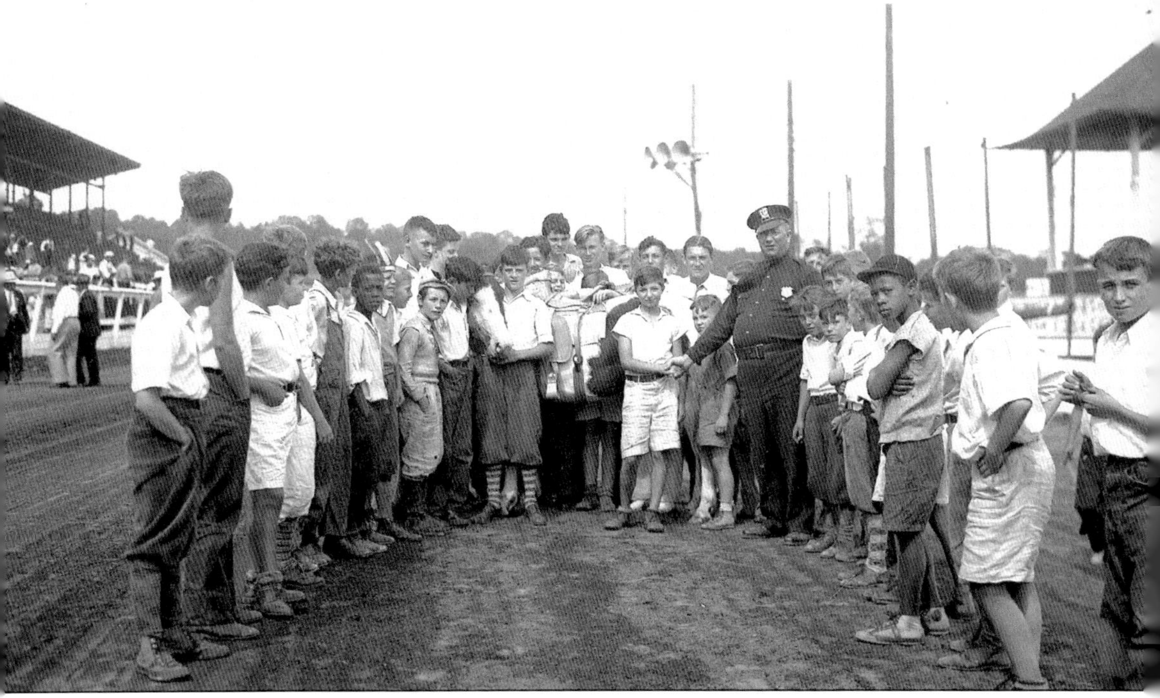

Every year in the 1930s, Middletown patrolman George Finn took a group of underprivileged boys to the Orange County Fair. Finn was appointed to the force on June 10, 1918, and wore shield No. 1 for many years.

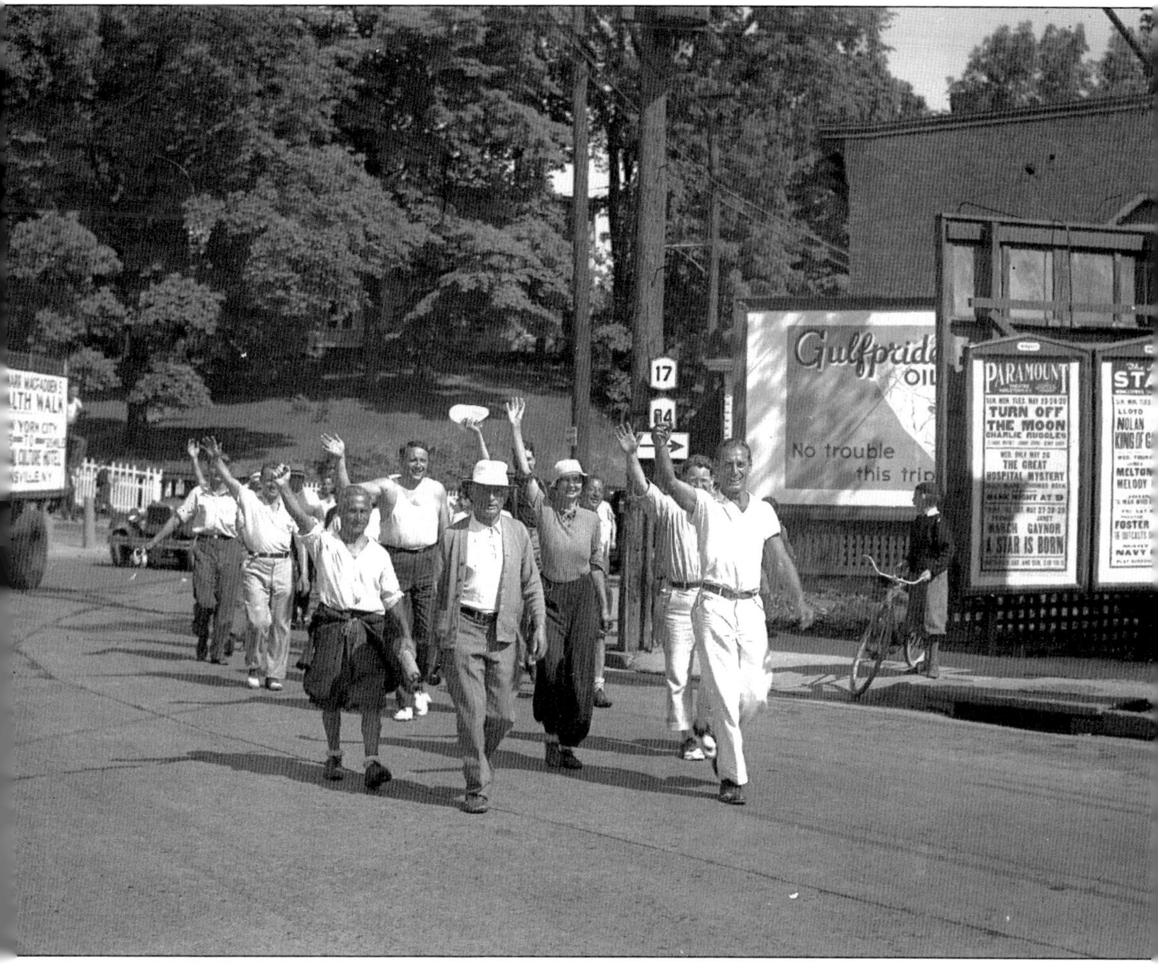

Bernarr Macfadden was an early health enthusiast and publisher of the national magazine *Physical Culture*. Macfadden leads a group from Academy Avenue into East Main Street as they pass through Middletown in 1937, on their way to the Physical Culture Hotel in Dansville, New York. The group walked about 30 miles a day, staying in hotels at night. Dansville is near Geneseo in the western part of New York State some 150 miles from Middletown.

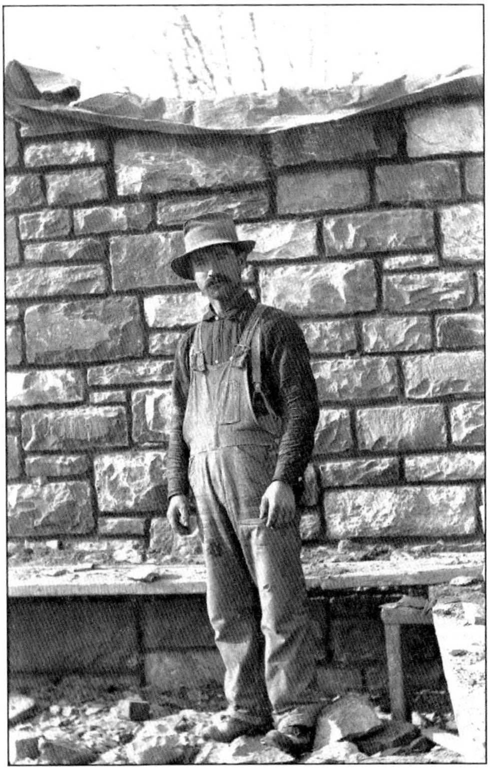

In 1913, an Italian stone mason poses for the camera of Margaret Moon, Truman Moon's daughter. A group of masons were brought here from Italy to help construct Webb Horton Memorial Church on East Main Street. Moon related that when she returned to give this man his photograph, the workmen had already returned to their homeland.

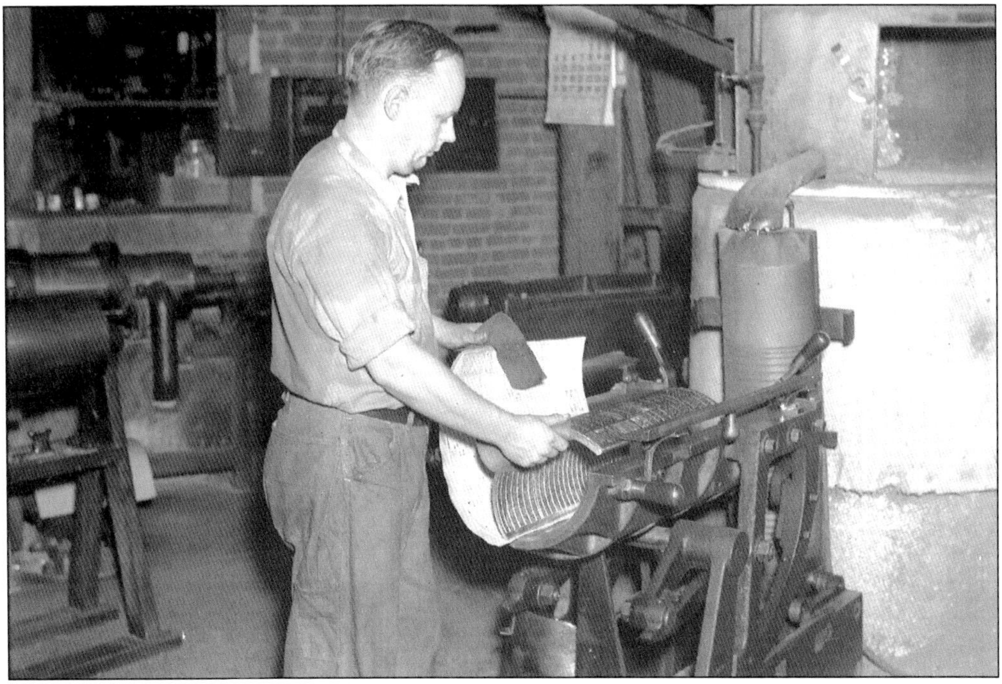

A *Middletown Times-Herald* pressman makes a matrix. The curved printing plate will go on the printing press. This was the final step in the hot lead process by which newspapers used to be printed.

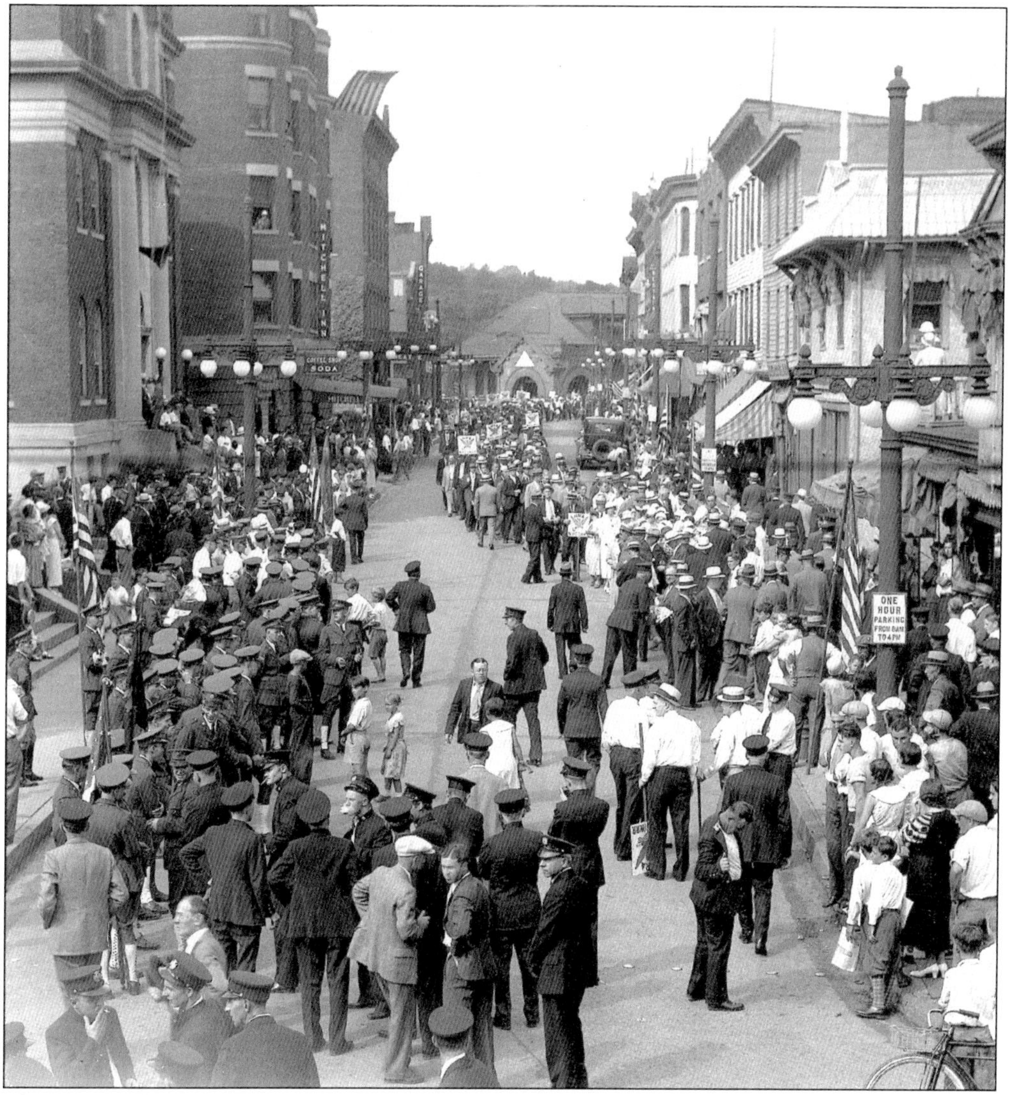

The National Recovery Administration (or NRA) was a Depression-era federal program. Its emblem was a blue eagle with the words "We Do Our Part." To promote the program, a parade was held in Middletown in 1934 and here it is seen on James Street.

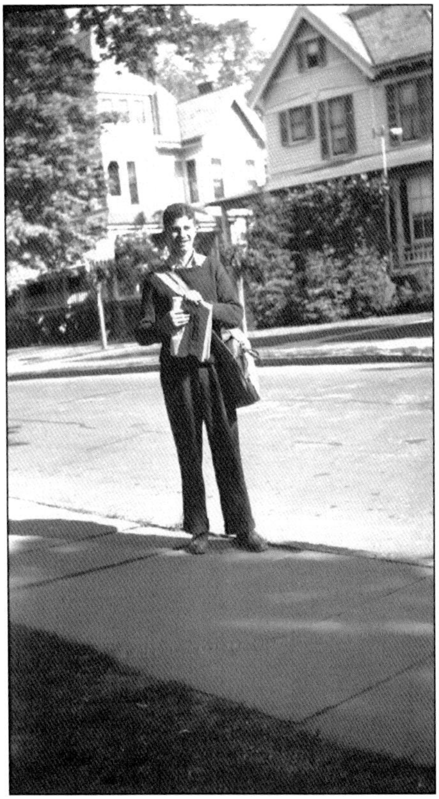

Truman Moon photographed Joe Guattery, *Middletown Times-Herald* newsboy, on West Main Street in 1938.

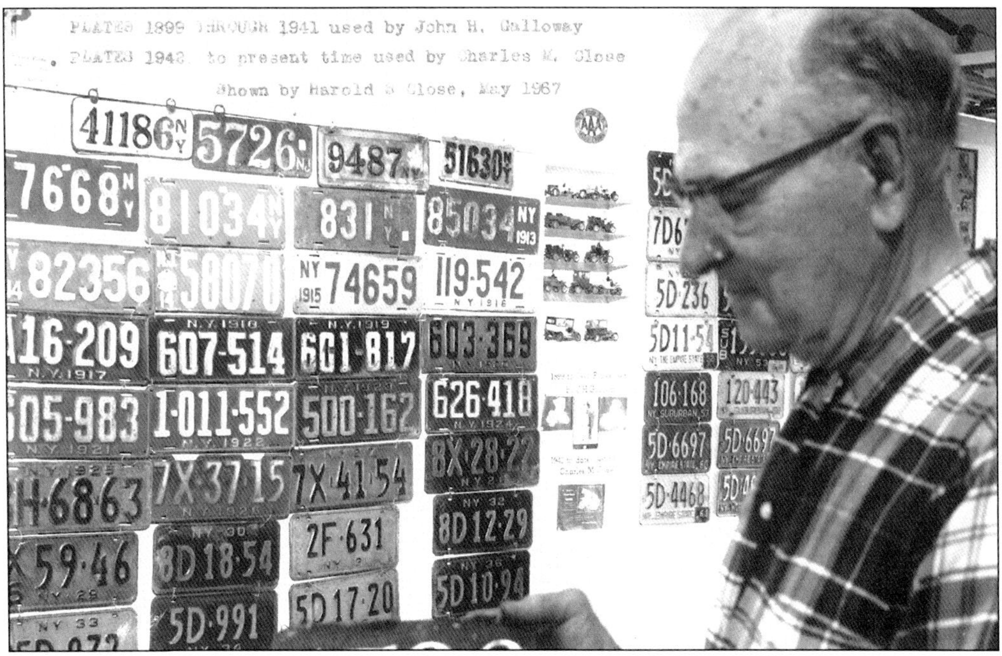

Harold S. Close, shown here, was president of Ayres and Galloway Hardware Company and a member of the Middletown Police Commission. His collection of license plates features many rare early editions. Charles M. Close was Harold's son.

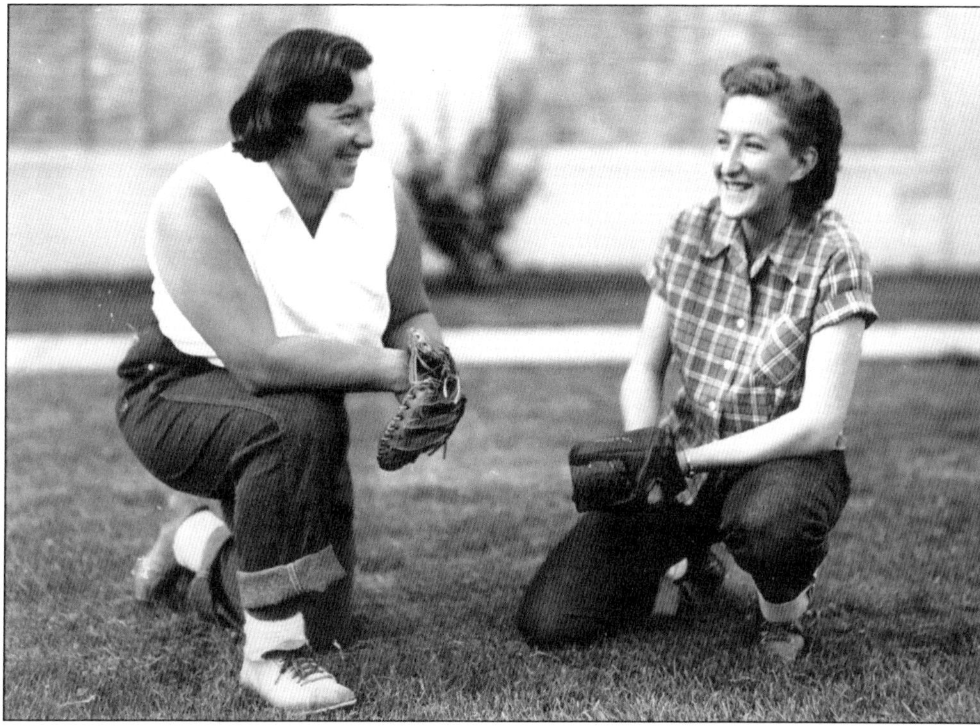

The Middletown Starlets, a women's softball team was active in 1954. Left is catcher Mary Diana with pitcher Ruth Bauer. Diana was a long time physical education instructor at Orange County Community College.

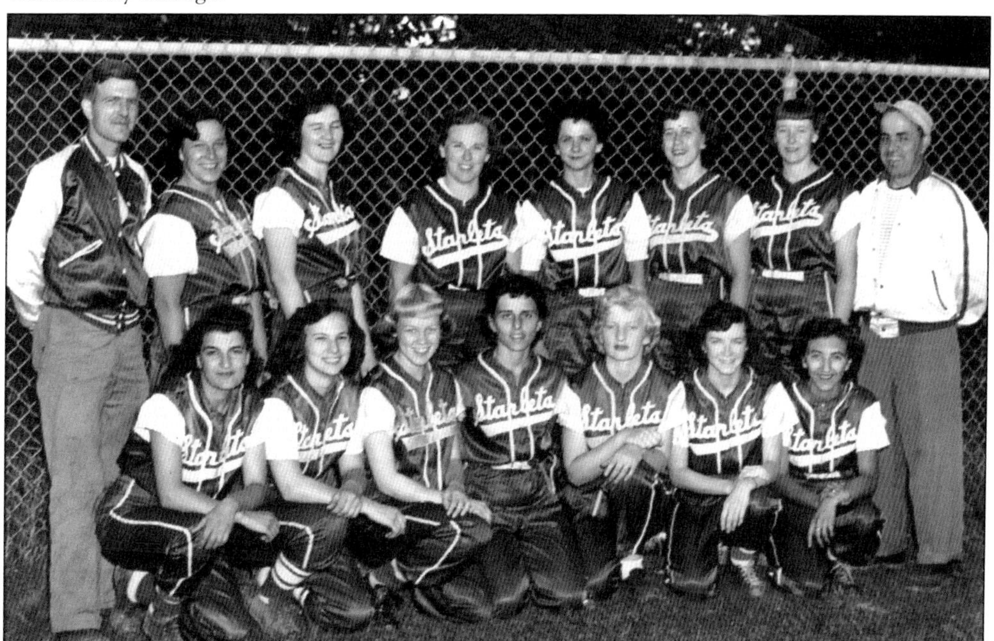

The Middletown Starlets are ready to participate in the one of the 1954 National Girl's Softball Conference title games. Coach Vince Dino is on the right.

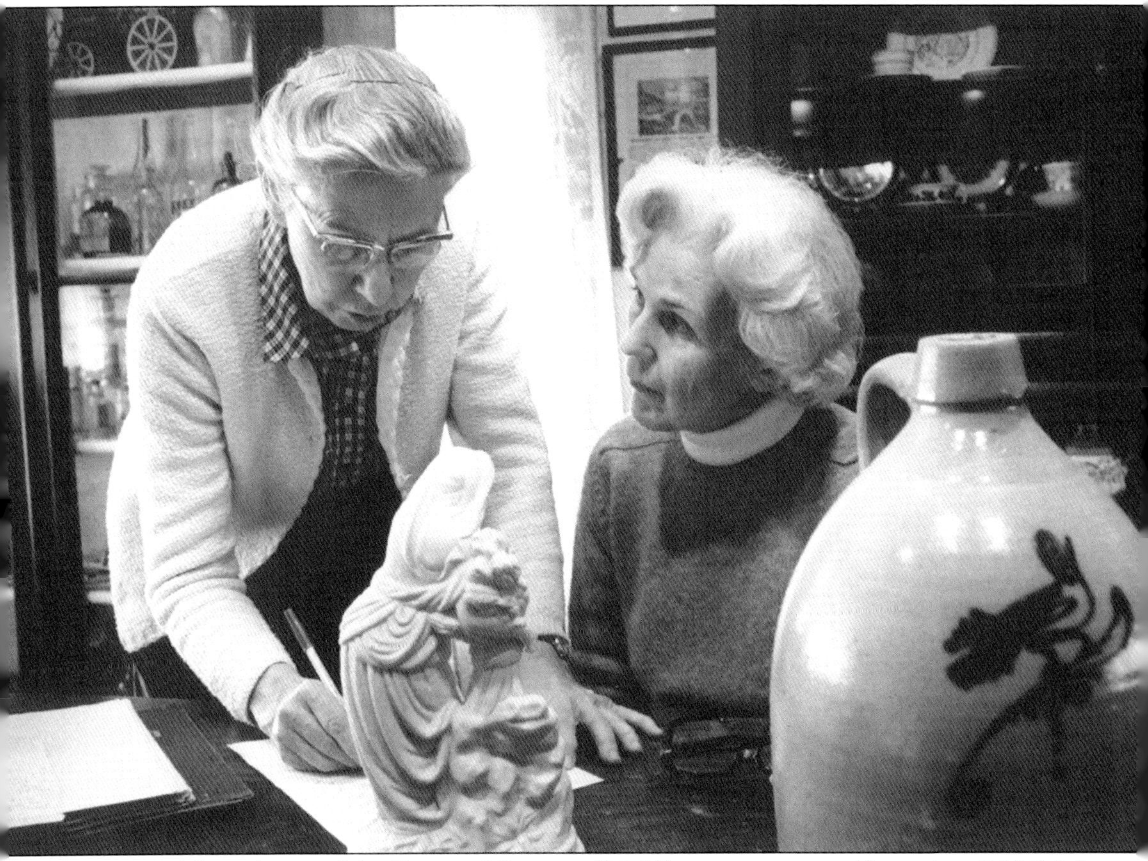

Two of the stalwarts of the Historical Society of Middletown are pictured here. Ann P. Vail, left, and Mary Catherine Kennedy examine two artifacts at the society's home in 1986. Ann Vail has been a volunteer at the Historical Society of Middletown for over 50 years. Mary Catherine Kennedy remains on the board of directors.

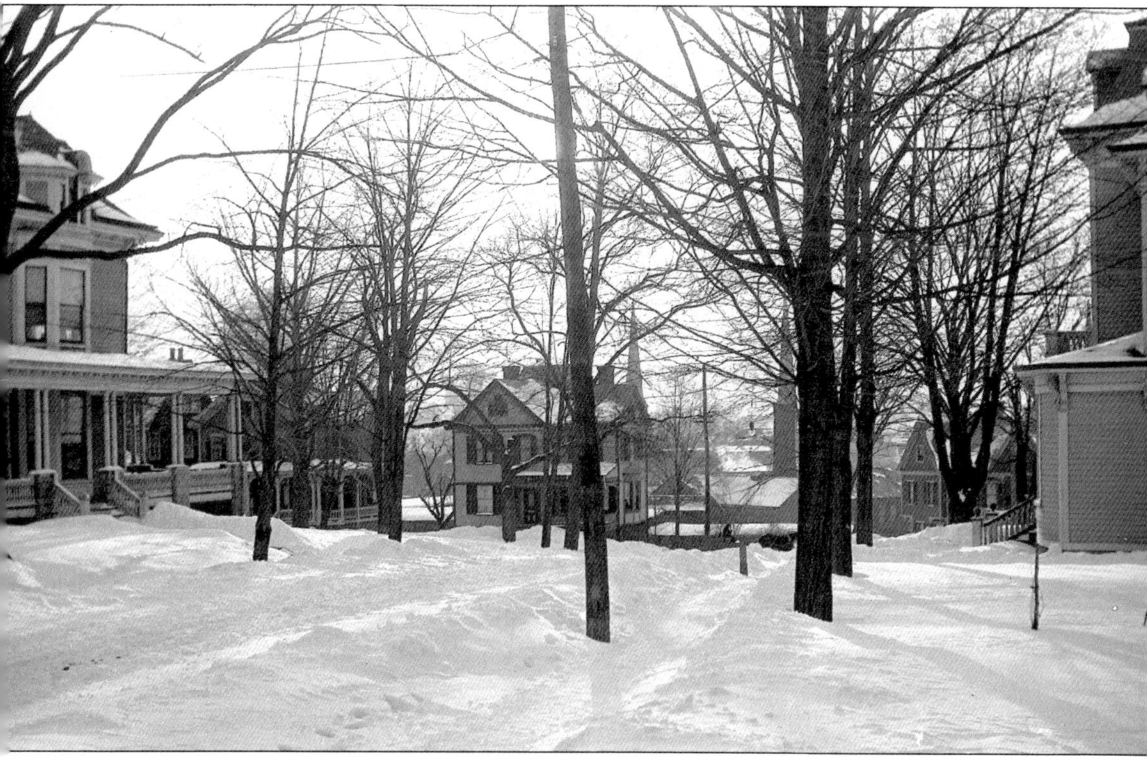

It is the morning of March 17, 1916, and Truman Moon is out with his camera. Shown is upper West Main Street. The city may not have cleared the streets of snow in those days, but householders definitely had to shovel their sidewalks.

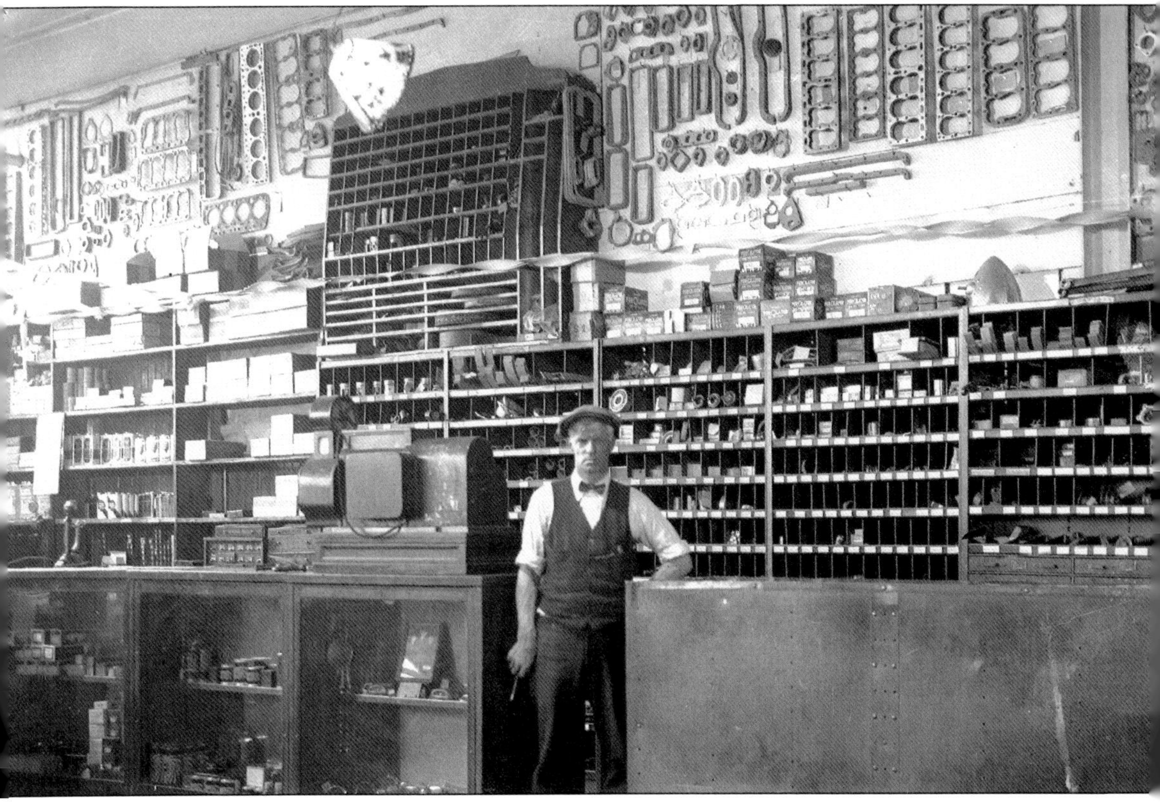

The parts department of the Samuel T. Randall Garage on Dolson Avenue is shown here on May 17, 1935. Edwin H. Simmons was parts manager at that time. It was said that Simmons always knew where his parts were at any time.

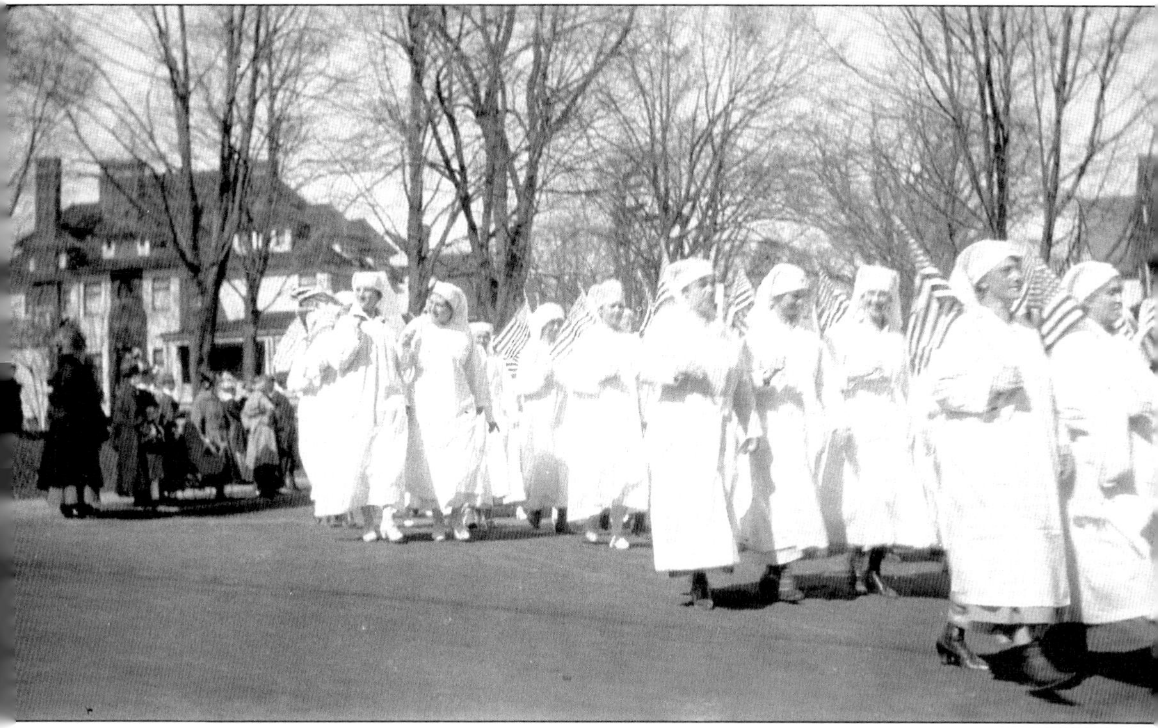

Ladies of the Red Cross participate in the Registration Day parade, June 5, 1917.

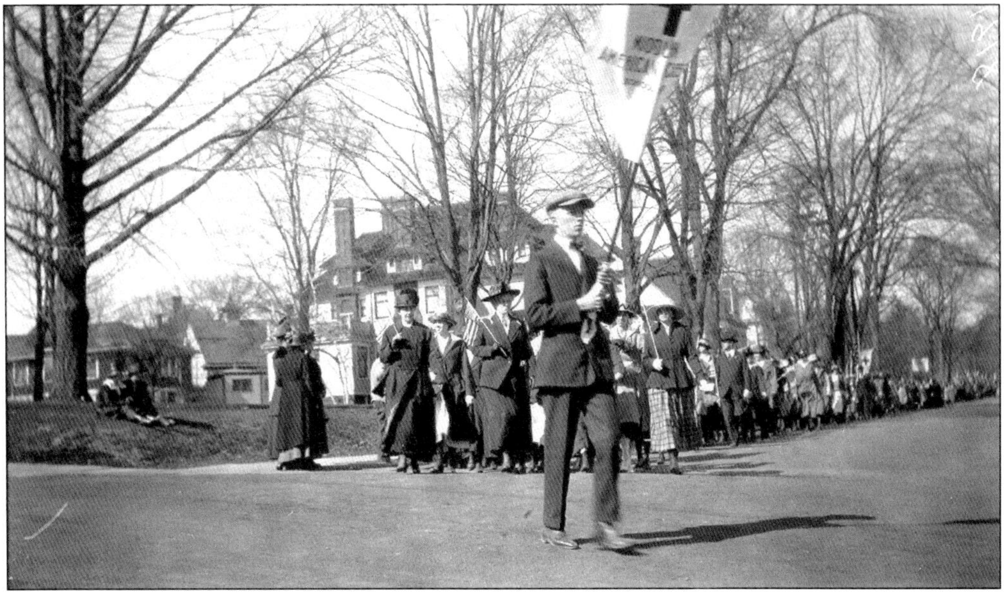

This is another view of the Registration Day parade shows Highland Avenue and West Main Street.

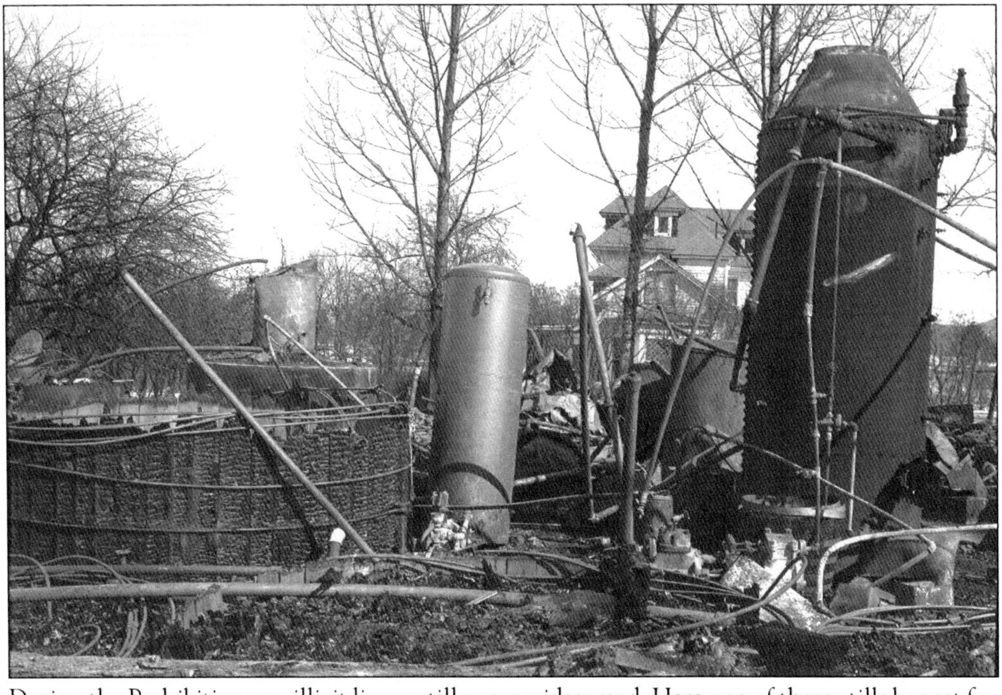

During the Prohibition era, illicit liquor stills were widespread. Here one of these stills has set fire to the barn that housed it. The local newspaper gave the location as Turkeytown.

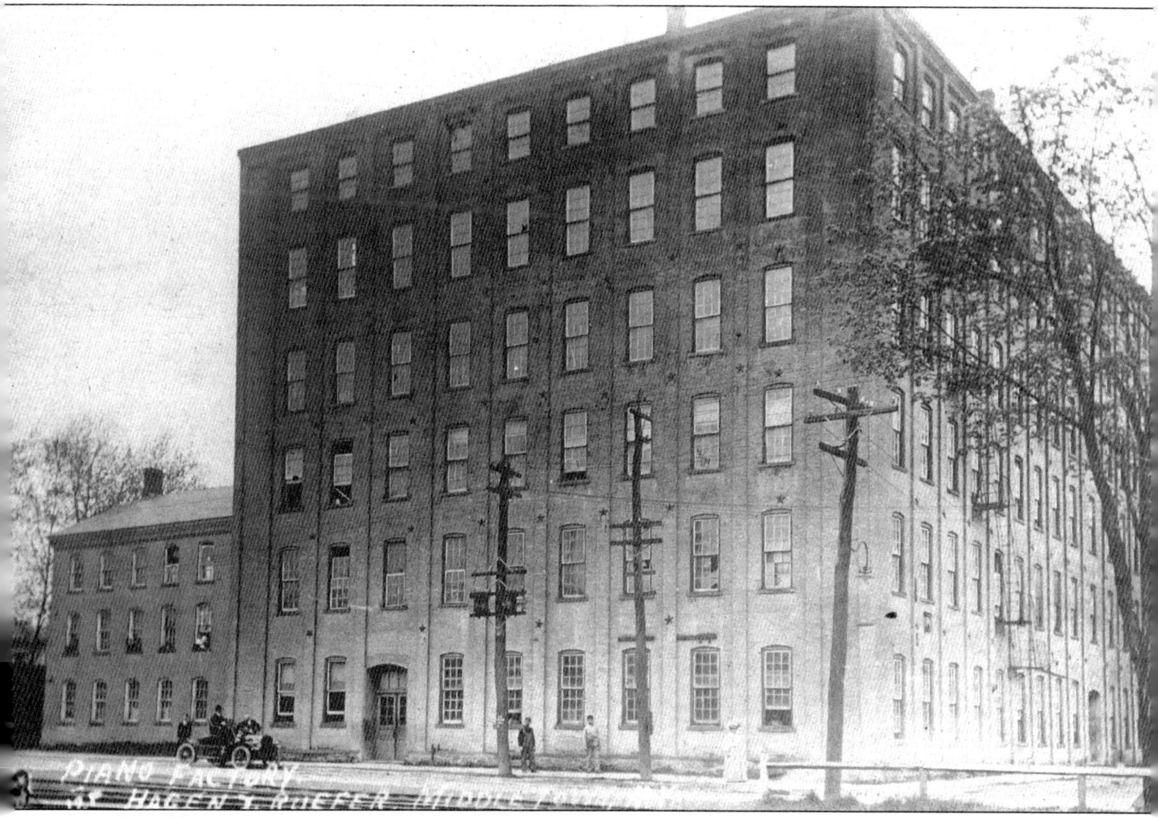

One of Middletown's largest buildings, the Hagen and Reufer Piano Key Company was located at the corner of Railroad Avenue and Grove Street. The structure was destroyed in a spectacular fire on April 26, 1911. The site today is a parking lot.

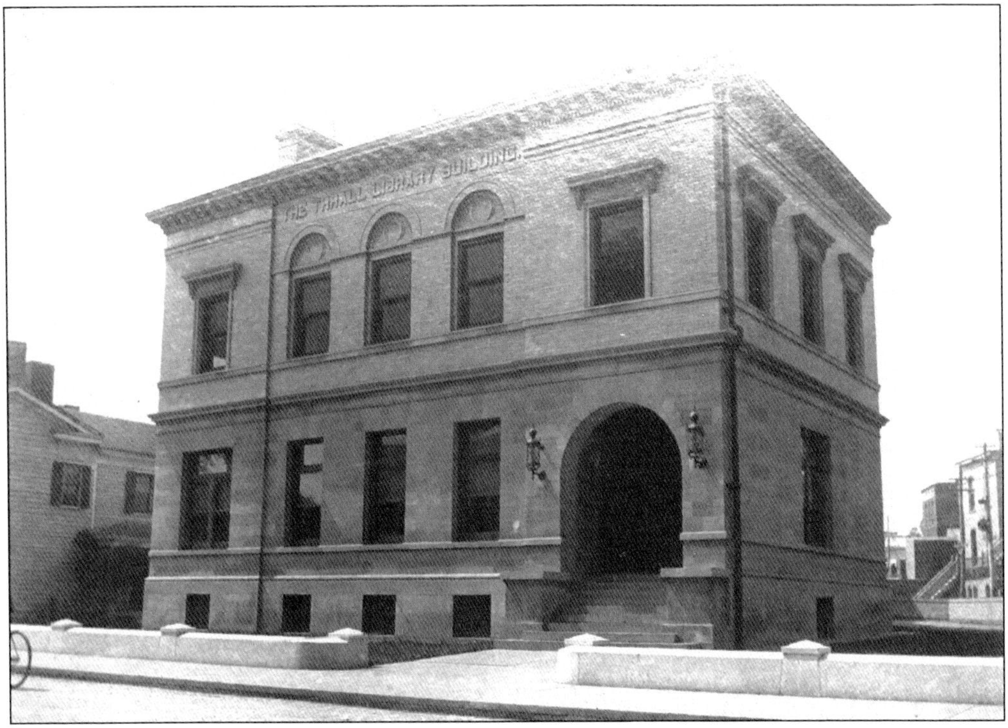

The Thrall Library, as originally built, is seen here. The building on Orchard Street now stands vacant.

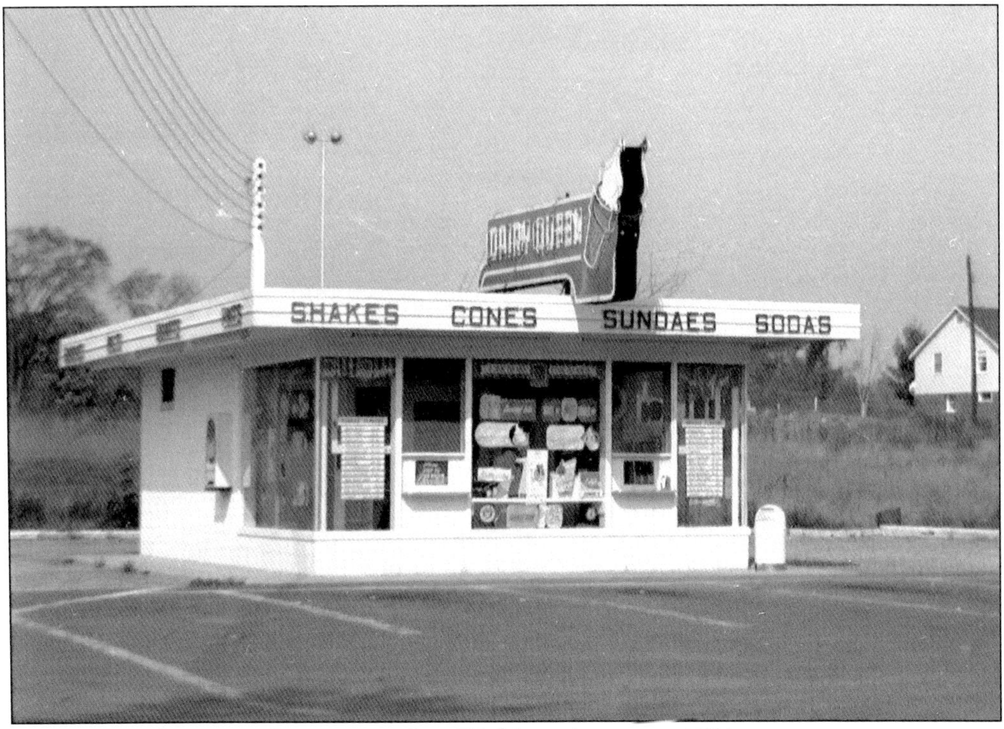

Middletown's first Dairy Queen opened on Wickham Avenue in 1954.

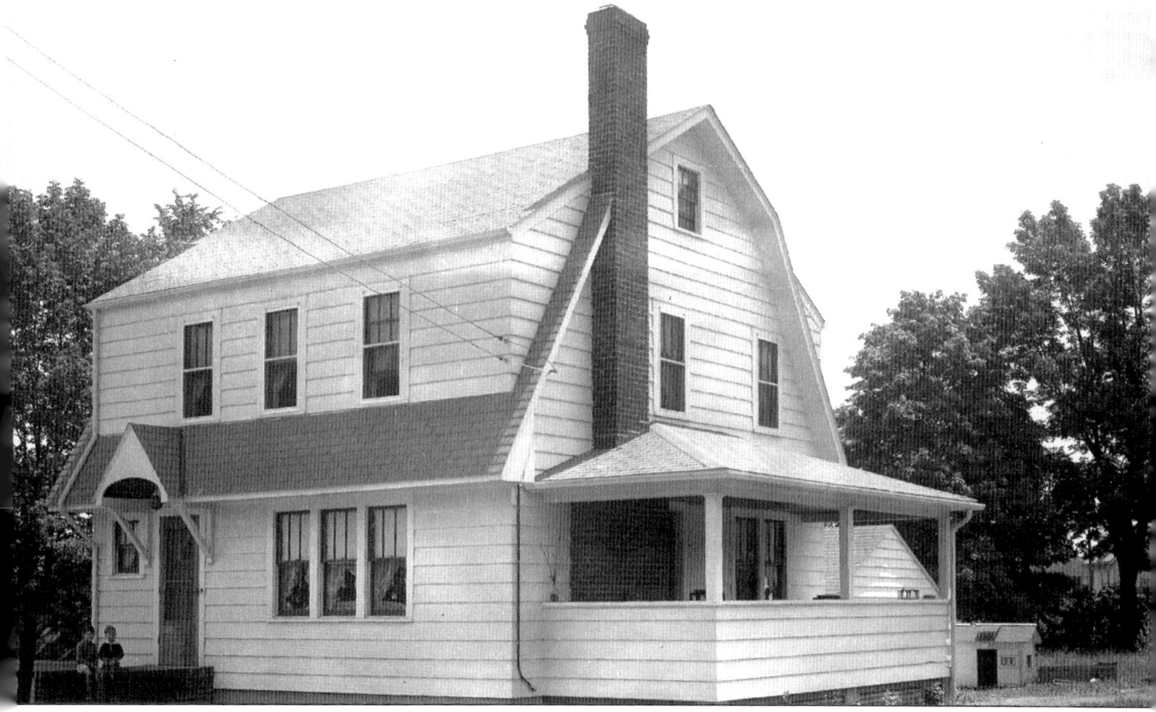

This home at 216 Highland Avenue was built in 1934 for George Curran.

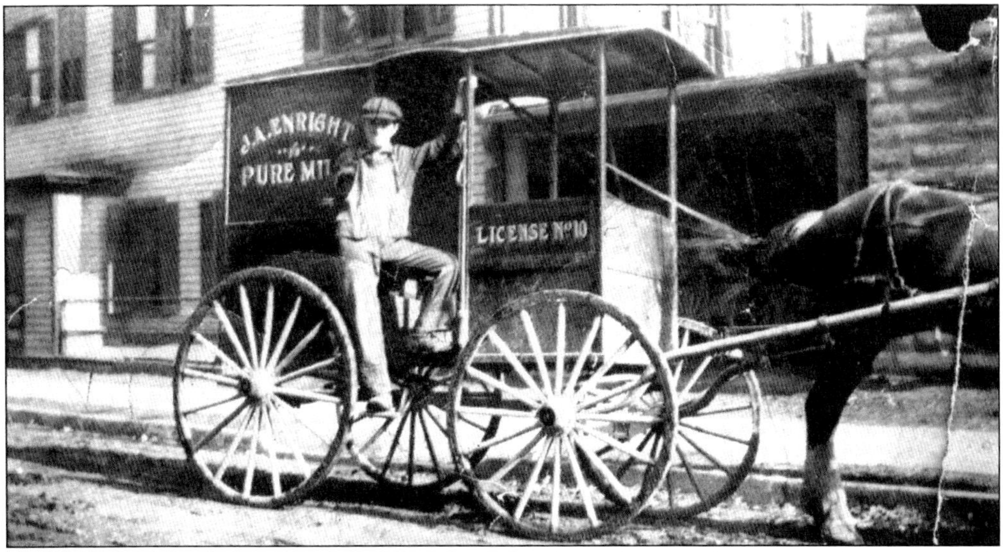

Joseph A. Enright had a dairy farm at 29½ Genung Street for over 50 years; in this photograph Enright is pictured with his horse and wagon.

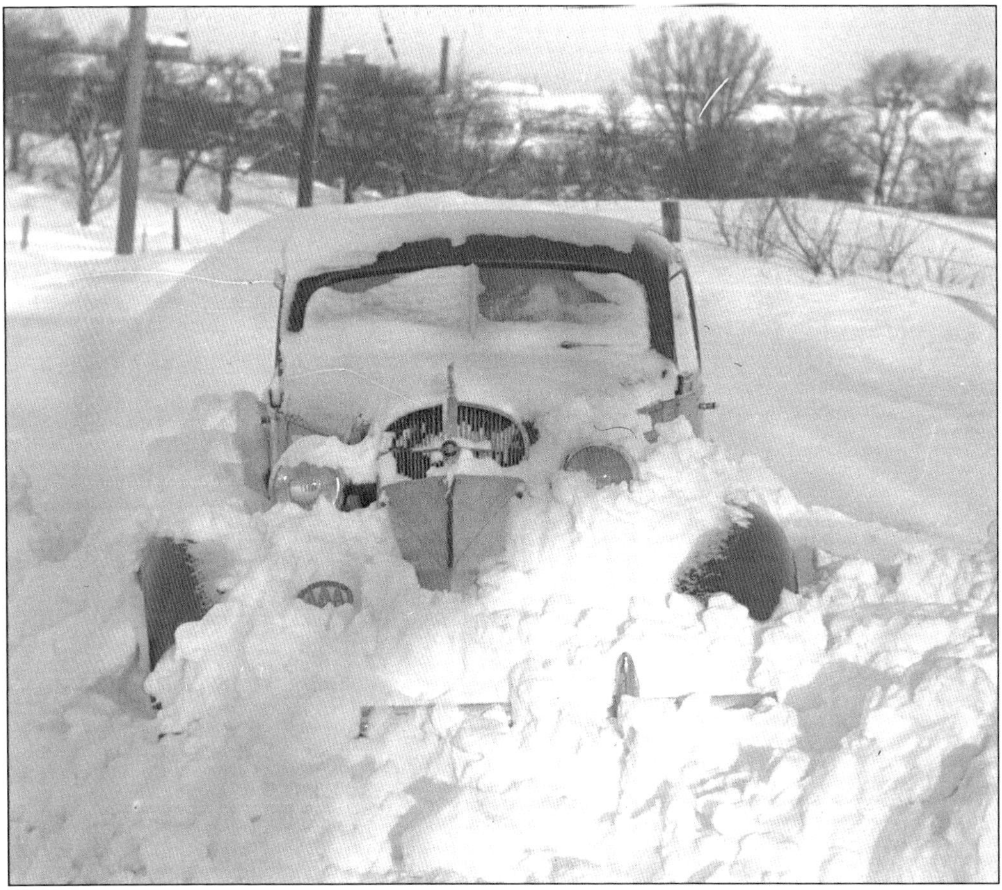

This 1935 Chevrolet is well buried in snow.

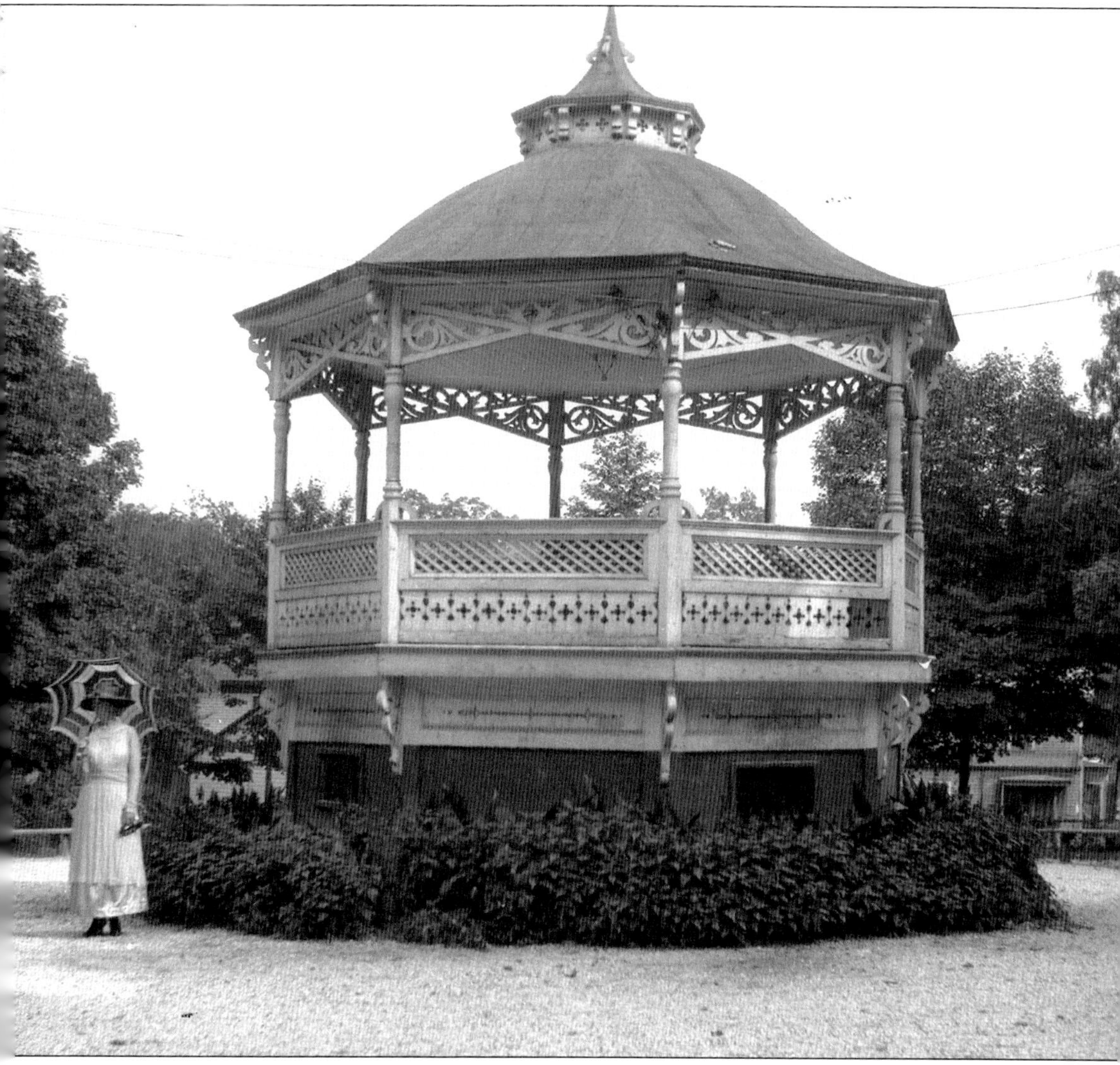

This bandstand once stood in Academy Avenue Park across the street from the high school. The young lady is Bertha Fellows.